Lecture Notes in Computer Science   3083

Commenced Publication in 1973
Founding and Former Series Editors:
Gerhard Goos, Juris Hartmanis, and Jan van Leeuwen

T0226085

Springer

Berlin
Heidelberg
New York
Hong Kong
London
Milan
Paris
Tokyo

Wolfgang Emmerich   Alexander L. Wolf (Eds.)

Component Deployment

Second International Working Conference, CD 2004
Edinburgh, UK, May 20-21, 2004
Proceedings

 Springer

Volume Editors

Wolfgang Emmerich
University College London
Dept. of Computer Science
Gower Street, London WC1E 6BT, UK
E-mail: w.emmerich@cs.ucl.ac.uk

Alexander L. Wolf
University of Colorado
Department of Computer Science
Boulder, Colorado, 80309-430 USA
E-mail: alw@cs.colorado.edu

Library of Congress Control Number: 2004105536

CR Subject Classification (1998): D.2, F.3, D.1, D.3, D.4

ISSN 0302-9743
ISBN 3-540-22059-3 Springer-Verlag Berlin Heidelberg New York

Springer-Verlag is a part of Springer Science+Business Media

springeronline.com

© Springer-Verlag Berlin Heidelberg 2004
Printed in Germany

Typesetting: Camera-ready by author, data conversion by Boller Mediendesign
Printed on acid-free paper   SPIN: 11009528   06/3142   5 4 3 2 1 0

Preface

This volume of the Lecture Notes in Computer Science series contains the proceedings of the second Working Conference on Component Deployment, which took place May 20–21, 2004, at the e-Science Institute in Edinburgh, Scotland, as a collocated event of the International Conference on Software Engineering.

Component deployment addresses what needs to be done *after* a component has been developed. Component deployment includes activities such as component customization, configuration, integration, activation, de-activation and decommissioning. The emerging research community that investigates component deployment concerns itself with the principles, methods and tools for deployment activities. The community held its first working conference in Berlin, Germany, in June 2002. The proceedings were published by Springer-Verlag as volume 2370 of the Lecture Notes in Computer Science series.

The program of this year's conference consisted of an invited talk and 16 technical paper presentations. The invited talk was given by Patrick Goldsack of Hewlett Packard Research Laboratories Bristol, UK. He presented the Smart-Frog component deployment framework that HP released as Open Source. The technical papers were carefully selected from a total of 34 submitted papers. Each paper was thoroughly peer reviewed by at least three members of the program committee and consensus on acceptance was achieved by means of an electronic PC meeting.

The conference and these proceedings would not have been possible without the help of a large number of people. Anthony Finkelstein, in his role as General Chair of ICSE, simplified our task considerably by arranging our use of the CyberChair electronic submission and reviewing service, as well as handling publicity and registration. We are indebted to ACM SIGSOFT and the UK e-Science Programme for generously providing support for the conference, and to Malcolm Atkinson and Dave Berry at the e-Science Institute for hosting CD 2004. Particular thanks go to Gill Mandy for handling the local arrangements. Richard van der Stadt of Borbala was always available and responded incredibly quickly whenever we needed him and, as a result, he eased the paper submission and review process considerably. Finally, we thank the members of the program committee for their hard work and careful reviews.

March 2004   Wolfgang Emmerich and Alexander L. Wolf

Program Committee

Table of Contents

A Tailorable Environment for Assessing the Quality of Deployment Architectures in Highly Distributed Settings

Marija Mikic-Rakic, Sam Malek, Nels Beckman, and Nenad Medvidovic

Computer Science Department
University of Southern California
Los Angeles, CA 90089-0781
{marija,malek,nbeckman,neno}@usc.edu

Abstract. A distributed software system's deployment architecture can have a significant impact on the system's properties. These properties will depend on various system parameters, such as network bandwidth, frequencies of software component interactions, and so on. Existing tools for representing system deployment lack support for specifying, visualizing, and analyzing different factors that influence the quality of a deployment, e.g., the deployment's impact on the system's availability. In this paper, we present an environment that supports flexible and tailorable specification, manipulation, visualization, and (re)estimation of deployment architectures for large-scale, highly distributed systems. The environment has been successfully used to explore large numbers of postulated deployment architectures. It has also been integrated with a middleware platform to support the exploration of deployment architectures of actual distributed systems.

Keywords. Software deployment, availability, disconnection, visualization, environment, middleware

1   Introduction

For any large, distributed system, multiple deployment architectures (i.e., distributions of the system's software components onto its hardware hosts, see Fig. 1.) will be typically possible. Some of those deployment architectures will be more effective than others in terms of the desired system characteristics such as scalability, evolvability, mobility, and dependability. Availability is an aspect of dependability, defined as the degree to which the system is operational and accessible when required for use [5]. In the context of distributed environments, where a most common cause of (partial) system inaccessibility is network failure [17], we define availability as the ratio of the number of successfully completed inter-component interactions in the system to the total number of attempted interactions over a period of time. In other words, availability in distributed systems is greatly affected by the properties of the network, including its reliability and bandwidth.

W. Emmerich and A.L. Wolf (Eds.): CD 2004, LNCS 3083, pp. 1-17, 2004.
© Springer-Verlag Berlin Heidelberg 2004

Maximizing the availability of a given system may thus require the system to be redeployed such that the most critical, frequent, and voluminous interactions occur either locally or over reliable and capacious network links. However, finding the actual deployment architecture that maximizes a system's availability is an exponentially complex problem that may take *years* to resolve for any but very small systems [11]. Also, even a deployment architecture that increases the system's current availability by a desired amount cannot be easily found because of the many parameters that influence this task: number of hardware hosts, available memory and CPU power on each host, network topology, capacity and reliability of network links, number of software components, memory and processing requirements of each component, their configuration (i.e., software topology), frequency and volume of interaction among the components, and so forth. A naive solution to this problem would be to keep redeploying the actual system that exhibits poor availability until an adequate deployment architecture is found. However, this would be prohibitively expensive. A much more preferable solution is to develop a means of modeling the relevant system parameters, estimating the deployment architecture based on these parameters in a manner that produces the desired (increase in) availability, and assessing the estimated architecture in a controlled setting, *prior* to changing the actual deployed system.

In this paper, we discuss a tailorable environment developed precisely for that purpose. The environment, called DeSi, supports specification, manipulation, visualization, and (re)estimation of deployment architectures for large-scale, highly distributed systems. DeSi allows an engineer to rapidly explore the space of possible deployments for a given system (real or postulated), determine the deployments that will result in greatest improvements in availability (while, perhaps, requiring the smallest changes to the current deployment architecture), and assess a system's sensitivity to and visualize changes in specific parameters (e.g., the reliability of a particular network link) and deployment constraints (e.g., two components must be located on different hosts). We have provided a facility that automatically generates large numbers of deployment scenarios and have evaluated different aspects of DeSi using this facility. DeSi also allows

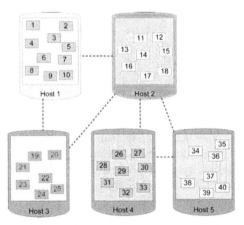

Fig. 1. Example deployment architecture: A software system comprising 40 components is deployed onto five hosts. The dotted lines represent host interconnectivity; filled lines represent software component interaction paths

one to easily integrate, evaluate, and compare different algorithms targeted at improving system availability [11] in terms of their feasibility, efficiency, and precision. We illustrate this support by showing the integration of six such algorithms.

DeSi also provides a simple API that allows its integration with any distributed system platform (i.e., middleware) that supports component deployment at runtime. We demonstrate this support by integrating DeSi with the Prism-MW middleware [10]. Finally, while availability has been our focus to date, DeSi's architecture is flexible enough to allow exploration of other system characteristics (e.g., security, fault-tolerance, and so on).

The remainder of the paper is organized as follows. Section 2 defines the problem of increasing the availability of distributed systems, and overviews six different algorithms we have developed for this purpose. Section 3 highlights the related work. Section 4 discusses the architecture, implementation, and usage of the DeSi environment. Evaluation of DeSi is presented in Section 5. The paper concludes with a discussion of future work.

2   Background

2.1   Problem Description

The distribution of software components onto hardware nodes (i.e., a system's software *deployment architecture*, illustrated in Fig. 1) greatly influences the system's availability in the face of connectivity losses. For example, components located on the same host will be able to communicate regardless of the network's status; components distributed across different hosts might not. However, the reliability (i.e., rate of failure) of connectivity among the hardware nodes on which the system is deployed may not be known before the deployment and may change during the system's execution. The frequencies of interaction among software components may also be unknown. For this reason, the current software deployment architecture may be ill-suited for the given state of the "target" hardware environment. This means that a *redeployment* of the software system may be necessary to improve its availability. The critical difficulty in achieving this task lies in the fact that determining a software system's deployment architecture that will maximize its availability for the given target environment (referred to as *optimal deployment architecture*) is an exponentially complex problem.

In addition to the characteristics of hardware connectivity and software interaction, there are other constraints on a system's redeployment, including the available memory on each network host, the required memory for each software component, the size of data exchanged between software components, the bandwidth of each network link, and possible restrictions on component locations (e.g., a component may be fixed to a selected host, or two components may not be allowed to reside on the same host). Fig.2 shows a formal model that captures the system properties and constraints, and a formal definition of the problem we are addressing. The mem_{comp} function captures the required memory for each component. The frequency of interaction between any pair of components is captured via the *freq* function, and the average size of data exchanged between them is captured via the *evt_size* function. Each host's available memory is captured via the mem_{host} function.

The reliability of the link between any pair of hosts is captured via the *rel* function, and the network bandwidth via the *bw* function. Using the *loc* function, deployment of any component can be restricted to a subset of hosts, thus denoting a set of allowed hosts for that component. Using the *colloc* function, constraints on collocation of components can be specified.

The definition of the problem contains the criterion function A, which formally describes a system's availability as the ratio of the number of successfully completed interactions in the system to the total number of attempted interactions. Function f represents the exponential number of the system's candidate deployments. To be considered valid, each candidate deployment must satisfy the four stated conditions. The first condition states that the sum of memories of the components deployed onto a given host may not exceed the host's available memory. The second condition states that the total volume of data exchanged across any link between two hosts may not exceed the link's *effective bandwidth*, which is the product of the link's actual bandwidth and its reliability. The third condition states that a component may only be deployed onto a host that belongs to a set of allowed hosts for that component,

---

Model

Given:

(1) a set C of n components ($n = |C|$) and three functions $freq : C \times C \to \Re$, $evt\_size : C \times C \to \Re$, and $mem_{comp} : C \to \Re$

$$freq(c_i, c_j) = \begin{pmatrix} 0 & if & c_i = c_j \\ frequency\ of\ communication\ between\ c_i\ and\ c_j & if & c_i \neq c_j \end{pmatrix} \quad evt\_size(c_i, c_j) = \begin{pmatrix} 0 & if & c_i = c_j \\ avg\ size\ of\ data\ c_i\ and\ c_j\ exchange & if & c_i \neq c_j \end{pmatrix}$$

$mem_{comp}(c) = required\ memory\ for\ c$

(2) a set H of k hardware nodes ($k = |H|$) and three functions $rel : H \times H \to \Re$, $bw : H \times H \to \Re$, and $mem_{host} : H \to \Re$

$$rel(h_i, h_j) = \begin{pmatrix} 1 & if & h_i = h_j \\ 0 & if & h_i\ is\ not\ connected\ to\ h_j \\ reliability\ of\ the\ link\ between\ h_i\ and\ h_j & if & h_i \neq h_j \end{pmatrix} \quad bw(h_i, h_j) = \begin{pmatrix} \infty & if & h_i = h_j \\ 0 & if & h_i\ is\ not\ connected\ to\ h_j \\ bandwidth\ of\ the\ link\ between\ h_i\ and\ h_j & if & h_i \neq h_j \end{pmatrix}$$

$mem_{host}(h) = available\ memory\ on\ host\ h$

(3) Two functions that restrict locations of software components $loc : C \times H \to \{0,1\}$ $colloc : C \times C \to \{-1,0,1\}$

$$loc(c_i, h_j) = \begin{pmatrix} 1 & if & c_i\ can\ be\ deployed\ onto\ h_j \\ 0 & if & c_i\ cannot\ be\ deployed\ onto\ h_j \end{pmatrix} \quad colloc(c_i, c_j) = \begin{pmatrix} -1 & if & c_i\ cannot\ be\ on\ the\ same\ host\ as\ c_j \\ 1 & if & c_i\ has\ to\ be\ on\ the\ same\ host\ as\ c_j \\ 0 & if & there\ are\ no\ restrictions\ on\ collocation\ of\ c_i\ and\ c_j \end{pmatrix}$$

Problem

Problem:
Find a function $f : C \to H$ such that the system's overall availability

A defined as $A = \dfrac{\sum_{i=1}^{n} \sum_{j=1}^{n} (freq(c_i, c_j) * rel(f(c_i), f(c_j)))}{\sum_{i=1}^{n} \sum_{j=1}^{n} freq(c_i, c_j)}$ is maximized, and the following four conditions are satisfied:

(1) $\forall i \in [1,k] \left(\forall j \in [1,n] \quad f(c_j) = h_i \ \bigg| \ \sum_j mem_{comp}(c_j)) \leq mem_{host}(h_i) \right)$

(2) $(\forall i \in [1,k] \quad \forall j \in [i+1,k]) \begin{pmatrix} (\forall l \in [1,n] \quad \forall m \in [l+1,n]) \\ where\ f(c_l) = h_i \wedge f(c_m) = h_j \\ \sum_{l,m} data\_vol(c_l, c_m) \leq effective\_bw(h_i, h_j) \end{pmatrix}$ where $data\_vol$ and $effective\_bw$ are defined as follows:

$data\_vol(c_x, c_y) = freq(c_x, c_y) * evt\_size(c_x, c_y)$ $effective\_bw(h_x, h_y) = rel(h_x, h_y) * bw(h_x, h_y)$

(3) $\forall j \in [1,n] \quad loc(c_j, f(c_j)) = 1$

(4) $\forall i \in [1,n] \quad \forall j \in [i+1,n] \quad (colloc(c_i, c_j) = 1) \Rightarrow (f(c_i) = f(c_j))$ $(colloc(c_i, c_j) = -1) \Rightarrow (f(c_i) \neq f(c_j))$

In the most general case, the number of possible functions f is k^n. However, note that some of these deployments may not satisfy one or more of the above four conditions.

Fig. 2. Formal statement of the problem

specified via the *loc* function. Finally, the fourth condition states that two components must be deployed onto the same host (or on different hosts) if required by the *colloc* function.

2.2   Algorithms

In this section we briefly describe six algorithms we have developed for increasing a system's availability by calculating a new deployment architecture. A detailed performance comparison of several of these algorithms is given in [11].

Exact Algorithm: This algorithm tries every possible deployment, and selects the one that has maximum availability and satisfies the constraints posed by the memory, bandwidth, and restrictions on software component locations. The exact algorithm guarantees at least one optimal deployment (assuming that at least one deployment is possible). The complexity of this algorithm in the general case (i.e., with no restrictions on component locations) is $O(k^n)$, where k is the number of hardware hosts, and n the number of software components. By fixing a subset of m components to selected hosts, the complexity reduces to $O(k^{n-m})$.

Unbiased Stochastic Algorithm: This algorithm generates different deployments by randomly assigning each component to a single host from the set of available hosts for that component. If the randomly generated deployment satisfies all the constraints, the availability of the produced deployment architecture is calculated. This process repeats a given number of times and the deployment with the best availability is selected. As indicated in Fig. 2, the complexity of calculating the availability for each valid deployment is $O(n^2)$, resulting in the same complexity of the overall algorithm.

Biased Stochastic Algorithm: This algorithm randomly orders all the hosts and all the components. Then, going in order, it assigns as many components to a given host as can fit on that host, ensuring that all of the constraints are satisfied. Once the host is full, the algorithm proceeds with the same process for the next host in the ordered list of hosts, and the remaining unassigned components in the ordered list of components, until all components have been deployed. This process is repeated a desired number of times, and the best obtained deployment is selected. Since it needs to calculate the availability for every deployment, the complexity of this algorithm is $O(n^2)$.

Greedy Algorithm: This algorithm incrementally assigns software components to the hardware hosts. At each step of the algorithm, the goal is to select the assignment that will maximally contribute to the availability function, by selecting the "best" host and "best" software component. Selecting the best hardware host is performed by choosing a host with the highest sum of network reliabilities with other hosts in the system, and the highest memory capacity. Similarly, selecting the best software component is performed by choosing the component with the highest frequency of interaction with other components in the system, and the lowest required memory. Once found, the best component is assigned to the best host, making certain that the four constraints are satisfied. The algorithm proceeds with searching for the next best component among the remaining components, until the best host is full. Next, the algorithm selects the best host among the remaining hosts. This process repeats until every component is assigned to a host. The complexity of this algorithm is $O(n^3)$ [11].

Clustering Algorithm: This algorithm groups software components and physical hosts into a set of component and host *clusters*, where all members of a cluster are treated as a single entity. For example, when a component in a given cluster needs to be redeployed to a new host, all of the cluster's member components are redeployed. The algorithm clusters components with high frequencies of interaction, and hosts with high connection reliability. Clustering can significantly reduce the size of the redeployment problem; it also has the potential to increase the availability of a system. For example, connectivity-based clustering in peer-to-peer networks improves the quality of service by reducing the cost of messaging [15].

Decentralized Algorithm: The above algorithms assume the existence of a central host with reliable connections to every other host in the system. This assumption does not hold in a wide range of distributed systems (e.g., ad-hoc mobile networks), requiring a decentralized solution. Our decentralized redeployment algorithm [8] leverages a variation of the auction algorithm, in which each hosts acts as an agent and may conduct or participate in auctions. Each host's agent initiates an auction for the redeployment of its local components, assuming none of its neighboring (i.e., connected) hosts is already conducting an auction. The auction initiation is done by sending to all the neighboring hosts a message that carries information about a component (e.g., name, size, and so on). The agents receiving this message have a limited time to enter a bid on the component before the auction closes. The bidding agent on a given host calculates an initial bid for the auctioned component, by considering the frequency and volume of interaction between components on its host and the auctioned component. In each bid message, the bidding agent also sends additional local information, including its host's network reliability and bandwidth with neighboring hosts. Once the auctioneer has received all the bids, it calculates the final bid based on the received information. The host with the highest bid is selected as the winner. If the winner has enough free memory and sufficient bandwidth to host the auctioned component, then the component is redeployed to it and the auction is closed. If this is not the case, then the winner and the auctioneer attempt to find a component on the winner host to be traded (swapped) with the auctioned component. The complexity of this algorithm is $O(k*n^3)$.

3   Related Work

This section briefly outlines several research areas and approaches relevant to our work on DeSi: software architectures, disconnected operation, software deployment, software visualization, and visual software environments.

Software architectures provide high-level abstractions for representing structure, behavior, and key properties of a software system [14]. They are described in terms of *components*, which describe the computations and state of a system; *connectors*, which describe the rules and mechanisms of interaction among the components; and *configurations*, which define topologies of components and connectors. DeSi leverages an architectural model of a distributed system, including its deployment information. In our approach, a component represents the smallest unit of deployment.

Disconnected operation refers to the continued functioning of a distributed system in the (temporary) absence of network connectivity. We have performed an extensive survey of existing disconnected operation approaches, and provided a framework for their classification and comparison [12]. One of the techniques for supporting disconnected operation is (re)deployment, which is a process of installing, updating, or relocating a distributed software system.

Carzaniga et. al. [1] provide an extensive comparison of existing *software deployment* approaches. They identify several issues lacking in the existing deployment tools, including integrated support for the entire deployment lifecycle. An exception is Software Dock [4], which has been proposed as a systematic framework that provides that support. Software Dock is a system of loosely coupled, cooperating, distributed components. It provides software deployment agents that travel among hosts to perform software deployment tasks. Unlike DeSi, however, Software Dock does not focus on visualizing, automatically selecting, or evaluating a system's deployment architecture.

UML [13] is the primary notation for the *visual modeling* of today's software systems. UML's deployment diagram provides a standard notation for representing a system's software deployment architecture. Several recent approaches extend this notation via stereotypes [3,7]. However, using UML to visualize deployment architectures has several drawbacks: UML's deployment diagrams are static; they do not depict connections among hardware hosts; and they do not provide support for representing and visualizing the parameters that affect the key system properties (e.g., availability). For these reasons, we have opted not to use a UML-based notation in DeSi.

There are several examples of *visual software development environments* that have originated from industrial and academic research. For example, AcmeStudio [16] is an environment for modeling, visualizing, and analyzing software architectures. Environments such as Visual Studio [9] provide a toolset for rapid application development, testing, and packaging. In our context, the role of the DeSi environment is to support tailorable, scalable, and platform-independent modeling, visualization, evaluation, and implementation of highly distributed systems. For these reasons we opted for using Eclipse [2] in the construction of DeSi. Eclipse is a platform-independent IDE for Java with support for plug-ins. Eclipse provides an efficient graphical library (Draw2D) and accompanying graphical editing framework (GEF), which we leveraged in creating visual representations of deployment architectures in DeSi.

4   The DeSi Environment

In this section, we discuss the architecture, implementation, and typical usage of the DeSi environment. We focus on the key architecture- and implementation-level decisions and the motivation behind them.

4.1   DeSi's Architecture

The overall architecture of the DeSi environment adheres to the model-view-controller (MVC) architectural style [6]. Fig 3 depicts the architecture. The centerpiece of the architecture is a rich and extensible *Model*, which in turn allows extensions to the *View* (used for model visualization) and *Controller* (used for model manipulation) subsystems. Each is discussed in more detail below.

Model: DeSi's *Model* subsystem is reactive and accessible to the *Controller* via a simple API. The *Model* currently captures three different system aspects in its three components: *SystemData*, *GraphViewData*, and *AlgoResultData*.

SystemData is the key part of the *Model* and represents the software system itself in terms of the parameters outlined in Section 2.1: numbers of components and hosts, distribution of

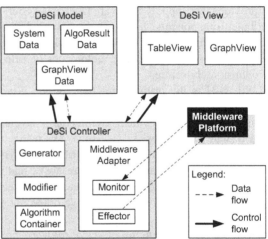

Fig. 3. DeSi's architecture

components across hosts, software and hardware topologies, and so on. *GraphViewData* captures the information needed for visualizing a system's deployment architecture: graphical (e.g., color, shape, border thickness) and layout (e.g., juxtaposition, movability, containment) properties of the depicted components, hosts, and their links. Finally, *AlgoResultData* provides a set of facilities for capturing the outcomes of the different deployment estimation algorithms: estimated deployment architectures (in terms of component-host pairs), achieved availability, algorithm's running time, estimated time to effect a redeployment, and so on.

View: DeSi's *View* subsystem exports an API for visualizing the *Model*. The current architecture of the *View* subsystem contains two components—*GraphView* and *TableView*. *GraphView* is used to depict the information provided by the *Model*'s *GraphViewData* component. *TableView* is intended to support a detailed layout of system parameters and deployment estimation algorithms captured in the *Model*'s *SystemData* and *AlgoResultData* components. The decoupling of the *Model*'s and corresponding *View*'s components allows one to be modified independently of the other. For example, it allows us to add new visualizations of the same models, or to use the same visualizations on new, unrelated models, as long as the component interfaces remain stable.

Controller: DeSi's *Controller* subsystem comprises four components. The *Generator*, *Modifier*, and *AlgorithmContainer* manage different aspects of DeSi's *Model* and *View* subsystems, while the *MiddlewareAdapter* component provides an interface to a, possibly third-party, system implementation, deployment, and execution platform (depicted as a "black box" in Fig 3). The *Generator* component takes as its input the desired number of hardware hosts, software components, and a set of ranges for system parameters (e.g., minimum and maximum network reliability, component interaction frequency, available memory, and so on). Based on this information, *Generator* creates a specific deployment architecture that satisfies the given input and stores it in *Model* subsystem's *SystemData* component. The *Modifier* component allows fine-grain tuning of the generated deployment architecture (e.g., by altering a single network link's reliability, a single component's required memory, and so on). Finally, the *AlgorithmContainer* component invokes the selected redeployment algorithms (recall Section **2.2**) and updates the *Model*'s *AlgoResultData*. In each case, the three components also inform the *View* subsystem that the *Model* has been modified; in turn, the *View* pulls the modified data from the *Model* and updates the display.

The above components allow DeSi to be used to generate automatically and manipulate large numbers of hypothetical deployment architectures. The *MiddlewareAdapter* component, on the other hand, provides DeSi with the same information from a running, *real* system. *MiddlewareAdapter*'s *Monitor* subcomponent captures the runtime data from the external *MiddlewarePlatform* and stores it inside the *Model*'s *SystemData* component. *MiddlewareAdapter*'s *Effector* subcomponent is informed by the *Controller*'s *AlgorithmContainer* component of the calculated (improved) deployment architecture; in turn, the *Effector* issues a set of commands to the *MiddlewarePlatform* to modify the running system's deployment architecture. The details of this process are further illuminated in Section 4.2.3.

4.2   DeSi's Implementation

DeSi has been implemented in the Eclipse platform [2] using Java 1.4. DeSi's implementation adheres to its MVC architectural style. In this section, we discuss (1) the implementation of DeSi's extensible model, (2) the visualizations currently supported by DeSi, and (3) its capabilities for generating deployment scenarios, assessing a given deployment, manipulating system parameters and observing their effects, and estimating redeployments that result in improved system availability.

4.2.1   Model Implementation
The implementations of the *SystemData* and *AlgoResultData* components of DeSi's *Model* are simple: each one of them is implemented as a single class, with APIs for

accessing and modifying the stored data. For example, *AlgoResultData*'s implementation provides an API for accessing and modifying the array containing the estimated deployment architecture, and a set of variables representing the achieved availability, algorithm's running time, and estimated time to change a given system from its current to its new deployment.

The *GraphViewData* component contains all the persistent data necessary for maintaining the graphical visualization of a given deployment architecture. It keeps track of information such as figure shapes, colors, placements, and labels that correspond to hardware hosts, software components, and software and hardware links. In our implementation of *GraphViewData*, each element of a distributed system (host, component, or link) is implemented via a corresponding *Figure* class that maintains this information (e.g., each host is represented as a single instance of the *HostFigure* class). Components and hosts have unique identifiers, while a link is uniquely identified via its two end-point hosts or components.

The *GraphViewData* component's classes provide a rich API for retrieving and modifying properties of individual components, hosts, and links. This allows easy runtime modification of virtually any element of the visualization (e.g., changing the line thickness of links). Furthermore, the information captured inside *GraphViewData* is not directly tied to the properties of the model captured inside *SystemData*. For example, the *color* property of *HostFigure* can be set to correspond to the amount of available memory or to the average reliability with other hosts in the system.

4.2.2   View Implementation

The *TableView* component of DeSi's *View* subsystem displays the *Deployment Control Window*, shown in Fig. 4. This window consists of five sections, identified by panel names: *Input*, *Constraints*, *Algorithms*, *Results*, and *Tables of Parameters*.

The *Input* section allows the user to specify different input parameters: (1) numbers of components and hosts; (2) ranges for component memory, frequency and event size; and (3) ranges for host memory, reliability and bandwidth. For centralized deployment scenarios we provide a set of text fields for specifying the properties of the central host. The *Generate* button on the bottom of this panel results in the (random) generation of a single deployment architecture that satisfies the above input. Once the parameter values are generated, they are displayed in the *Tables of Parameters* section, which will be discussed in more detail below.

The *Constraints* section allows specification of different conditions for component (co-)location: (1) components that must be deployed on the same host, (2) components that may not be deployed on the same host, and (3) components that have to be on specific host(s). The three buttons on the right side of the *Constraints* panel correspond to these conditions. Consecutive clicks on the *Use Mapping* button, located on the bottom right side of the panel, enable and disable the above three buttons.

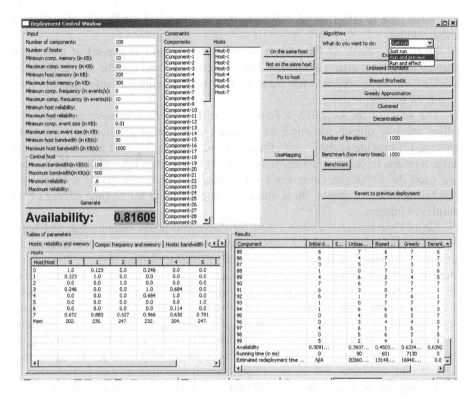

Fig. 4. DeSi's Deployment Control Window

The *Algorithms* section allows the user to run different redeployment estimation algorithms by clicking the corresponding algorithm's button. Running the algorithms requires the existence of a deployment architecture, which can be generated by clicking on the *Generate* button of the *Input* panel. There are three provided options for running the algorithms (depicted in the drop-down menu at the top of the *Algorithms* section in Fig.4): (1) *Just run*, which runs the algorithm and displays the result in the *Results* panel, (2) *Run and preview*, which runs the algorithm and displays the results both in the *Results* panel and in the graphical view (discussed further below), and (3) *Run and effect*, which, in addition to actions described in option 2, also updates *SystemData* to set the current deployment to the output of the selected algorithm. The latter action can be reversed by clicking on the *Revert to previous deployment* button.

We have provided a benchmarking capability to compare the performance of various algorithms. The user can specify the number of times the algorithms should be invoked. Then, the user triggers via the *Benchmark* button a sequence of automatic random generations of new deployment architectures and executions of all algorithms.

The *Results* section displays the outcomes of different algorithms. For each algorithm, the output consists of (1) a new mapping of components to hosts, (2) the system's achieved availability, (3) the running time of the algorithm, and (4) the estimated time to effect the new deployment. Section 4.2.3 details the calculation of these results.

Finally, the *Table of Parameters* section provides an editable set of tables that display different system parameters. The user can view and edit the desired table by clicking on the appropriate tab from the tab list. The editable tables support fine-tuning of system parameters.

The goals of the *GraphView* component of DeSi's *View* subsystem were to (1) allow users to quickly examine the complete deployment architecture of a given system, (2) provide scalable and efficient displays of deployment architectures with large numbers of components and hosts, and (3) be platform independent. To this end we used the Eclipse environment's GEF plug-in, which consists of a library for displaying different shapes, lines, and labels and a facility for runtime editing of the displayed images.

GraphView provides a simple API for displaying hosts, components, and links. For example, displaying two connected hosts requires two consecutive calls of the *createHost* method, followed by the *createH2HLink* method. Fig. 5 illustrates a deployment architecture with 100 components and 8 hosts. Network connections between hosts are depicted as solid lines, while dotted lines between pairs of hosts denote that some of the components on the two respective hosts need to communicate, but that there is no network link between them. Clearly, the existence of dotted lines indicates a decrease in the system's availability. Therefore, just by observing the number of dotted lines one can reason about the quality of a given deployment architecture.

For systems with large numbers of hosts and components, visualizing the system and its connectivity becomes a challenge. For this reason, *GraphView* supports zooming in and out (see Fig. 5), and provides the ability to "drag" hosts and components on-screen, in which case all relevant links will follow them. For the same reason, we do not display connections between components residing on different hosts. If such connections exist, the components will have thicker borders. A thin

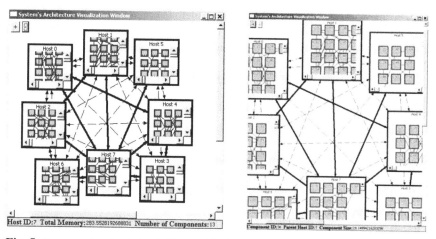

Fig. 5. Two zooming levels in DeSi's graphical visualization of a deployment architecture with 8 hosts and 100 components

border on a component denotes that it does not communicate with remote components.

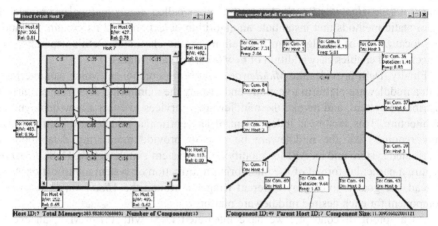

Fig. 6. Detailed view of (a) a single host and (b) a single component in DeSi

GraphView has several other features that allow users to easily visualize and reason about a given deployment architecture. A user can get at-a-glance information on any of the hosts and components in the system. Selection of a single graphical object displays its information in the status bar at the bottom of the window (see Fig. 5). The displayed information can easily be changed or extended through simple modifications to *GraphView* to include any (combination) of the information captured in the *SystemData* component. Detailed information about a host or component can be displayed by double-clicking on the corresponding graphical object. The *DetailWindow* for a host, shown in Fig. 6a, displays the host's properties in the status bar, the components deployed on the host, the host's connections to other hosts, and the reliabilities and bandwidths of those connections. Similarly, the *DetailWindow* for a component, shown in Fig. 6b, displays the component's properties and its connections to other components.

4.2.3   Controller Implementation

The implementation of DeSi *Controller*'s *Generator* component provides methods for (1) generating random deployment problems, (2) producing a specific (initial) deployment that satisfies the parameters and constraints of a generated problem, and (3) updating DeSi *Model*'s *SystemData* class accordingly. This capability allows us to rapidly compare the different deployment algorithms discussed in Section 2.2. *Generator* is complemented by the class implementing the *Controller*'s *Modifier* component. *Modifier* provides facilities for fine-tuning system parameters (also recall the discussion of editable tables in Section 4.2.2), allowing one to assess the sensitivity of a deployment algorithm to specific parameters in a given system.

Each deployment algorithm in DeSi *Controller*'s *AlgorithmContainer* component is encapsulated in its own class, which extends the *AbstractAlgorithm* class.

AbstractAlgorithm captures the common attributes and methods needed by all algorithms (e.g., *calculateAvailability*, *estimateRedeploymentTime*, and so on). Each algorithm class needs to implement the abstract method *execute*, which returns an object of type *AlgorithmResult*. A bootstrap class called *AlgorithmInvoker* provides a set of static methods that instantiate an algorithm object and call its *execute* method. The localization of all algorithm invocations to one class aids DeSi's separation of concerns and enables easy addition of new (kinds of) algorithms.

Finally, DeSi provides the *Middleware Controller* component which can interface with a middleware platform to capture and display the monitoring data from a running distributed system, and invoke the middleware's services to enact a new deployment architecture. This facility is independent of any particular middleware platform and only requires that the middleware be able to provide monitoring data about a distributed system and an API for modifying the system's architecture. DeSi does not require a particular format of the monitoring information or system modification API; instead, the goal is to employ different wrappers around the *Middleware Controller* component for each desired middleware platform.

As a "proof of concept", we have integrated DeSi with Prism-MW, an event-based, extensible middleware for highly distributed systems [10]. Prism-MW provides support for centralized deployment. It provides pluggable monitoring capabilities. It also provides a special-purpose *Admin* component residing on each host. The *Admin* component is in charge of gathering the monitoring information, sending it to the central host, and performing changes to the local subsystem by migrating components. Prism-MW also provides a *Deployer* component residing on the central host. The *Deployer* component controls the redeployment process, by issuing events to remote *Admin* components to perform changes to their local configurations. We have wrapped DeSi's *Middleware Controller* as a Prism-MW component that is capable of receiving events with the monitoring data from Prism-MW's *Deployer* component, and issuing events to the *Deployer* component to enact a new deployment architecture. Once the monitoring data is received, *Middleware Controller* invokes the appropriate API to update DeSi's *Model* and *View* subsystems. This results in the visualization of an actual system, which can now be analyzed and its deployment improved by employing different algorithms. Once the outcome of an algorithm is selected, *Middleware Controller* issues a series of events to Prism-MW's *Deployer* component to update the system's deployment architecture.

5   Discussion

The goal of DeSi is to allow visualization of different characteristics of software deployment architectures in highly distributed settings, the assessment of such architectures, and possibly their reconfiguration. In this section we evaluate DeSi in terms of four properties that we believe to be highly relevant in this context: tailorability, scalability, efficiency, and ability to explore the problem space. Each property is discussed in more detail below.

5.1   Tailorability

DeSi is an environment intended for exploring a large number of issues concerning distributed software systems. As discussed above, to date we have focused on the impact a deployment architecture has on a system's availability. However, its MVC architecture and component-based design allow it in principle to be customized for visualizing and assessing arbitrary system properties (e.g., security, fault-tolerance, latency). All three components of DeSi's *Model* subsystem (*SystemData*, *GraphViewData*, and *AlgoResultData*) could be easily extended to represent other system properties through the addition of new attributes and methods to the corresponding classes. Another aspect of DeSi's tailorability is the ability to add new *Views* or modify the existing ones. Clear separation between DeSi *View* and *Model* components makes creating different visualizations of the same model easy. DeSi also enables quick replacement of the *Control* components without modifying the *View* components. For example, two *Control* components may use the *GraphView's* API for setting the thickness of inter-host links differently: one to depict the reliability and the other to depict the available bandwidth between the hosts. Finally, DeSi also provides the ability to interface with an arbitrary middleware platform.

5.2   Scalability

DeSi is targeted at systems comprising many components distributed across many hosts. DeSi supports scalability in the (1) size of its *Model*, (2) scalability of its *Views*, and (3) scalability of the *Controller*'s algorithms. *Model*s of systems represented in DeSi can be arbitrarily large since they capture only the subset of system properties that are of interest. Furthermore, the centralization of the *Model* simplifies access and maintenance of the relevant system properties.

Another aspect of DeSi's scalability are *Controller*'s algorithm implementations: with the exception of the *ExactAlgorithm*, all of the algorithms are polynomial in the number of components. We have tested DeSi *Model*'s scalability by generating random models with hundreds of hosts and thousands of components, and *Controller*'s scalability by successfully running the algorithms on these models. Finally, the combination of the hierarchical viewing capabilities of the DeSi *View* subsystem (i.e., system-wide view, single host view, single component view), the zooming capability, and the ability to drag components and hosts to view their connectivity, enables us to effectively visualize distributed systems with very large numbers of components and hosts.

5.3   Efficiency

A goal of this work was to ensure that DeSi's scalability support does not come at the expense of its performance. As a result of developing the visualization components using Eclipse's GEF, DeSi's support for visualizing deployment architectures exhibits much better performance than an older version that was implemented using Java Swing libraries. We also enhanced the performance of the *GraphView* component by repainting only parts of the screen that correspond to the modified parts of the model. As discussed in Section 4.2.2, we also provide three options for running the redeployment algorithms. This enables us to customize the overhead associated with running the algorithms and displaying their results. Finally, while the efficiency and complexity of the redeployment algorithms is not the focus of this paper, with the exception of the exact algorithm, all of the provided algorithms run in polynomial time [11].

5.4   Exploration Capabilities

The nature of highly distributed systems, their properties, and the effects of their parameters on those properties is not well understood. This is particularly the case with the effect a system's deployment architecture has on its availability [11]. The DeSi environment provides a rich set of capabilities for exploring deployment architectures of distributed systems. DeSi provides side-by-side comparison of different algorithms along multiple dimensions (achieved availability, running time, and estimated redeployment time). It also supports tailoring of the individual parameters of the system model, which allows quick assessment of the sensitivity of different algorithms to these changes. Next, DeSi provides the ability to tailor its random generation of deployment architectures to focus on specific classes of systems or deployment scenarios (e.g., by modifying desired ranges of certain parameters such as minimum and maximum frequency of component interactions). DeSi supports algorithm benchmarking by automatically generating, assessing, and comparing the performance of different algorithms for a large number of randomly generated systems. DeSi's extensibility enables rapid evaluation of new algorithms. Finally, through its *MiddlewareAdapter*, DeSi provides the ability to visualize, reason about, and modify an *actual* system.

6   Conclusion

A distributed software system's deployment architecture can have a significant impact on the system's properties. In order to ensure the desired effects of deployment, those properties need to be assessed. They will depend on various system parameters (e.g., reliability of connectivity among hosts, security of links between hosts, and so on). Existing tools for visualizing system deployment (e.g., UML [13]) depict only distributions of components onto hosts, but lack support for specifying, visualizing, and analyzing different factors that influence the quality of a deployment.

This paper has presented DeSi, an environment that addresses this problem by supporting flexible and tailorable specification, manipulation, visualization, and (re)estimation of deployment architectures for large-scale, highly distributed systems. The environment has been successfully used to explore large numbers of postulated deployment architectures. It has also been integrated with the Prism-MW software architecture implementation and deployment platform to support the exploration of deployment architectures of *actual* distributed systems.

Our experience to date with DeSi has been very promising. At the same time, it has suggested a number of possible avenues for further work. We plan to address issues such as tailoring DeSi for use in exploring other non-functional system properties (e.g., security), improving existing DeSi visualizations (e.g., planarizing the graphs of hosts and components), making DeSi into an Eclipse plug-in, creating new views (e.g., visually displaying the performance of different algorithms), and integrating DeSi with other middleware platforms (e.g., different implementations of CORBA).

7   References

1. A. Carzaniga et. al. A Characterization Framework for Software Deployment Technologies. Technical Report, Dept. of Computer Science, University of Colorado, 1998.
2. Eclipse. http://eclipse.org/
3. J. Greenfield (ed.). UML Profile for EJB. *Public Review Draft JSR-000026*, Java Community Process, 2001.
4. R. S. Hall, D. Heimbigner, and A. L. Wolf. A Cooperative Approach to Support Software Deployment Using the Software Dock. *21st International Conference on Software Engineering (ICSE'99)*, pp. 174-183, Los Angeles, CA, May 1999.
5. IEEE Standard Computer Dictionary: *A Compilation of IEEE Standard Computer Glossaries*. New York, NY: 1990.
6. G. E. Krasner and S. T. Pope. A Cookbook for Using the Model-View-Controller User Interface Paradigm in Smalltalk-80. *Journal of Object-Oriented Programming*, 1(3):26-49, August/September 1988.
7. Luer, and D. Rosenblum. UML Component Diagrams and Software Architecture - Experiences from the Wren Project. *1st ICSE Workshop on Describing Software Architecture with UML*, pages 79-82, Toronto, Canada, 2001.
8. S. Malek et. al. A Decentralized Redeployment Algorithm for Improving the Availability of Distributed Systems. Technical Report *USC-CSE-2004-506*, 2004.
9. Microsoft Visual Studio. http://msdn.microsoft.com/vstudio/
10. M. Mikic-Rakic and N. Medvidovic. Adaptable Architectural Middleware for Programming-in-the-Small-and-Many. *Middleware 2003*, Rio De Janeiro, June 2003.
11. M. Mikic-Rakic, et. al. Improving Availability in Large, Distributed, Component-Based Systems via Redeployment. Technical Report *USC-CSE-2003-515*, 2003.
12. M. Mikic-Rakic and N. Medvidovic. Toward a Framework for Classifying Disconnected Operation Techniques. *ICSE Workshop on Architecting Dependable Systems*, Portland, Oregon, May 2003.
13. Object Management Group. The Unified Modeling Language v1.4. Tech. report, 2001.
14. D.E. Perry, and A.L. Wolf. Foundations for the Study of Software Architectures. *Software Engineering Notes*, Oct. 1992.
15. L.Ramaswamy, et. al. Connectivity Based Node Clustering in Decentralized Peer-to-Peer Networks. *Peer-to-Peer Computing* 2003.
16. B. Schmerl, and D. Garlan. AcmeStudio: Supporting Style-Centered Architecture Development. *ICSE 2004*, Edinburgh, Scotland, 2004.
17. J. Weissman. Fault-Tolerant Wide-Area Parallel Computing. *IPDPS 2000 Workshop*, Cancun, Mexico, May 2000.

Customizing Component-Based Architectures by Contract

Orlando Loques[1] and Alexandre Sztajnberg[2]

[1] Instituto de Computação - Universidade Federal Fluminense (UFF)
Rua Passo da Pátria, 156 - Bloco E - 3o. andar
São Domingos, Niterói - RJ, CEP 24.210-240
loques@ic.uff.br
[2] Instituto de Matemática e Estatística - Universidade do Estado
do Rio de Janeiro (UERJ)
Rua São Francisco Xavier, 524 - 6018-D
Maracanã, Rio de Janeiro - RJ, CEP 22.550-900
alexszt@ime.uerj.br

Abstract. This paper presents an approach to describe, deploy and manage component-based applications having dynamic functional and non-functional requirements. The approach is centered on architectural descriptions and associated high-level contracts. The latter allow the non-functional requirements to be described separately at design time, and during the running time are used to guide architecture customizations required to enforce these requirements. This helps to achieve separation of concerns, facilitating the reuse of modules that implement the application in other systems. The infrastructure required to manage the contracts follows an architectural pattern, which can be directly mapped to specific components included in a supporting reflective middleware. This feature allows designers to write a contract and to follow a standard recipe to insert the extra code required to its enforcement in the supporting middleware.

1 Introduction

The current software development technology offers a rich diversity of options to specify the interfaces and write the functional code of program components. Once built and made available, these components can be used to compose different applications, having specific non-functional requirements, that should be deployed in diverse operating environments. However, the specification of non-functional requirements and the implementation of the corresponding management strategies are, generally, embedded in the code of the components in an ad-hoc manner, mixed with the applications specific code. This lack of modularity makes component reuse difficult, also making difficult verification and debugging tasks. In this context, there is a growing interest for handling non-functional aspects in a specific abstraction level [2, 5, 11]. This approach would allow to single out the resources to be used and the specific mechanisms that

W. Emmerich and A.L. Wolf (Eds.): CD 2004, LNCS 3083, pp. 18–34, 2004.
© Springer-Verlag Berlin Heidelberg 2004

will be required to support the non-functional aspects, and, if possible, turn automatic the configuration and management of those resources.

Besides requirements normally associated to communication system level performance, non-functional (sometimes called QoS) requirements (or aspects) include characteristics such as availability, reliability, security, real-time, persistency, coordination and debugging support. Such kind of aspect can be handled by reusable services provided by middleware infrastructures or native systems support. This approach makes feasible to design a software system based on its architectural description, which includes the functional components, the interactions among those components and also the non-functional requirements, which depend on the properties of the supporting infrastructure. To this end, it has to be provided a means to specify those requirements in the context of the applications architecture description and, also, there is to be available an environment that allows to deploy those requirements over the system resources even during running time.

Among the available techniques to specify non-functional constraints, we highlight the concept of contract [7]. A contract establishes a formal relationship between two or more parts that use or provide resources, where rights, obligations and negotiation rules over the used resources are expressed. For instance, a parallel computing application can have a contract defining rules to replicate processing resources, in order to guarantee a maximum execution time constraint.

In the previous context, this work presents the CR-RIO framework (*Contractual Reflective - Reconfigurable Interconnectable Objects*) [5, 1] conceived to specify and support non-functional contracts, associated to the architectural description of an application. The approach helps to achieve separation of concerns [10] facilitating the reuse of components that implement the functional computation in other application systems, and allows the non-functional requirements to be handled separately during the system design process. The framework includes a contract description language, which allows the definition of a specialized view of a given software architecture. The supporting infrastructure required to impose the contracts during running time follows an architectural pattern that can be implemented by a standard set of components included in a middleware. The results of our investigation point out that the code generation of these components can be automated, unless of some explicit parts of code related to specific contract and resources classes.

In the rest of this paper, we initially describe the key elements of the framework including the architecture description language with support to contracts. Next, we present the supporting infrastructure and demonstrate the validity of the framework through an example. Complementing the article we present some related proposals and provide some conclusions.

2   Basic Framework

The CR-RIO framework integrates the software architecture paradigm, which is centered in an architecture description language (ADL), with concepts such as reflection and dynamic adaptation capability [10], which are generally provided in an isolated fashion in middleware proposals described in the literature. This integration facilitates the achievement of separation of concerns, software component reuse and dynamic adaptation capability of applications. CR-RIO includes the following elements (see Figure 1):

a) CBabel, an ADL used to describe the functional components of the application and the interconnection topology of those components. CBabel also caters for the description of non-functional aspects, such as coordination, distribution and different types of QoS requirements. A CBabel specification corresponds to a meta-description of an application that is available in a repository and is used to deploy the architecture in a given operating environment; these descriptions can be submitted to formal verification procedures [3].

b) An architecture-oriented component model, that allows programming the software configuration of the application; (i) Modules (or components), which encapsulate the application's functional aspects; (ii) Connectors, used in the architecture level to define relationships between modules; in the operation level connectors mediate the interaction between modules; and (iii) Ports, which identify access points through which modules and connectors provide or require services. This component model can be mapped to available implementation technologies; in our experiments components were mapped to Java and CORBA objects.

c) A simple software design methodology that stimulates the designer to follow a simple meta-level programming discipline, where functional aspects are concentrated in modules (base level) and non-functional aspects are encapsulated in connectors (meta-level). It is worth to point out that some QoS requirements can be directly mapped into connectors, which are equivalent to meta-level components, and can be configured in an applications architecture.

d) The Configurator, a reflective element that provides services to instantiate, execute and manage applications with distributed configurations. The Configurator provides two APIs: configuration and architectural reflection, through which these services are used, and a persistent architecture description repository, where the two APIs reflect their operations. A specialized module can consult the architecture's description repository and decide to make adaptations, for instance, in face of changes in the QoS support level.

To specify non-functional aspects CBabel employs the concept of architectural contract. In our approach, an architectural contract is a description where two parts express their non-functional requirements, through services and parameters, negotiation rules and adaptation policies for different contexts. The CR-RIO framework provides the required infrastructure to impose and manage the contracts during running time. Regarding QoS aspects we propose an architectural pattern that simplifies the design and coding of the components of the supporting infrastructure, consistently establishing the relationship between the Configurator and the QoS contract supporting entities.

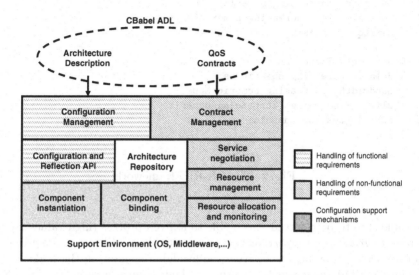

Fig. 1. The CR-RIO framework

3   The QoS Contract Language

In our proposal a functional service of an application is considered a specialized activity, defined by a set of architectural components and theirs interconnection topologies; with requirements that generally do not admit negotiation [2]. Non-functional services are defined by restrictions to specific non-functional activities of an application, and can admit some negotiation including the used resources. A contract regulating non-function aspects can describe, at design time, the use of shared resources the application will make and acceptable variations regarding the availability of these resources. The contract will be imposed at run-time by an infrastructure composed by a set of components that implement the semantics of the contract. Our proposal incorporates concepts from the QML (QoS Markup Language) [7], which were reformulated for the context of software architecture descriptions [5]. A QoS contract includes the following elements:

a) QoS Categories are related to specific non-functional aspects and described separately from the functional components. For example, if processing and communication performance characteristics are critical to an application, associated QoS categories, *Processing* and *Transport*, could be described as in Figure 2.

The *Processing* category (lines 1-7) represents processor and memory resources where the *cpuUse* property is the used percentage of the total CPU time (low values are preferred - *decreasing*), the *cpuSlice* property represents

```
01   QoScategory Processing {
02      cpuUse: decreasing numeric %;
03      cpuSlice: increasing numeric %;
04      priority: increasing numeric;
05      memAvaliable: increasing numeric Mbytes;
06      memReq: increasing numeric Mbytes;
07   }
08   QoScategory Transport {
09      delay: decreasing numeric ms;
10      bandwidth: increasing numeric Mbps;
11      slidingWindowSize: increasing numeric;
12      MSS: increasing numeric;
13   }
```

Fig. 2. The CR-RIO framework

the time slice to be reserved / available to a given process (high values are pre-ferred - *increasing*), *priority* represents a priority for its utilization, *memAvaliable* and *memReq* represent, respectively the available memory in the node and the memory (to be) requested for a process. The *Transport* category (lines 8-13) represents the information associated to transport resources used by clients and servers. The *bandwidth* property represents the available/required bandwidth for network connections and the *delay* property represents the transmission delay of one bit between two peer components. The use of those categories, and of the other elements of the language to be described next, is presented in Section 4.

b) A QoS profile quantifies the properties of a QoS Category. This quantifica-tion restricts each property according to its description, working as an instance of acceptable values for a given QoS Category. A component, or a part of an architecture, can define QoS profiles in order to constrain its operational context.

c) A set of services can be defined in a contract. In a service, QoS constraints that have to be applied in the architectural level are described, and can be asso-ciated to either (i) the applications components or (ii) the interaction mechanism used by these components. In that way, a service is differentiated from others by the desired / tolerated QoS levels required by the application, in a given operational context. A QoS constraint can be defined by associating a specific value of a property to an architecture declaration or associating a QoS profile to that declaration.

d) A negotiation clause describes a negotiation policy and acceptable opera-tional contexts for the services described in a contract. As a default policy, the clause establishes a preferred order for the utilization of the services. Initially the preferable service is used. According to the described in the clause, when a preferable service cannot be maintained anymore, the QoS supporting infras-tructure tries to deploy a service less preferable, following the described order. The supporting infrastructure can deploy a more preferable service again if the necessary resources are again available.

3.1 Support Architecture

CR-RIO supporting middleware follows an architectural pattern composed by a set of components, namely: one Global Contract Manager (GCM), and Local Contract Managers (LCMs), Contractors and QoS Agents (see Figure 9). The conceptual basis for this pattern is described in [5]; a more pragmatic view is presented in [1]. Here we present a brief description of CR-RIO middleware components. This middleware uses CBabel described architectures and QoS contracts, which are available as meta-level information, to instantiate an application and to manage its associated contract.

The GCM represents the main authority; it can fully interpret and manage contract descriptions and knows their service negotiation state machine. When a negotiation is initiated the GCM identifies which service will be negotiated first and sends the related configuration descriptions, to each participating node, and the associated QoS profiles to the LCM. Each LCM is responsible for interpreting the local configuration and activating a *Contractor* to perform actions such as resource reservation and method requests monitoring.

If the GCM receives a positive confirmation from all LCM involved, the service being negotiated can be attended and the application can be instantiated with the required quality. If not, a new negotiation is attempted in order to deploy the next possible service. If all services in the negotiation clause are tried with no success, an *out-of-service* state is reached and a contract violation message is issued to the application level. The GCM can also initiate a new negotiation when it receives a notification informing that a preferred service became available again.

For each particular contract, a specific Contractor instance is created. It has several responsibilities: (a) to translate the properties defined by the QoS profiles into services of the support system and convey the request of those services (with adequate parameters) to the QoS Agents; (b) when required, to map each defined interaction scheme (*link*) into a connector able to match the required QoS for the actual interaction, and (c) to receive *out-of-spec notifications* from the QoS Agents. The information contained in a notification is compared against the profile and, in some cases, the Contractor can try to make (local) adjustments to the resource that provides the service. For instance, the priority of a streamer could be raised in order to maintain a given frame generation rate. In a case where this is not possible an *out-of-profile* notification is sent to the LCM.

QoS Agents encapsulate the access to system level mechanisms, providing adequate interfaces to perform resource requests, initialize local system services and monitor the actual values of the required properties. According to the thresholds to be monitored, registered by the Contractor, a QoS Agent can issue an *out-of-spec* notification indicating that a resource is not available or does not meet the specification defined in the profile.

4   Example

During our research we developed some prototype examples to evaluate and refine the framework. A virtual terminal in a mobile machine was used to evaluate security and communication aspects in the context of a mobile network [6]. In [1] we presented a video on demand application, an application with fault tolerance requirements, and the application with timing requirements, which will be detailed in the next subsections.

4.1   Data Acquisition-Processing Application

Let us consider a data acquisition system, which periodically receives data and image coming in batches from one or more sensors. The received image and data have to be processed and filtered before being stored in a data base. This basic architecture can be used in different application contexts and run on different support environments. For example, a simple application, with a single data source, can run on a single processor, provided that enough processing power is available to execute the required pre-processing activities within the required time interval for data acquisition. A complex application, where data comes from many geographically-distributed sensors, as well as where more complex and time consuming processing and filtering activities are performed, will require more processing power in order to meet the timing restrictions. Yet, a more complex application could have its processing requirements changing considerably along its running time; e.g., because an increase in the amount of input data triggered by the occurrence of an external event.

In such changing scenario, it is desirable to provide concepts and mechanisms to allow the basic architecture to be gracefully adapted in order to cater for the requirements of each different application context. For example, for the simple application a CPU reservation scheme would be enough to guarantee the processing power required for the application. For the complex application, assuming that it is parallelizable, a solution would be to distribute the execution, for example using a master-worker architecture. Such parallel architecture could be deployed on a grid of processors provided that some operational requirements are met in order to not hinder the application's performance; e. g., the allocated nodes should have enough resources and their message transport time to the master should be lower than a given limit. Moreover, considering that the processing requirements can increase or decrease along the application running time, the number of parallel workers can be dynamically configured. Thus, when the processing demand increases, the number of parallel workers could be increased in order to reduce each one individual computation time, aiming to achieve an overall speed-up. Accordingly, the number of workers can be reduced in order to free system resources when the processing demands decreases.

We highlight that components of our architectural contract support framework can encapsulate the access to different available resource management services, in order to obtain the information required to enforce the architectural adaptations. In a related work we used the contract approach to express and implement contracts related to multimedia distributed applications based on services provided by the OpenH323 framework [12]. For the architectural contracts presented in this paper we consider parameters such as CPU reservation / monitoring, CPU availability, network bandwidth, and resource discovery that can be provided by available platforms such as the WNS framework [14].

In the example presented in this section we demonstrate how our approach using software architecture and contract concepts can be used to: (a) describe the applications components and respective topology configuration; (b) describe the policies on resource usage required to comply with the processing constraints imposed by the application and (c) effectively deploy the application with the support of middleware components included in the framework.

4.2 Basic Configuration

The basic configuration of the application is depicted in Figure 3. A client module collects the data from the sensors and sends them to the server for pre-processing. As soon as the pre-processing procedure is finished the server signals the client, which then can send a new data sample to be processed. The interaction between the client and the server (or servers) modules is explicitly mediated by a connector that will help to implement the application contract.

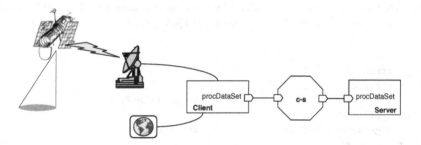

Fig. 3. Data Acquisition-Processing Application

Figure 4 presents the CBabel description of the applications architecture, composed by a client (*client* - line 3), a server (*server* - line 4), and their connection topology; interaction is performed through the clients *procDataSet* out port and the servers *procDataSet* in port (line 6). Note that this interconnection could be statically defined using a specific connector to mediate the client-server interaction, encapsulating the required communication or interaction mechanism. However, as the non-functional requirements include communication, processing and replication aspects, the use of connectors in the architecture will be defined separately in a contract or automatically selected by the contract support middleware.

In an initial context we assume that the *client* and *server* components are deployed in the same node, and that the client execution requirements are easily

```
01  module Client_Server {
02    port procDataSet;
03    module Client {out port procDataSet;} client;
04    module Server {in  port procDataSet;} server;
05    instantiate client, server;
06    link client.procDataSet to server.procDataSet;
07  } capture_images;
08  start capture_images;
```

Fig. 4. CBabel description of the applications architecture

met. In this case, to attend the applications requirements, processing and storage resources have just to be reserved for the *server* module. The QoS contract regarding such requirement is described in Figure 5. The *prioProc* service (lines 14-16) states that the instantiation of the *server* module at the *host1* node is associated to the *ProcMem* processing QoS profile (lines 19-22). In that case, the *server* module instantiation is conditioned to the availability of enough storage capability (at least 200 Mbytes) and of a processing slice of at least 0.25 (25

The Contractor is responsible for translating the requirements regarding the storage and processing resources described in the contract (in this case, `Processing.cpuSlice >= 0.25; Processing.memReq >= 200;`), into parameters that can be passed to the *Processing* QoS Agent.

```
13  contract {
14    service {
15      instantiate server at host1 with profile ProcMem;
16    } prioProc;
17    negotiation {prioProc -> out-of-service;};
18  } oneServer;
19  profile {
20    Processing.cpuSlice >= 0.25;
21    Processing.memReq >= 200;
22  } ProcMem;
```

Fig. 5. *oneServer* contract description

In this first context, the requirements are static and if the *Global Contract Manager* receives a service violation notification, an out-of-service state is reached and no other service is attempted according the associated QoS contract (line 17). Thus, the application cannot execute given the lack of resources.

4.3   Second Configuration - Distributed Parallel Workers

In a second context the servers are replicated though a master-worker architecture in order to distribute the processing load, based on a slightly modified *Master-Slave* design pattern [4]. To this end a *Replication* QoS category (Figure 6) is introduced. When this category is used, a special connector is selected to provide the services related to group communication and maintenance, according to the value of the *groupComm* property (line 20). The *numberOfReplicas* and *maxReplicas* properties (lines 17-18) describe respectively the number of replicas to be deployed and the maximum number of replicas allowed. This last property can be used with *replicaMaint* (line 19) in the case of a contract that will handle dynamically creation of replicas. The *distribPolicy* property (line 21) indicates a policy to be adopted for the distribution of replicas (in this case, driven by the best memory, CPU or transport operating status, or an optimization of these parameters).

```
16   QoScategory Replication {
17     numberOfReplicas: increasing numeric;
18     maxReplicas: numeric;
19     replicaMaint: enum (add, remove, maintain);
20     groupComm: enum (p2p, multicast, broadcast);
21     distribPolicy: enum (bestMem, bestCpu, bestTransp, optim);
22   }
```

Fig. 6. *Replication* QoS category

Again, the preprocessing performed in each server should be concluded before a new data-set is produced by the client. Here, the communication system transport time becomes a relevant performance parameter. As the data-set has to be sampled at a given rate, the deadline within which the server task has to be performed is known beforehand. So, in a distributed environment, where the communication with the server adds to the total preprocessing execution time, the overall deadline should include this parameter. Thus, in order to express this fact, we consider in the contract a message transport time parameter (line 29, fig.7); the latter aggregated with the previous processor reservation parameter will provide a trustful means to impose the application timing requirement at run time. The corresponding contract is represented in Figure 7.

According to the *repProc* contract each replica will only be instantiated if the *ProcMem* and *Preplic* profiles properties are satisfied. The number of replicas and the distribution policy described in the *Preplic* profile (lines 24-27) are controlled by the GCM. A number of five replicas were selected (line 25) and the distribution policy will try to optimize resources (line 26). Additionally, it can be observed that replicating the *server* module in different processing nodes implies in creating instances of this module. This task is also initiated by the

```
13  contract {
14    service {
15      instantiate server with profile ProcMem, Preplic;
16      link client to server with profile Pcom;
17    } repProc;
18    negotiation {repProc -> out-of-service;};
19  } repServer;
20  profile {
21    Processing.cpuSlice >= 0.25;
22    Processing.memReq >= 200;
23  } ProcMem;
24  profile {
25    Replication.numOfReplicas = 5;
26    Replication.distribPolicy = optim;
27  } Preplic;
28  profile {
29    Transport.delay < 5;
30    Replication.groupComm = multicast;
31  } Pcom;
```

Fig. 7. QoS contract for the replication configuration

GCM as soon as it establishes the service, delegating the actual configuration of the instances to the *Configurator*. In this case, the GCM forwards a list of nodes were the replicated modules have to be created and the *Configurator* executes an instantiation batch such as:

```
instantiate Server as repl1 at node1;
link client.procDataSet to repl1.procDataSet by groupCon;
instantiate Server as repl2 at node2;
link client.procDataSet to repl2.procDataSet by groupCon;
...
```

The execution of this batch connects the *client* module to each replica of the *server* (*repl1*, *repl2*,) by a connector composition (*groupCon*) that provides the group communication mechanisms (multicast, in this case - line 30). The *Configurator* dynamically manages the naming of the replicas and makes this information consistent for the GCM. For all the established client-replica interconnection this connector is used to provide the client-server interaction style and the group communication. This configuration is robust but still static. If any of the processing or transport properties of any replica is out of specification the respective LCM is notified by the QoS Agent, which forwards this notification to the GCM. As no other service is provided in the contract, the application is terminated.

4.4   Third Configuration - Dynamic Processing Requirements

Finally, in a third context, it is assumed that the processing requirements change dynamically, either increasing or decreasing. Thus, we add to the contract specification three new profiles (maintReplica, addReplica, removeReplica) which indirectly capture this behavior, allowing to optimize the number of processors processing the application, and also cater for the processing time deadline. These profiles include upper and lower bounds to the execution time, which are used to control the number of worker replicas. The final contract is presented in Figure 8.

In the *dynRepServer* contract three services are described. The *Smaint* service (lines 14-17) is the preferred one, where the execution time meets the application requirements and no replicas need to be created (profile *maintReplica* - lines 38-41). If the execution time (execution_time property was added to the *Processing* category) is greater than the upper bound, the *Smaint* service is discontinued and the *Sadd* service (lines 18-21) is tried. In this case, the *addReplica* profile is imposed and one or more replicas are created (line 43), but the number of replicas is limited by the *Pmax* profile Replication.maxReplica = 10 property. If this limit is reached no more replicas can be created and the service cannot be provided. On the other way, if the execution time gets bellow the lower bound, the *Sremove* service (lines 22-24) is deployed in order to release resources, removing one or more replicas. The calculation of the actual number of replicas to be added or removed can be performed by the GCM using some heuristic based on the information regarded to resource availability collected from the LCMs.

According to the negotiation clause, where the switching modes for the services are described, when the *Sadd* or *Sremove* services are effective they are renegotiated while the measured execution time is out of the required range (i.e, < 500 or > 600). When this value fits again in the preferred range, the establishment of the *Smaint* service is again negotiated. Similarly, if any property of the involved profiles is invalidated during operation, a new negotiation can be initiated. In the worst case, when the *Sadd* (or Smaint) service is selected, and no configuration of replicas can fulfill the contract profiles, an *out-of-service* state is reached and the application is terminated. In the next section we discuss how the described configurations could be deployed using our framework.

4.5   Implementation Details

Each participant node (Figure 9) has instances of the *LCM*, of the specific *Contractor* for the application and of the *QoS Agents* associated to the resources to be controlled in each specific platform. The *groupCon* connector only takes part of the configuration when the replication services are deployed. As the first step, the GCM retrieves the applications contract (for the explanation, we consider the third configuration only) and creates instances of the LCM in the nodes where the application components are to be instantiated. Next, it selects the

```
13  contract {
14    service {
15      instantiate server with profile maintReplica, ProcMem;
16      link client to server with profile Pcom;
17    } Smaint; // basically the same service as repProc
18    service {
19      instantiate server with profile addReplica, ProcMem, Pmax;
20      link client to server with profile Pcom;
21    } Sadd;
22    service {
23      remove server with profile removeReplica;
24    } Sremove;
25
26    negotiation {
27      Smaint -> ((Sremove -> Sremove) || (Sadd -> Sadd));
28      Sremove -> Smaint;
29      Sadd -> Smaint;
30      Sadd -> out-of-service;
31      Smaint -> out-of-service;
32    };
33  } dynRepServer;
34
35  profile {
36      Replication.maxReplica = 10;
37  } Pmax;
38  profile {
39    Replication.Maint = maint;
40    Processing.execution_time >= 500 ms <= 600 ms;
41  } maintReplica;
42  profile {
43    Replication.Maint = add;
44    Processing.execution_time > 600 ms;
45  } addReplica;
46  profile {
47    Replication.Maint = remove;
48    Processing.execution_time < 500 ms;
49  } removeReplica;
```

Fig. 8. QoS contract for the dynamic replication configuration

preferred service (*Smaint*) to be used and initializes a negotiation activity, sending to the LCMs the information related to this service, including the associated QoS profiles (*ProcMem*, *Pcom* and *maintReplica*). Each LCM instantiates (a) the QoS Agents that provide the interfaces (management and event generation) to the resources used by the service, and (b) the application specific Contractor, that will interpret the service information and will interact with the QoS Agents to impose the desired properties.

In the server node, the LCM identifies the processing resources that have to be managed (`instantiate` that creates an instance of the *server* - QoS contract, line 15). Also, based on the `link` primitive that interconnects the *client* module to the *server* module (QoS contract, line 16), the LCM in the clients node identifies the need of a group communication connector and makes the necessary arrangements to manage the transport resources. When the LCM instantiates a Contractor it also sends to it the profiles that have to be attended. In the sequence, the Contractor interacts with the QoS Agents to request resources and to receive relevant events regarding the status of the resources. In this example, the *Processing* QoS Agent associated to a server node is responsible for reserving and monitoring the CPU time slice (*cpuSlice*) and memory (*memReq*) for the server module. Also, observe that in addition to monitor the communication *delay* the client-server communication channel could optionally use some kind of resource reservation (e.g., the RSVP protocol) put in effect through the *Transport* QoS Agent. After the initial phase, if the required QoS profiles were imposed, a Contractor notifies the success to its associated LCM that, by its turn, forwards a corresponding notification to the GCM. If all involved LCMs did return a positive confirmation, the GCM concludes that the negotiation was successful and that the *Smaint* service can be established.

In steady state, if a significant change in the monitored values is detected, the QoS Agents notifies the registered Contractors. If the reported values do not violate the active QoS profiles, nothing has to be done. If there is a violation, the Contractor can try to locally readapt the resource in order to keep the service; for instance, passing new parameters to the QoS Agent. If it is not possible to readapt, the Contractor sends an *out-of-profile* notification to the LCM and, in the sequence, another service can be negotiated.

To exemplify an operation, lets suppose that while the *Smaint* service is operational the *Processing* QoS Agent in the client node observes that the measured `execution_time` value rises beyond the upper bound defined by the *maintReplica* profile (> 600). The *Processing* QoS Agent notifies the Contractor triggering a new negotiation. The servers Contractor verifies that a property is out of the *ProcMem* profile specification and sends the respective LCM an *out-of-profile* notification. This information is then propagated to the GCM, along with an *out-of-service* notification. Then the GCM selects the *Sadd* service and starts the actions required to create a new replica.

The described infrastructure can be adapted to different support environments, currently we are working in a prototype using the WNS framework [14]. Many optimizations are also feasible. For instance, when a Contractor sends an *out-of-profile* notification this could be followed by the set of QoS profiles that could be attended at that moment. Receiving this composed information the GCM could select the next service to be negotiated, immediately discarding the services with associated profiles out of the set. Another point of interest is having resource re-adaptation locally managed by a Contractor, using the interface provided by the QoS Agents. This would be suitable for resources that have embedded re-adaptation policies and mechanisms. For example, considering the

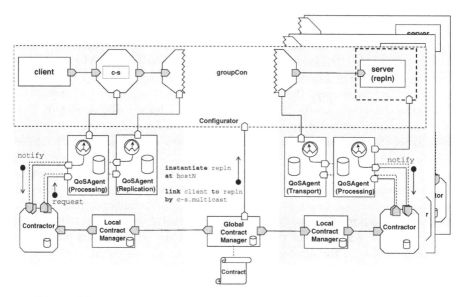

Fig. 9. Mapping the application contract in the architectural pattern

Processing.cpuSlice property, the Contractor could try to raise the priority of the local server process to maintain this property within the profile specification. We are investigating how to specify this kind of concern at the contract level.

5 Related Works and Conclusions

The reflective middleware approach [9] allows for the provided services to be configured to meet the non-functional properties of the applications. However, the approach does not provide clear abstractions and mechanisms to help the use of such requirements in the design of the architectural level of an application. This leads to the middleware services to be used in an ad-hoc fashion, usually through pieces of code intertwined to the applications program. The proposal described in [8] includes basic mechanisms to collect status information associated to non-functional services. It also suggests an approach to manage non-functional requirements in the architectural level, in a way quite similar to ours. CR-RIO complements this proposal providing an explicit methodology based on contracts and proposing extra mechanisms to deploy and manage these contracts. More detailed comparisons are available in [1].

Our approach helps to achieve separation of concerns and component reuse by allowing non-functional aspects of an application to be specified separately using high-level contracts expressed in an extended ADL. Part of the codification, related to a non-functional requirement, can be encapsulated in connectors, which can be (re)configured during running time in order to cater for the impositions defined by the associated contract. The infrastructure required to enforce a contract follows an architectural pattern that is implemented by a standard set of components. We think that making these structures explicit and available to designers, the task of mapping architecture-level defined contracts to implementations can be simplified. The approach has been evaluated through case studies that showed that the code of the supporting components can be automatically generated, excepting some localized pieces related to specificities of the particular QoS requirement under consideration. However, we should notice that the treatment of low-level details always has to be considered in any QoS aware application. Our approach can help to identify the intervening hot spots and make the required adaptations more rapidly.

In our proposal, the composition of contracts can be specified combining in a unique clause the negotiation clauses of the involved contracts [6]. Contracts regarding different non-functional aspects can be orthogonal and cause no interference with each other. Contract conflicts can be handled applying a suitable decision policy; already assigned resources could then be retaken in order to satisfy the preferred contracts. We are also investigating the specification of individual contracts for clients and servers [13]. Besides providing the flexibility to support more dynamic architectures, this would allow to manage contract composition conflicts through lower granularity interventions.

Acknowledgments Sidney Ansaloni and Romulo Curty, M.Sc. students, provided the examples and valuable insights that helped us to present this text. Orlando Loques and Alexandre Sztajnberg are partially supported by CNPq (grants PDPG-TI 552137/2002 e 552192/2002, respectively). Alexandre Sztajnberg is also partially supported by Faperj (grant E-26/171.430/2002).

References

1. Ansaloni, S., An Architectural Pattern to Describe and Implement Qos Contracts, Masters Dissertation, Instituto de Computao, UFF, May, 2003.
2. Beugnard, A., Jzquel, J.-M., Plouzeau, N., Watkins, D., Making Components Contract Aware, IEEE Computer, 32(7), July, 1999.
3. Braga, C. e Sztajnberg, A., Towards a Rewriting Semantics to a Software Architecture Description Language, 6th Workshop on Formal Methods, Campina Grande, Brasil, October, 2003.
4. Buschman, F., et alli, Pattern-Oriented Software Architecture - a System of Patterns (POSA1), John Willey and sons, Chichester, ISBN 0-471-95869-7, UK, 1996.
5. Curty, R., "A Methodology to Describe and Implement Contracts for Services with Differentiated Quality in Distributed Architectures ", Masters Dissertation, Instituto de Computao, UFF, 2002.
6. Curty, R., Ansaloni, S., Loques, O.G. e Sztajnberg, A., Deploying Non-Functional Aspects by Contract, 2nd Workshop on Reflective and Adaptive Middleware, Middleware2003 Companion, pp.90-94, Rio de Janeiro, Brasil, June, 2003.
7. Frolund, S. e Koistinen, J., "Quality-of-Service Specifications in Distributed Object Systems", Distributed Systems Engineering, IEE, No. 5, pp. 179-202, UK, 1998.
8. Garlan, D., Schmerl, B. R. and Chang, J., Using Gauges for Architecture-Based Monitoring and Adaptation, Working Conference on Complex and Dynamic Systems Architecture, December, 2001.

9. Kon, F. et alli, The Case for Adaptive Middleware, Communications of the ACM, pp. 33-38, Vol. 45, No. 6, June, 2002.

10. Loques, O., Sztajnberg, A., Leite, J., Lobosco, M., On the Integration of Configuration and Meta-Level Programming Approaches, in Reflection and Software Engineering V. 1826, LNCS, pp. 191-210, Springer-Verlag, Heidelberg, Germany, June, 2000.

11. Loyall, J. P., Rubel, P., Atighetchi, M., Schantz, R., Zinky, J. Emerging Patterns in Adaptive, Distributed Real-Time, Embedded Middleware, 9th Conference on Pattern Language of Programs, Monticello, Il., September, 2002.

12. Open H323, Quicknet Technologies, http://www.OpenH323.org, 2004.

13. Sztajnberg, A. and Loques, O., Bringing QoS to the Architectural Level, ECOOP 2000 Workshop on QoS on Distributed Object Systems, Cannes France, June, 2000.

14. Wolski, R., Spring, Neil T. and Hayes, J., The Network Weather Service: A Distributed Resource Performance Forecasting Service for Metacomputing, Future Generation Computer Systems", vol. 15, No. 5-6, pp. 757-768, 1999.

Deploying CORBA Components on a Computational Grid: General Principles and Early Experiments Using the Globus Toolkit

Sébastien Lacour, Christian Pérez, and Thierry Priol

IRISA / INRIA
Campus de Beaulieu
35042 Rennes, France
{Sebastien.Lacour, Christian.Perez, Thierry.Priol}@irisa.fr

Abstract. The deployment of high bandwidth wide-area networks has led computational grids to offer a very powerful computing resource. In particular, this inherently distributed resource is well-suited for multi-physics applications. To face the complexity of such applications, the software component technology appears to be a very adequate programming model. However, to take advantage of the computational power of grids, component-based applications should be *automatically deployed* in computational grids. Based on the CORBA component specifications for the deployment of components, which seem to currently be the most complete, this paper proposes a detailed process for component deployment in computational grids. It also reports on early experiments on deploying CORBA components in a computational grid using the Globus Toolkit 2.4.

1 Introduction

Networks have been growing very quickly for several years in terms of bandwidth, as stated by Gilder's law claiming that network bandwidth increases much faster than processors' power. The bandwidth of the currently deployed wide-area networks has reached a level allowing several distributed computing resources to be used together within a grid to handle complex applications in various domains such as scientific computing. In particular, grid infrastructures are very valuable for the execution of new scientific applications which require a huge amount of computing power or physical resources which do not exist in a single physical location. Multiphysics applications, combining several simulation codes, are examples of such new demanding applications. They aim to simulate complex phenomena which require the simulation of various physics: computational fluid dynamics and structural analysis can be combined to improve the design of aircrafts; simulating the behavior of the ocean jointly with the atmosphere can provide more accurate weather forecast. They are just a few examples of a growing number of coupled applications. Usually such applications are programmed with tools designed for parallel computing (like MPI). Several *ad-hoc*

W. Emmerich and A.L. Wolf (Eds.): CD 2004, LNCS 3083, pp. 35–49, 2004.

code couplers have been developed to couple simulation codes together and to run them on either parallel machines or grid infrastructures. However such an approach lacks genericity and requires each simulation code to be adapted to a specific code coupler. Modularity and encapsulation are provided at their lowest level, making the re-usability of codes very limited. Programming models allowing assembly and re-usability of pieces of software have been investigated for some time. However, few attempts have been made to apply such models to scientific computing either due to the lack of efficiency of these models or the quasi absence of appropriate software environments (including deployment) on high-performance computers. It is even more acute in grid infrastructures.

State of the art work in programming models suggests that programming models based on the software component model [1] provide many benefits. For instance, the component model emphasizes the development of an application by assembling (composing) existing pieces of software. Hence, not only is the development time reduced, but code can be reused and the resulting application presents more modularity. Several component models are available like Enterprise Java Beans (EJB) by SUN [2], Web Services [3], the CORBA Component Model (CCM) [4] or the Common Component Architecture (CCA) [5]. In particular, these models differ with respect to deployment. Web Services as well as CCA do not specify how components should be deployed, while EJB and CCM do. The CCM deployment model supersedes the model proposed by EJB because CCM allows for the deployment of a set of interconnected components on a set of distributed machines. Thus, we choose to work with CCM as it presents the most complete deployment model. In previous work, we have shown that high performance communication is possible using CORBA [6] and that high performance computing can be brought to CORBA by extending its specification with the concept of parallel component [7]. The results obtained from this research show clearly there is no obstacle in using CORBA for high-performance computing.

As already mentioned, computational grids can yield a potentially huge computational power, federating resources spread all over the world [8]. However, access to this computational power has a price. A computational grid can consist of very heterogeneous resources, such as compute nodes with different architectures and operating systems, networks with various performance characteristics, storage resources of different sizes, *etc.* Reliable measures must be taken to enforce security, involving authentication, authorization, data encryption for confidentiality, *etc.* Thus, a middleware is necessary to solve those issues so that users can actually, easily access computational grids. The Globus Toolkit [9, 10] is such a wide-spread and well-established middleware, as exemplified by TeraGrid [11].

The remaining issue is to deploy components in a grid environment. Our objective is to be able to *automatically* deploy CORBA components in a computational grid, thus marrying the advantages of both worlds: distributed computing provides the ease of programming using CORBA components while grid computing provides the tools to effectively, securely deploy applications in computational grids. The *actual* deployment of components is essential for the success of the component programming model, and it must be as *automatic* as possible for the wide acceptance of the model. Automatic deployment means that the client should not have to worry about the compute nodes which will execute the component-based application. Ideally, the client should not have to be a computer scientist, but a physicist, a chemist, a biologist, *etc.* Thus the deployment phase should be very simple and merely require a pointer to a computational grid which the client has access to plus a packaged component-based application.

This paper presents how we envision the deployment process of CORBA components on a computational grid managed by the Globus Toolkit and mentions a number of issues encountered at deployment time. Section 2 introduces the CORBA component model. The Globus Toolkit is presented in Section 3. Section 4 deals with the deployment of CORBA components in a grid: it shows how both software components from the world of distributed computing and grid access middleware from the world of grid computing can be used in combination. The early experiments we carried out are detailed in Section 5. Before concluding, some related works are presented in Section 6.

2   Overview of the CORBA Component Model

The CORBA Component Model [4] (CCM) is part of the latest CORBA [12] specifications (version 3). The CCM specifications allow the deployment of components into a distributed environment, that is to say that an application can deploy interconnected components on different heterogeneous servers in one operation. Figure 1 presents the general picture of CCM. The component life-cycle is divided into two parts. First, the creation of the component requires to define the component interface, to implement it and then to package it so as to obtain a component package, *i.e.* a component. The second part consists in (optionally) linking together several components into a component assembly and in deploying it. CCM provides a model for all theses phases. For example, the CCM abstract model deals with the external view of a component, while the Component Implementation Framework (CIF) provides a model to implement a component. There are also models for packaging and deploying a component, as well as for the runtime environment of a component. In this section, we briefly introduce the abstract model, the execution model and the deployment model.

2.1   Ccm Abstract Model

A CORBA component is represented by a set of ports described in the Interface Definition Language (IDL) of CORBA 3 defined by the OMG. The IDL of CORBA 3 is an extension of the IDL of CORBA version 2 by the OMG. There are five kinds of ports as shown in Figure 2. *Facets* are named connection points that provide services available as interfaces while *receptacles* are named connection points to be connected to a facet. They describe the component's ability to use a reference supplied by some external agent. *Event sources* are named connection points that emit typed events to one or more interested event consumers, or to an event channel. *Event sinks* are named connection points into which events of a specified

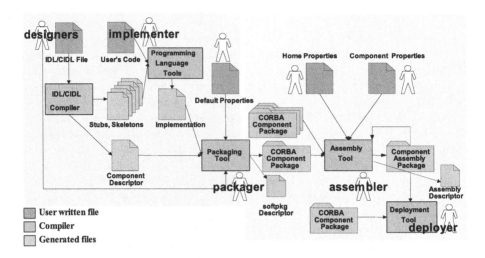

Fig. 1. Overview of the CORBA Component Model

type may be pushed. *Attributes* are named values exposed through accessor (read) and mutator (write) operations. Attributes are primarily intended to be used for component configuration, although they may be used in a variety of other ways. Figure 3 shows an example of component definition using IDL3.

Facets and receptacles allow a synchronous communication model based on the remote method invocation paradigm. An asynchronous communication model based on data transfer is implemented by the event sources and sinks.

A component is managed by an entity named *home*. A home provides factory and finder operations to create and/or find a component instance. For example, a home exposes a `create` operation which locally creates a component instance.

2.2   Ccm Execution Model

CCM uses a programming model based on containers. Containers provide the run-time environment for CORBA components. A container is a framework for integrating transactions, security, events, and persistence into a component's behavior at runtime. Containers provide a standard set of services to a component, enabling the same component to be hosted by different container implementations. All component instances are created and managed at runtime by its container.

2.3   Ccm Deployment Model

The deployment model of CCM is fully dynamic: a component can be dynamically connected to and disconnected from another component. For example,

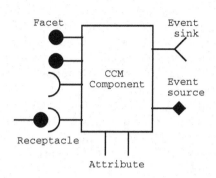

```
// Interface Average definition
typedef sequence<double> Vector;
interface Average {
  double compute(in Vector v);
};
// Component A definition
component aComponent {
  attribute string   name;
  provides   Average avgPort;
  uses       Display dspPort;
};
```

Fig. 2. A CCM component

Fig. 3. A component IDL definition

```
aComponent ref = ServerComp->provide_avgPort();
ClientComp->connect_avgClientPort(ref);
```

Fig. 4. Example of code to connect two components

Figure 4 illustrates how a component **ServerComp** can be connected to a component **ClientComp** through the facet **FacetExample**: a reference is obtained from the facet and then it is given to a receptacle. Moreover, the model supports the deployment of a static application. In this case, the assembly phase has produced a description of the initial state of the application. Thus, a deployment tool can deploy the components of the application according to the description. It is worthwhile to remark that it is just the initial state of the application: the application can change it by modifying its connections and/or by adding/removing components.

The deployment model relies on the functionality of some fabrics to create component servers which are hosting environments of component instances. The issues of determining the machines where to create the component servers and how to actually create them are *out of the scope* of the CCM specifications.

3   The Globus Toolkit: a Grid Access Middleware

The Globus Toolkit [9, 10] is an open source software toolkit used for building grids. ("Globus Toolkit" is a trademark of the University of Chicago.) It includes software for security enforcement, resource, information, and data management, portability. This middleware is wide-spread and well-established, as exemplified by many projects relying on the Globus Toolkit, such as GriPhyN (the Grid Physics Network, [13]), the American DOE Science Grid [14], the European DataGrid project [15], TeraGrid [11]: see [16] for a list of software installed on TeraGrid machines, the *Common TeraGrid Software Stack* (CTSS), including the Globus Toolkit.

The Globus Toolkit uses the Grid Security Infrastructure (GSI, [17]) for enabling secure *authentication* and *communication* over the grid network. GSI is based on public key encryption (X.509 certificates) and the Secure Sockets Layer (SSL) communication protocol. Globus users can initialize proxies, which are certificates signed by the user: proxies provide a convenient alternative to constantly entering passwords when submitting many jobs.

The resource management module of the Globus Toolkit relies on GRAM (Globus Resource Allocation Manager) and GASS (Global Access to Secondary Storage). GRAM [18] supports remote job submission and control using GSI for mutual authentication of both users and remote resources: GRAM's authorization mechanism is based on GSI identities and a mechanism to map GSI identities to local user accounts (see the `grid-mapfile` configuration file of the Globus Toolkit). GRAM understands the RSL (Resource Specification Language, [19]) which provides an interchange language to describe grid resource requirements and to submit a job. GASS [20] provides basic access to remote files, allowing file staging before and after the execution of a job on a grid node.

The Grid Information Service (GIS) of the Globus Toolkit is implemented in MDS (Monitoring and Discovery Service, [21]). It includes robust authentication mechanisms using GSI. MDS allows for flexible, hierarchical, distributed (scalable), extensible information storage; it is based on an LDAP directory. MDS also supports dynamic sources of information, such as the Network Weather Service (NWS, [22, 23]).

Finally, the data management module of the Globus Toolkit provides the ability to access and manage data in a grid environment. It includes GridFTP [24, 25], which is used to move files between grid-enabled storage systems. GridFTP is a high-performance, secure (using GSI), reliable data transfer protocol optimized for high-bandwidth wide-area networks: it allows parallel transfers, third-party transfers, partial file transfers.

A grid middleware system like the Globus Toolkit provides features to access and control grid resources. It does *not* provide any programming model.

4   Deployment Process of CORBA Components in a Computational Grid

This section describes how we envision the general deployment process of CORBA components *in a computational grid*. This process complies with the deployment and configuration process [26] as specified by the Object Management Group (OMG, [27]).

4.1   Initial Assumptions

Before the deployment takes place, we assume that the computational grid has already been built and deployed on the computing resources. This is a reasonable hypothesis as we rely on the Globus Toolkit for its widespread adoption. The grid access middleware as well as the ORB have been installed on the resources of the grid.

We also assume that the user's authentication certificate has already been obtained, installed and signed by a certificate authority (CA) attached to the target computational grid. The user's grid identity must be mapped to a user identity (Unix username) on each resource of the grid. An authentication proxy must also have been initialized to access the computational grid resources.

The accurate resource description of the computational grid must already be compiled and available. This resource description can typically be included in the information service of the grid access middleware, such as the MDS of the Globus Toolkit. The resource description should be precise enough to describe compute node characteristics (architecture, memory size, operating system, CPU speed, *etc.*), network topology (interconnection links, firewalls, *etc.*) and performance properties (bandwidth, latency, jitter, loss), storage capacities, *etc.*

Finally, we assume that the component or component assembly to be deployed has already been packaged in a ZIP file: according to the CCM specification, component packages should have a `.zip` extension, and component assembly packages should have a `.aar` extension.

4.2   Starting Point

Ideally, *automatic* deployment should allow the client user to run a component-based application on a grid which he has access to by simply typing a command line in his terminal. This command (the "deployment tool", executed on a computer which we call the "deployment client") merely requires:

- a CCM component assembly package (`.aar`), or a component package (`.zip`), or a pointer (URL) to such a file;
- a pointer to the information service describing the resources available in the computational grid; in the Globus Toolkit's terminology, that would be a "base distinguished name" in the MDS tree.

This command should return a handle to steer (get status, suspend, restart, terminate) the component-based program's execution. The actions of this magic command are described in the following subsections.

4.3   Planning the CORBA Component Deployment

The goal of this phase is to determine on which compute nodes the component-based application will run. More precisely, it will determine which component will execute on which particular compute resource of the computational grid.

First, we need to extract information out of the archive (component or assembly package) provided on the command line or downloaded from the location given on the command line. According to the CCM specification, the archive is self-described, since it contains a package descriptor file (or a pointer to such a package descriptor). The component or assembly package contains deployment constraints such as the following.

Architecture and operating system. The component(s) in a package have been compiled for a specific computer architecture and under a specific operating system, so they will have to run on their target architectures under the proper operating system. A package may contain various components compiled for different architectures and operating systems.

Dependencies. A component may have environmental or other dependencies: the component deployment tool must make sure those dependencies will be satisfied at execution time. The dependencies may be on libraries, executables, JAVA classes: if necessary, they must be staged in on the compute node running the component prior to execution.

Host or process collocation. The CCM specification allows the components of a component assembly to be partitioned: components may be free or partitioned to a single process or a single host, meaning that a group of component instances will have to be deployed in the same process or on the same compute node.

There is a possibility to enrich the constraints attached to a component package or a component assembly package using the `extension` XML element, yielding still more deployment tool-specific constraints. Those constraints could concern network technology requirements for performance, desired completion time, *etc.* but this is out of the scope of this paper.

A component assembly package may also contain various implementations (possibly using different programming languages) of the same component interface.

After gathering all the information pertaining to deployment plus the description of the grid resources, the second step consists in *automatically mapping* the component(s) to the computing resources where they will execute. This part is not the focus of this paper, and research has already been conducted on this topic [28, 29, 30] (*cf.* related works in Section 6).

4.4 Preparing Execution and Launching Processes on a Computational Grid

The previous phase resulted in a *deployment plan* which specifies which components must be launched on which nodes of the computational grid.

Using the grid access middleware, we stage in to the execution nodes the input data files and component dependencies (libraries, JAVA classes, *etc.*). Ideally, the automatic determination of the deployment plan should have selected nodes close to each other for communication efficiency. The locality of the selected nodes may allow various file staging strategies. For instance, instead of transferring files twice from a remote repository to two compute nodes close to each other, we may prefer to transfer files once from the remote repository to one of the compute nodes, which will then forward the files to the other node in close neighborhood. Depending on the information services describing the grid resources, we may be able to detect that two selected compute nodes share a common file system (*e.g.*, NFS): in this case, another possible strategy would consist in staging in input data to the common file system just once. Then both compute nodes could access the read-only input data through the shared file system.

Now the component servers can be launched as regular processes on the compute nodes selected in the deployment plan. Each component server returns a CORBA reference (IOR) to the deployment tool invoked from the deployment client: this IOR will be necessary to control the component server. Then CORBA containers get created within the component servers to install the CORBA homes objects, and the homes create the components as stated by the deployment plan: all those newly created objects return IOR references for the deployment tool to be able to control the newly created entities.

If we want an actual control over the application, the IORs must be returned to the deployment tool using a secure channel and as soon as the objects which they reference get created. In particular, they must be returned before the application completion. This conversational mode of communication between the deployment client (which submits the job to execute) and the various processes of the running application is rather unusual in grid computing. Most often, grid computing applications do not need to exchange messages with the deployment client during execution: the input data is transfered all at once *prior to* execution, and the output data is retrieved *after* execution is completed. Of course, this does not mean that the subtasks of the application do not communicate with each other during execution.

This conversational mode is also necessary for the following reason. As we consider a grid environment, we do not own the resources we use, so we assume that each compute session (*i.e.*, each application deployment) is independent of all other sessions, should they be initiated by the same user or by another user of the computational grid. In practice, the component servers, containers, components, *etc.* register to a name service (this is out of the CORBA specification). This name service must be operational *before* the components get launched because they need the IOR of (or any sort of reference to) the name service. However, we cannot count on a persistent name service running for multiple compute sessions, and the name service should be deployed first by the deployment tool. Here again, we see that we have a conversation-like operation mode, where the deployment client launches a process on a compute node, this process answers with an IOR, and this answer triggers another action on the deployment client's side.

The location of the name service would be completely up to the deployment tool, but a reasonable strategy would choose a compute node close to as many compute nodes hosting the application components as possible.

4.5   Configuration and Start of Execution

The last phase of deployment consists in connecting together the components of an assembly and configuring the components. To do that, the deployment tool may need once again CORBA references (IORs) to the components which have been launched (or a reference to the name service if those components registered to it). Usually, client requests start the server components' execution.

4.6   Execution Control

Control means that the deployment tool can get the status (active, completed, *etc.*) of the running application, cancel, suspend or restart its execution. Thus the deployment tool can cleanly deallocate the resources it uses to run the application. This control may also be useful for application re-deployment, or dynamic visualization component connection: those two issues are out of the scope of this paper. See [31] for algorithms which dynamically remap the subtasks of a running application.

The component servers are launched as regular grid processes. The latter return a handle to the grid access middleware, which is not aware that it is launching CORBA processes: this handle allows the grid access middleware to monitor and control its processes. Thus, the deployment tool has two ways to steer the application execution: the CORBA IORs plus the grid middleware handles for each executing process.

5   Early Experiments with MicoCCM and the Globus Toolkit

The grid access middleware we use is the Globus Toolkit version 2.4.3. We rely on this version since it is now well established and stable. We did not rely on version 3 of the Globus Toolkit because it lacks maturity and its future is currently uncertain. Version 4 of the Globus Toolkit is not available yet, but migration to this future version should not be an issue. The ORB we utilize is MicoCCM version 2.3.11, a fully compliant implementation of CORBA, including the CORBA component model (CCM).

As mentioned in Subsection 4.1, we assume that we have a valid, already packaged component or component assembly (using Frank Pilhofer's Assembly Toolkit [32]), as well as the list of hosts which will execute the components. Currently, we have no deployment planner implemented, so the resources are selected in a round-robin manner, as provided by the MDS. However, we acknowledge that deployment planning is a very important phase in a grid environment, and it should be designed carefully, since it can have a huge impact on execution performance. This work is unavoidable in a near future.

In our current implementation, input data files and component dependencies are staged in to each compute node directly from their repositories: the subtle strategies evoked in Subsection 4.4 have not been implemented yet, all the more so as the necessary information is not available in the grid information system (MDS).

The very first step consists in launching the Mico name service daemon on one of the selected compute nodes and retrieve its CORBA reference (IOR). Once the name service's IOR has been obtained, the component servers are launched on the grid resources in the same way as the name service daemon is started: the component servers may also return their IOR to the deployment tool (even if this is not mandatory, since the component servers' IORs can be retrieved using the name service). Once the component servers have been launched, the Globus Toolkit need not create any more processes: the components can be created by thread creation within the component servers, possibly several components per component server depending on the process collocation constraints expressed in the component assembly package descriptor. The component creations can be initiated from the client side (CORBA component creation requests executed in the deployment tool) or from the server side (creation requests within the component server). We initiate remote component creations from the deployment tool (client side) to avoid modifying already existing component server programs. As the component creation gets initiated from the client side, then it is better to have the component servers send their IOR directly to the deployment tool, rather than having the deployment tool poll the name service until it holds the component servers' IORs. This is done using a simple wrapper program around the component server.

More specifically, the deployment process of the name service is exactly the same as of a component server. The deployment tool first creates a Globus GASS server which will receive the IOR of the remotely created object (name service daemon or component server) over a secured channel. The URL (hostname and port) where the GASS server is listening is retrieved by the deployment tool. Then it launches the remote process (name service daemon or component server) using GRAM remote job submission facility, passing to the remote process the URL of the GASS server among other arguments (including CORBA or MicoCCM specific arguments). The RSL script used for job submission specifies the list of files (input data, component dependencies, *etc.*) which must be staged in to the remote node prior to process execution. Using GridFTP, third-party transfers are permitted to stage in those files directly from a repository within the grid, which may not be located on the deployment client. If the process creation succeeds on the compute node selected to execute a component server or a name service daemon, the IOR of the newly created object is sent back to the deployment client using the GASS contact URL, and the GRAM job submission function in the deployment tool returns a handle, *i.e.* a Globus job ID useful to control the processes created by GRAM.

Thus the deployment tool possesses both Globus job IDs and CORBA IORs to control the processes (name service daemon and component servers) on the remote machines. For instance, an application can be stopped using the CORBA way and IORs (by calling the `ComponentServer::remove()` method) or using the Globus way and job IDs (by calling `globus-job-cancel`). Eventually, these control handles may permit a re-deployment of a component-based application or they may allow to dynamically plug visualization components to the running application.

All the data transfers using GridFTP and GASS are reliable and secured using GSI authentication and authorization mechanisms.

6   Related Work

ICENI (the Imperial College e-Science Networked Infrastructure [33, 34]) is a service oriented, integrated grid middleware which provides a component programming model to aid the application developer in constructing grid applications. The main focus of ICENI is meta-data information (performance, behavior) on component implementations in order to select and map the component implementations (corresponding to given interfaces) best-suited to the available computing resources of a grid. The selection and mapping are constrained by user-level (pricing, quality of service) and application-level requirements [28, 29]. The ICENI project currently supports deployment using *Fork* (using the Unix secure shell ssh) and plans to eventually resort to the Globus Toolkit, Condor, Sun GridEngine in unspecified ways [35, 36]. Currently, the deployment using the Globus Toolkit or Condor are not implemented [37].

The *Partitionable Services Framework* (PSF) and its deployment module *Smock* assume that so-called "wrappers" have already been deployed on each node [38]; the way those wrappers get deployed and how components get uploaded to the execution servers are not specified: their experiments are conducted using an emulated network. PSF also includes *Sekitei* [30], a planner implementing an algorithm to choose component implementations, link the components together and map them to computing resources: the placement algorithm is evaluated using simulation, with no actual deployment of processes.

The *Common Component Architecture* [39, 5] (CCA) proposes a component model similar to the abstract model of CORBA. It does not provide any detail on the automatic deployment process in grid environments [40]. A recent work [41] has focused on merging the CCA component model with the OGSI framework. It is different from our work since we support both CORBA and Globus communication models.

The *Assembly and Deployment Toolkit* [32] provided by Frank Pilhofer makes it very easy to configure and create component archives and component assembly archives. However the deployment feature is limited to a *single machine* already running a MicoCCM daemon *manually launched* by the user of the toolkit, with no security enforced, so it is ill-suited for deployment in grid environments.

The *Concerto* [42] platform aims to support the deployment of parallel components [7] on *clusters of workstations*: as this project does not envisage deployment on computational grids, it does not face the problem of heterogeneity inherent to computational grids, nor does it need to enforce security (authentication, authorization, encryption) because it assumes a trusted environment and trusted users.

7   Conclusion and Future Work

The deployment of high bandwidth wide-area networks has led computational grids to offer a very powerful computing resource. In particular, this inherently distributed resource is well-suited for multiphysics applications. To face the complexity of such applications as well as the heterogeneity and volatileness of grids, the software component technology appears to be a very adequate programming model. We choose to work with the CORBA component model because its deployment model is very complete: it specifies the deployment of a set of components on a set of distributed (component) servers. However, it specifies neither how to select those nodes, nor how to create the component servers. On the other hand, a grid access middleware, such as the Globus Toolkit, deals with security enforcement, resource, information, data management, and portability.

This paper studies the deployment of CORBA component-based applications in a computational grid using the Globus Toolkit. Its main result is that both models are complementary, not conflicting. This result seems to be generalizable to other component models and grid middleware systems. CCM does not specify how machines are to be selected, nor how component servers (processes) should be created whereas the Globus Toolkit only encompasses the start of remote processes. Moreover, grid services like data management are very useful to stage in component binaries. We have validated our analysis by actual experiments on our private computational grid. The deployment tool is currently hand-written and specific to our test case.

Our future works can be divided into three issues. The first issue is to integrate a planner for *automatically* selecting the machines on which the components will be deployed. The second issue concerns the extension of existing grid information services: while information related to compute *nodes* (CPU speed, memory size, operating system, *etc.*) is properly described in currently available resource information systems, the *network* topology and its characteristics are generally not described in a satisfactory, simple, synthetic and complete way. The last issue will be to support Grid Services. As we try not to have only one model for the component model and the grid middleware model, it should be straightforward to migrate to a web service enabled Globus Toolkit like GT4.

References

[1] Szyperski, C.: Component Software: Beyond Object-Oriented Programming. First edn. Addison-Wesley / ACM Press (1998)
[2] Sun Microsystems: Enterprise JavaBeans Specification (2001)
[3] Cerami, E.: Web Services Essentials. 1st edn. O'Reilly & Associates (2002)
[4] Open Management Group (OMG): CORBA components, version 3. Document formal/02-06-65 (2002)
[5] Armstrong, R., Gannon, D., Geist, A., Keahey, K., Kohn, S., McInnes, L., Parker, S., Smolinski, B.: Toward a common component architecture for high-performance scientific computing. In: Proc. of the 8th IEEE International Symposium on High Performance Distributed Computing (HPDC'99), Redondo Beach, CA (1999) 115–124
[6] Denis, A., Prez, C., Priol, T.: Towards high performance CORBA and MPI middlewares for grid computing. In Lee, C.A., ed.: Proc. of the 2nd International Workshop on Grid Computing. Number 2242 in LNCS, Denver, CO, Springer-Verlag (2001) 14–25 held in conjunction with SuperComputing 2001 (SC'01).
[7] Prez, C., Priol, T., Ribes, A.: A parallel CORBA component model for numerical code coupling. The International Journal of High Performance Computing Ap-

plications (IJHPCA) **17** (2003) 417–429 Special issue Best Applications Papers from the 3rd International Workshop on Grid Computing.

[8] Foster, I., Kesselman, C.: Computational Grids. In: The Grid: Blueprint for a New Computing Infrastructure. Morgan Kaufmann, San Francisco, CA (1998) 15–51

[9] The Globus Alliance web site: http://www.Globus.org/ (URL)

[10] Foster, I., Kesselman, C.: The Globus Project: a status report. In: Proc. of the 7th Heterogeneous Computing Workshop, held in conjunction with IPPS/SPDP'98, Orlando, FL (1998) 4–18

[11] The TeraGrid web site: http://www.TeraGrid.org/ (URL)

[12] Open Management Group (OMG): Common Object Request Broker Architecture (CORBA/IIOP). Document formal/02-11-03 (2003)

[13] The Grid Physics Network (GriPhyN) web site: http://www.GriPhyN.org/ (URL)

[14] The DOE Science Grid web site: http://DOEScienceGrid.org/ (URL)

[15] The DataGrid Project web site: http://www.eu-datagrid.org/ (URL)

[16] The Common TeraGrid Software Stack (CTSS): http://www.TeraGrid.org/userinfo/guide_software.html (URL)

[17] Foster, I.T., Kesselman, C., Tsudik, G., Tuecke, S.: A security architecture for computational grids. In: Proc. of the 5th ACM Conference on Computer and Communications Security, San Francisco, CA, ACM Press, New York, NY (1998) 83–92

[18] Czajkowski, K., Foster, I., Karonis, N., Kesselman, C., Martin, S., Smith, W., Tuecke, S.: A resource management architecture for metacomputing systems. In: Proc. of the IPPS/SPDP'98 Workshop on Job Scheduling Strategies for Parallel Processing. Volume 1459 of LNCS. (1998) 62–82

[19] Resource Specification Language (RSL) version 1.0: http://www-fp.globus.org/gram/rsl_spec1.html (URL)

[20] Bester, J., Foster, I., Kesselman, C., Tedesco, J., Tuecke, S.: GASS: A data movement and access service for wide area computing systems. In: Proc. of the 6th Workshop on Input/Output in Parallel and Distributed Systems (IOPADS), Atlanta, GA, ACM Press (1999) 78–88

[21] Czajkowski, K., Fitzgerald, S., Foster, I., Kesselman, C.: Grid information services for distributed resource sharing. In: Proc. of the 10th IEEE International Symposium on High-Performance Distributed Computing (HPDC-10), San Francisco, CA (2001) 181–194

[22] Wolski, R.: Forecasting network performance to support dynamic scheduling using the network weather service. In: Proc. of the 6th International Symposium on High-Performance Distributed Computing (HPDC-6'97), Portland, OR (1997) 316–325

[23] Swany, M., Wolski, R.: Representing dynamic performance information in grid environments with the network weather service. In: Proc. of the 2nd IEEE/ACM International Symposium on Cluster Computing and the Grid (CCGrid'02), Berlin, Germany (2002) 48–56

[24] The Globus Project: GridFTP: Universal data transfer for the grid. White paper, http://www.globus.org/datagrid/deliverables/C2WPdraft3.pdf (2000)

[25] The Globus Project: GridFTP update. Technical report, http://www.globus.org/datagrid/deliverables/GridFTP-Overview-200201.pdf (2002)

[26] Object Management Group (OMG): Deployment and configuration of component-based distributed applications specification. Draft Adopted Specification ptc/03-07-02, http://www.OMG.org/cgi-bin/apps/doc?ptc/03-07-02.pdf (2003)

[27] The Object Management Group (OMG) web site: http://www.OMG.org/ (URL)
[28] Furmento, N., Mayer, A., McGough, S., Newhouse, S., Field, T., Darlington, J.: Optimisation of component-based applications within a grid environment. In: Proc. of the 2001 ACM/IEEE conference on Supercomputing, Denver, CO, ACM Press, New York, NY, USA (2001) 30
[29] Furmento, N., Mayer, A., McGough, S., Newhouse, S., Darlington, J.: A component framework for HPC applications. In: Proc. of the 7th International Euro-Par Conference. Volume 2150 of LNCS., Manchester, UK (2001) 540–548
[30] Kichkaylo, T., Ivan, A.A., Karamcheti, V.: Constrained component deployment in wide-area networks using AI planning techniques. In: Proc. of the 17th International Parallel and Distributed Processing Symposium (IPDPS'2003), Nice, France (2003) 3
[31] Maheswaran, M., Siegel, H.J.: A dynamic matching and scheduling algorithm for heterogeneous computing systems. In: Proc. of the 7th Heterogeneous Computing Workshop, held in conjunction with IPPS/SPDP'98, Orlando, FL (1998) 57–69
[32] Pilhofer, F.: Assembly and deployment toolkit (URL) http://www.fpx.de/MicoCCM/Toolkit/.
[33] The ICENI web site at the London e-Science Centre: http://www.lesc.ic.ac.uk/iceni/ (URL)
[34] Furmento, N., Mayer, A., McGough, S., Newhouse, S., Field, T., Darlington, J.: ICENI: Optimisation of component applications within a grid environment. Journal of Parallel Computing **28** (2002) 1753–1772
[35] Furmento, N., , Lee, W., Newhouse, S., Darlington, J.: Test and deployment of ICENI, an integrated grid middleware on the UK e-Science grid. In: Proc. of the UK e-Science All Hands Meeting, Nottingham, UK (2003) 192–195
[36] Young, L., McGough, S., Newhouse, S., Darlington, J.: Scheduling architecture and algorithms within the ICENI grid middleware. In: Proc. of the UK e-Science All Hands Meeting, Nottingham, UK (2003) 5–12
[37] ICENI Research Group: Imperial college e-Science networked infrastructure. User's guide, The London e-Science Centre (2004) http://www.lesc.ic.ac.uk/iceni/downloads/guide.pdf.
[38] Ivan, A.A., Harman, J., Allen, M., Karamcheti, V.: Partitionable services: A framework for seamlessly adapting distributed applications to heterogeneous environments. In: Proc. of the 11th IEEE International Symposium on High Performance Distributed Computing (HPDC-11), Edinburgh, Scotland (2002) 103–112
[39] The CCA Forum web site: http://www.CCA-forum.org/ (URL)
[40] Bramley, R., Chiu, K., Diwan, S., Gannon, D., Govindaraju, M., Mukhi, N., Temko, B., Yechuri, M.: A component based services architecture for building distributed applications. In: Proc. of the 9th IEEE International Symposium on High Performance Distributed Computing (HPDC'00), Pittsburgh, PA (2000) 51–59
[41] Govindaraju, M., Krishnan, S., Chiu, K., Slominski, A., Gannon, D., Bramle, R.: Merging the CCA component model with the OGSI framework. In: Proc. of the 3rd International Symposium on Cluster Computing and the Grid (CCGrid2003), Tokyo, Japan (2003) 182–189
[42] Courtrai, L., Guidec, F., Sommer, N.L., Maho, Y.: Resource management for parallel adaptive components. In: Proc. of the 5th International Workshop on Java for Parallel and Distributed Computing (JPDC), held in conjunction with the 17th International Parallel and Distributed Processing Symposium (IPDPS'2003), Nice, France (2003) 134–140

Asynchronous, Hierarchical, and Scalable Deployment of Component-Based Applications

Vivien Quéma[1], Roland Balter[2], Luc Bellissard[2],
David Féliot[2], André Freyssinet[2], and Serge Lacourte[2]

[1] INPG - LSR-IMAG-INRIA - projet Sardes
INRIA Rhône-Alpes, 655 av. de l'Europe, 38334 Saint-Ismier Cedex, France
[2] ScalAgent Distributed Technologies

Abstract. The deployment of distributed component-based applications is a complex task. Proposed solutions are often centralized, which excludes their use for the deployment of large-scale applications. Besides, these solutions do often not take into account the functional constraints, i.e. the dependences between component activations. Finally, most of them are not fault-tolerant. In this paper, we propose a deployment application that deals with these three problems. It is hierarchical, which is a necessary feature to guarantee scalability. Moreover, it is designed as a distributed workflow decomposed into tasks executing asynchronously, which allows an "as soon as possible" activation of deployed components. Finally, the proposed deployment application is fault-tolerant. This is achieved by the use of persistent agents with atomic execution. This deployment application has been tested and performance measurements show that it is scalable.

1 Introduction

Context and Objectives As underlined by Emmerich in [1], it was claimed for a long time that object-orientation was the solution to software reusability. Nevertheless, the large number of fine grained classes generated during object-oriented modelling induces a large number of dependencies between them, thus making it difficult to take classes out of the context in which they were developed. To overcome these problems, component models were elaborated. "A component is a unit of composition that can be deployed independently and is subject to composition by a third party." [2]

First component models like COM or JavaBeans had their execution limited to just one machine. These component models have been extended to allow for distributed execution across multiple machines: .NET or EJB. These distributed technologies have induced a new approach of software development that is often referred to as component-based development (CBD). CBD raises numerous challenges, such as distribution management, component discovery, integration of components with legacy software modules, etc. One of the major, not yet solved challenge is the deployment of distributed component-based systems.

W. Emmerich and A.L. Wolf (Eds.): CD 2004, LNCS 3083, pp. 50–64, 2004.

According to Carzaniga and al. [3], deployment is a collection of interrelated activities that form the deployment life-cycle. In this paper, we focus on the steps preliminary to the application's launching, that is: installation, instantiation, binding, and finally activation of the components. In existing component technologies, these steps are often reduced to software delivery: the component code located on one server node is first sent to n customer sites and then activated. Such a deployment process does take into account neither the *applicative logic*, nor the *physical constraints* of the physical environment where the application is to be deployed. A distributed application encompasses a set of components that interact with each other in a complex way, thus making them interdependent. To run consistently components require the availability of other (possibly legacy) components. These dependencies must be carefully taken into account to ensure a consistent activation of each of the components. This issue is referred to as the application logic enforcement. On the other hand the deployment process must be fault tolerant, even in the case of large-scale applications executing on numerous heterogeneous devices with varying operational conditions (i.e. network failures, disconnected mode, etc.). This issue is referred to as the physical constraints enforcement.

Approach The paper addresses the two above-mentioned challenges. Application logic enforcement is achieved through the use of an architecture description language (ADL) to describe the distributed application to be deployed. This description relies on a hierarchical component model which is general enough to allow the description of most of component-based systems. Physical constraints enforcement is achieved by designing the deployment process as a scalable and fault tolerant distributed application. Scalability requires that the deployment process is distributed. This is achieved through a hierarchical structure of the deployment process in close connection with the component hierarchy of the application to be deployed. In addition, we propose to implement the deployment application on top of an asynchronous reliable runtime system, to meet the fault tolerance objective.

This paper is structured as follows: section 2 describes the hierarchical component model, and its associated architecture description language is introduced in section 3. Section 4 presents the deployment application. We describe its implementation in section 5 and performance figures are presented in section 6. Related work in addressed in section 7, before concluding the paper in section 8.

2   A Hierarchical Component Model

In this section, we present the component model that is used to model applications to be deployed. Our main objective was that the component model be general enough to allow modeling most of the component-based systems. It is inspired by previous work made on distributed component-based applications [4]. It shares similarities with Fractal [5], a recent component model, which also aims at modeling component-based systems. An application is represented by a hierarchical assembly of components. Every component is made of two parts: a *functional part* and a *control part*. Moreover, components are bound using *connectors*.

The Functional Part The functional part of a component corresponds to the services it provides to other components and the services it requires from other components. These services are accessed via functional interfaces defined by:

- An *identifier*: a name which is valid in the context of the component that owns the interface,
- A *role* specifying whether the considered interface is a client or a server interface,
- A *signature*: a collection of method signatures. Interface signatures are embodied as usual Java interfaces.
- A *contingency* used to specify whether a client interface is mandatory or optional (i.e. if it must be bound or not at runtime).

The Control Part A component also owns control interfaces which are server interfaces that embody the control behavior associated with the component. In particular, the control part allows the management of the component's lifecycle (start, stop, activate and deactivate). Decoupling the control part from the functional part is required for administration applications to easily manage component-based applications. For instance, we will show in the paper that the deployment application requires an activation interface.

Composite Components The component model is hierarchical: a set of components can be manipulated as a component, called *composite*. Composite components are useful to represent hierarchical applications. A composite usually encapsulates components that cooperate to provide a functionality. Similarly to primitive components, composite components own functional and control interfaces. Nevertheless, we distinguish internal interfaces that can be bound to encapsulated components and external interfaces that can be bound to components outside the composite.

Connectors A functional interface can be bound to one (or several) other functional interface(s) using a connector. There exist several connectors: local and remote procedure calls, asynchronous message passing, etc. A connector is instantiated by a connector factory. Each factory must provide a `create` method, whose parameters are the identifiers of the interfaces to be bound. Note that binding two functional interfaces requires that the components owning these interfaces are encapsulated within the same composite.

Example Figure 1 represents the architecture of an application that conforms to the component model. For readability purpose, some connectors have been omitted. The application is represented by the `Application` composite. It encapsulates two primitive components `Client 1` and `Client 2`, and a composite component `Topic`. Each client owns two client interfaces — `subscribe` to subscribe to the topic, and `publish` to publish a message on the topic —, and a server interface `receive` to receive messages broadcasted by the topic. The `Topic` composite component owns three external interfaces and three internal interfaces that are bound to two primitive components.

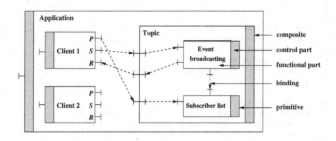

Fig. 1. Example of application following the model.

3   An Architecture Description Language

To manipulate the above described component model, we have defined an architecture description language (ADL). In this paper, we will only show how this ADL is used to deploy applications. Note that it is also used for other purposes [6]. Like other ADLs [7], it aims at describing an application as an assembly of interacting components. It is inspired by previous work made on the Olan configuration language [8]. It allows the description of:

- the *functional* part of the application, i.e. the set of (possibly legacy) involved components and their interactions.
- the *non functional* part of the application, i.e. the location of components to be deployed and the order in which they must be activated.

Components and connectors involved in the application are described in a file called *description*. The description of a primitive component specifies its functional interfaces, its control interfaces and its implementation (Java class, binary file, etc.). Similarly, the description of a composite component gives its interfaces (internal and external) and its implementation. Moreover, it describes its internal architecture, that is the set of encapsulated components, their locations, their bindings using connectors and their dependences in term of activation.

As for components, two kinds of connectors may be used: *primitive* and *composite* connectors. Primitive connector descriptions only specify the connector factory to be used. Composite connectors are described as assemblies of interacting components bound by primitive connectors. This makes the description of a composite connector comparable to that of a composite component.

```
Composite Application {

  *** No functional interfaces ***
  *** Control interfaces ***
  Activation controller {
    signature = fr.application.Activation ;
  }
  ...

  *** Implementation ***
  Implementation Application {
    type = java ;
    funct_part = void ;
    contr_part = fr.application.ApplicationControl ;
  }

  *** Encapsulated components ***
  Client client1 = new Client (zirconium.inria.fr);
  Client client2 = new Client (argent.inria.fr);
  Topic topic = new Topic (strontium.inria.fr);

  *** Connector factory ***
  Rmi rmiF = new Rmi (zirconium.inria.fr) ;

  *** Component bindings ***
  client1.abonnement => topic.abonnement using rmiF ;
  ...

  *** Activation dependencies ***
  (client1, client2) depend on topic ;

}
```

Fig. 2. Description of the `Application` composite.

Figure 2 depicts the description of the `Application` composite. It gives its control interfaces and its implementation. For legacy components, the implementation field is replaced by a description of the component location. Furthermore, encapsulated components and connector factories are specified with the keyword **new**, with in parameter the site where they have to be deployed. Bindings between components are specified with the symbol => and with the keyword **using** that is used to indicate the connector factory to be used. Finally, the order of component activations is specified: it is mentioned that the two client component activations depend on the topic activation.

4   The Deployment Application

The deployment application uses the ADL description to instantiate and bind application components. Our goal is twofold: (1) to use the ADL description to ensure the respect of functional constraints and (2) to exploit the hierarchical structure of the application to distribute the deployment intelligence. To reach our goal, the deployment application is implemented as a *distributed workflow* decomposed in *tasks*. Tasks execute in parallel or sequentially. They are responsible for the various deployment operations: instantiation, binding, activation. These tasks execute within hierarchically organized entities called *deployment controllers*. We first show how the controller hierarchy is built. We then describe the architecture of controllers.

4.1   Deployment Controller Hierarchy

Recall that the component model requires that two bound components be encapsulated in the same composite. As a consequence, an application built using this model has always a tree-like architecture: nodes of the tree are composite components, whereas leafs are primitive components. The deployment controllers' hierarchy follows this treelike hierarchy: each composite is associated with a controller. Figure 3 illustrates this concept: a deployment controller is associated to each of the four composites C_1, C_2, C_3 and C_4.

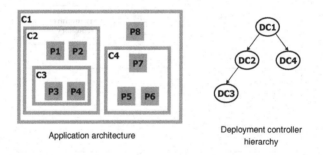

Application architecture

Deployment controller
hierarchy

Fig. 3. Applicative hierarchy.

However, it is also possible to extend this hierarchy by creating controllers in charge of a subset of components. Such an example is depicted on figure 4: components P_1 , P_2 and P_5, P_6 are associated to controllers $DCBis_1$ and $DCBis_2$, respectively. This consists in creating "virtual" composites, without functional and control code. This extension possibility is interesting for applications built using flat component models such as the Corba Component Model (CCM [9]), or Sun'S EJB model [10].

4.2   Deployment Controller Architecture

Principle Except for the root deployment controller, each controller is created by its parent controller. To communicate, two controllers must establish a session. This session is used to exchange control messages.

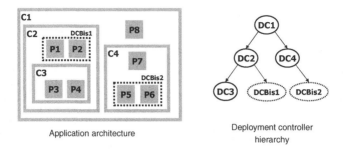

Application architecture

Deployment controller
hierarchy

Fig. 4. Extended hierarchy.

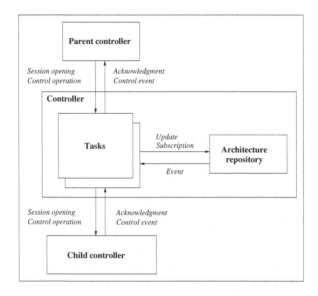

Fig. 5. Architecture of a controller.

As depicted on figure 5, each controller hosts a set of tasks responsible for various aspects of the deployment. These tasks can either be created by other tasks hosted by the controller or by tasks executing within the parent controller (creation orders are propagated using the session established between the two controllers). Tasks store their results in an architecture repository. Each time the repository is updated, it sends an event reporting the update to interested tasks, which react by either executing local operations, or creating other tasks.

Tasks We distinguish four kinds of tasks:

– *Creation tasks* are in charge of creating components. Their code depends on the type of component to be instantiated (Java, C, etc.). Moreover, in the case of composite components, the creation task creates the controller associated with the composite and opens a session that takes as parameter the ADL description of the composite to be deployed. This session is used by other tasks to send control orders. At the end of this task, the architecture repository is updated with references to the created component and its functional interfaces. Note that in the case of a "virtual" composite, stored references are those of its encapsulated components.

- *Integration tasks* are in charge of integrating legacy components. These are retrieved using information stored in the ADL description. The architecture repository is then updated with information about the component references.
- *Binding tasks* are in charge of binding components. Their code depends on the type of connector to be instantiated. Nevertheless they follow the same pattern: they first create the connector factory using information stored in the ADL description; then, they create the connector by calling the `create` method with appropriate parameters. These parameters are retrieved from the architecture repository.
- *Activation tasks* are in charge of activating components. For primitive components, this only consists in calling the `activate` method provided by the `Activation` control interface. For composite components, this task uses the session established with the child controller to send an activation order. Once the order is completed, the session with the child controller is closed.

Organization of Tasks Tasks are created by a controller according to the ADL description of the composite to be deployed. One creation (or integration) task and one activation task are created for each encapsulated component. Moreover, one binding task is created for each connector to be built. Note that in the case of a "virtual" composite, only connectors between encapsulated components are managed by the controller. Indeed, the bindings between encapsulated and other components are done by the parent controller.

Tasks within a controller execute independently. They synchronize through events generated by the repository upon updates. Tasks execute either in parallel or sequentially according to their type and the components they work on: all the creation and integration tasks execute in parallel. On the other hand, a binding task depends on the creation and integration tasks in charge of the components to be bound. Finally, an activation task executes after both all the component's required services have been bound and all the components it depends on have been activated. This organization of tasks guarantees an "as soon as possible" activation of each component. This would not be the case if all the creation tasks were delayed until all the binding tasks complete, themselves being delayed until the completion of all the creation tasks.

4.3   Fault Tolerance

Like every large-scale distributed application, the deployment application can be subject to node crashes, network breakdowns, disconnected sites, etc. It is thus necessary to discover and handle these faults.

Fault Detection Two kinds of faults may happen: either a task is blocked — for example, a component creation does not complete —, or a network or a machine crashes. In the latter case, the tasks interacting with this machine will block. Thus, each fault causes one or several tasks to block. Two fault discovering strategies are possible: the first one consists in setting bounds to the execution times of the different tasks. Once a bound has been raised, an error message is propagated. This method is not viable for the deployment of large-scale applications, since it is very difficult to determine realistic bounds.

The strategy we have adopted is "optimistic": no error message is propagated. Instead, every controller owns a supplementary task, called *monitoring task* whose role is to observe other tasks' progression. This task collects events produced by the repository, filters them and forwards interesting events to the monitoring task executing within the parent controller. All these events are received by the monitoring task executing within the root controller. This task is used by the application administrator to check the deployment progression.

Fault Handling Faults are handled following a two steps process: all or part of the controllers are stopped. Then, a new deployment order is given. Between these two steps, a site can be restarted, the ADL description can be modified, etc. Stopping a deployment controller is made possible by sending a stop order using the session established with its parent controller. This causes the different tasks executing within the controller to stop. Redeploying the application is made possible by opening new sessions along with the (possibly modified) ADL description. Stopped tasks are restarted (sometimes recreated). The repository is also restarted and used to determine the operations that remain to be done. It is important to note that for this mechanism to work correctly, it is required (1) that repositories and tasks have persistent states, and (2) that communications between them be reliable.

5 Implementation

The deployment application has been implemented using the ScalAgent middleware [11], a fault-tolerant platform that combines asynchronous communications with a distributed programming model based on persistent software entities called *agents*.

The Agent Paradigm Agents are autonomous reactive objects executing concurrently, and communicating through an event-reaction pattern. An event is a typed data structure used for exchanging information with other agents. Once an agent receives an event, it reacts accordingly, thus changing its state and/or communicating with other agents. Agents are persistent, which means that the agent lifetime is not bounded to the duration of the execution. However, persistence is not sufficient for retrieving a consistent state after failure. Also, agent reactions are atomic. This property ensures that a reaction is either fully executed or not executed at all.

The Execution Infrastructure This event-reaction model is based on a MOM which guarantees the reliable, causal delivery of messages. The MOM is represented by a set of agent servers organized in a bus architecture. Each server is made up of two components, the *local bus* and the *engine*. The local bus conveys messages. It is made of a *channel* in charge of routing messages and several networks that implement the basic message-based communication layers. The engine is responsible for the creation and execution of agents. It behaves according to their event-reaction model. It performs a set of instructions in a loop, getting the next message from the channel and making the proper agent react.

Implementing the Deployment Application Controllers, tasks, as well as repositories are implemented using agents. At session creation time, the agent implementing the child controller is created. This controller agent creates the agent responsible for the repository and uses the ADL description to create the agents responsible for the various tasks: a creation task and an activation task by encapsulated component, and a binding task for each binding to be established. Fault tolerance is made possible by the atomic execution of agents, which guarantees that restarted tasks and architecture repositories are in a consistent state.

6   Evaluation

Performance measurements have been done to validate the proposed deployment application. They have been performed on a 216 PCs cluster equipped with 733MHz Intel Pentium III processor and 256Mo RAM. Tests consisted in deploying applications, whose architecture follows the pattern represented on figure 6. Application components are implemented using Java objects communicating using the ScalAgent middleware.

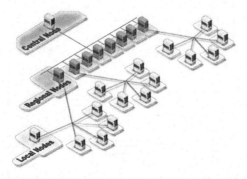

Fig. 6. Architecture of the test application.

Recall that deployed applications have always a tree-like hierarchy. The test application hierarchy is made of three levels: a central site connected to n composite components, each one encapsulating a regional composite connected to m local composites. Every local composite encapsulates 10 primitive components. Every regional composite encapsulates 10 primitive components as well as local composites. The measured metric is the average deployment completion time. We varied several parameters:

- The number of physical machines that host application components. This number ranges from 11 to 151.
- The number of local composites. This number ranges from 1 to 7000. In the case of the test application, each local composite execute within a Java process. As a matter of fact, the more the number of local composites increases, the more the required power on the machine is significant.
- The number of regional composites. This number ranges from 1 to 50. Note that increasing the number of regional composites decreases the number of local composites that each one encapsulates.

6.1   Distribution Impact Evaluation

To evaluate the distribution impact, the number of regional and local composites remains constant ($m = 10$ and $n = 100$), whereas the number of machines that host application components varies (from 20 to 111). Such applications involve 110 Java processes, each one hosting approximately 10 components. Obtained results are presented on figure 7. The average completion time ranges from 45 to 55. We can see that up to a certain number of machines, the decentralization increases the deployment performances. This is mainly due to the fact that each machine hosts less Java processes. Nevertheless, a too large number of machines increases the use of remote communications, thus reducing the deployment performances.

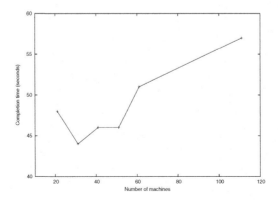

Fig. 7. Distribution impact evaluation.

6.2   Architectural Impact Evaluation

This test aims at evaluating the impact of the composite hierarchy. Recall that the application is represented by a central composite encapsulating m regional composites, each one encapsulating — besides its own primitive components —, $n = m$ local composites. Figure 8 shows that, for both a fixed number of machines (= 60) and a fixed number of local composites ($n = 500$), the deployment completion time is minimum for $m = 10$ regional composites (i.e. $n = m = 50$). This arises from the deployment application architecture which associates a controller to each composite. An increase of the number of controllers induces a parallelization of the deployment. Nevertheless, this number must be kept reasonable, since too large of a number causes each controller to handle a large number of sessions, which slows down the deployment process. This experience shows that the hierarchical structure of the application architecture has an impact on the deployment performances, which opens research perspectives towards tools to help determining an application's optimal architecture with regard to its deployment.

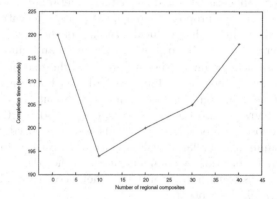

Fig. 8. Architectural impact evaluation.

6.3   Scalability Evaluation

This test is the most important. It aims at verifying that the proportional increase of parameters (n, m and the number of machines) does not cause an exponential increase of the deployment completion time. Figure 9 shows that this time remains linear, with n ranging from 10 to 450, m from 1 to 45, and the number of machines from 3 to 91.

7   Related Work

Deployment has been an increasing area of interest this last 10 years. Work has been done on the SOFA component model [12]. Similarly to our approach,

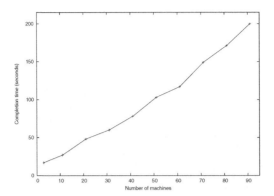

Fig. 9. Scalability assesment.

they use an ADL (CDL for Component Definition Language) which allows the description of the application to be deployed as a hierarchical assembly of components. Nevertheless, the proposed deployment process is centralized and does not take advantage from the hierarchical structure of the application. Indeed, a centralized server uses the ADL to propagate creation and binding orders.

[13] focuses on a deployment specific problem: the one of component discovery. The authors propose a trading service based both on the type of the component interfaces and on semantic information about the component. This tool has been integrated into the Corba component model (CCM) deployment process. The proposed protocol is synchronous and centralized, which we think is not a viable approach for large-scale applications. Such a tool could be integrated into our proposition as complementary to the ADL. It would be used by the different tasks to retrieve information they need, thus allowing dynamic evolution of the ADL description.

Researchers at University of Colorado have proposed a reconfiguration system for the Sun's EJB component model [14]. BARK (*Bean Automatic Reconfiguration FrameworK*) is designed to facilitate all the tasks in the deployment lifecycle for EJBs. It provides functions to download component packages over the Internet and load them into the EJB container. It also manipulates the component package descriptors to provide control over component bindings. In that sense, BARK may be compared to an ADL. BARK is composed of a set of Application Server Modules (ASM) that work in cooperation with EJB application servers. A central Repository is used for storing component software packages. Finally, a tool determines the scripts to be executed by each ASMs. The proposed deployment process shares similarity with ours since it uses an ADL-like description of EJBs. However, deployment orders are centralized and synchronous.

Hall et al. have worked on software deployment [15]. The architecture they propose, called *Software Dock*, is composed of a set of servers, or *docks*. These *docks* help registering software releases and software consumer configurations. They are used by *agents* that are in charge of a specific deployment task. Agents can migrate from *dock* to *dock* and communicate using a wide-area event system. Similarly to our approach, this system uses asynchronous communications and agents. However, this system is not dedicated to component deployment. As a matter of fact, the deployment is not hierarchical and it does not allow an "as soon as possible" activation of part of the components. Finally, agents do not execute atomically, which precludes fault tolerance.

We conclude this related work survey with work conducted by the Grid community. *proactive* [16] is an active object-based distributed programming model. One of the designers' goal is to remove any reference to physical machines, repositories, etc. from the code of objects. This is achieved by using *virtual structures*. They are mapped onto physical structures using XML descriptors. Proactive shares our goal of separating functional code from deployment-related data. Nevertheless, this system targets lowlevel software deployment like Java virtual machines, while we are focused on component-based applications.

8 Conclusion and Future Work

The deployment of distributed applications is one of the challenges raised by the *component-based development*. Existing solutions are often centralized and only consist in software delivery. Such deployment processes have several drawbacks: their centralized control excludes the deployment of large-scale distributed applications. Moreover, these processes do not take into account the *applicative logic*: the activation is often unnecessarily delayed and they do not propose to integrate legacy components with deployed applications. Finally, they do not take into account the *physical constraints* of the system on which the application is to be deployed: as a consequence, most of them do not tolerate faults.

In this paper, we have proposed a deployment application that solves these three challenges. (1) There is no centralized control: the deployment application is hierarchically organized according to the application's architecture. This hierarchical organization avoids bottlenecks and makes the deployment scalable. (2) The asynchronous and parallel execution of tasks allows an "as soon as possible" activation of deployed components. Indeed, every task synchronizes only with tasks it depends on. Dependency knowledge is made available by the ADL description of the application. (3) Finally, the proposed deployment application is fault tolerant. This is achieved by the use of persistent agents with atomic execution.

Future work: first performance measurements are an excellent encouragement to pursue our work. First, we plan to refine the experiments we have done in order to evaluate the computational and memory overheads of the deployment controllers. Second, we plan to provide the deployment application with support for high availability. As a matter of fact, while allowing a great deal of parallelism, the hierarchy of deployment controllers is still amenable to single points of failure. We are currently adding replication capabilities to the ScalAgent MOM; this will allow duplicating the deployment controllers, thus improving the availability of the deployment application.

References

[1] W. Emmerich. Distributed Component Technologies and their Software Engineering Implications. In *Proceedings of the 24th International Conference on Software Engineering (ICSE'02)*, pages 537 – 546, Orlando, Florida, May 2002.

[2] C. Szyperski. *Component Software: Beyond Object-Oriented Programming*. Addison-Wesley, 1998.

[3] A. Carzaniga, A. Fuggetta, R. Hall, A. van der Hoek, D. Heimbigner, and A. Wolf. A Characterization Framework for Software Deployment Technologies. Technical Report 857-98, Department of Computer Science, University of Colorado, 1998.

[4] L. Bellissard, S. Ben Atallah, F. Boyer, and M. Riveill. Distributed Application Configuration. In *Proceedings of the International Conference on Distributed Computing Systems (ICDCS'96)*, pages 579–585, Hong-Kong, May 1996.

[5] E. Bruneton, T. Coupaye, and J.-B. Stefani. Recursive and Dynamic Software Composition with Sharing. In *Proceedings of the 7th ECOOP International Workshop on Component-Oriented Programming (WCOP'02)*, Spain, June 2002.

[6] Vivien Quéma and Emmanuel Cecchet. The Role of Software Architecture in Configuring Middleware: the ScalAgent Experience. In *Proceedings of the 7th International Conference on Principles of Distributed Systems*, France, 2003.

[7] N. Medvidovic and R. N. Taylor. A Classification and Comparison Framework for Software Architecture Description Languages. *IEEE Transactions on Software Engineering*, 26(1), January 2000.

[8] R. Balter, L. Bellissard, F. Boyer, M. Riveill, and J.Y. Vion-Dury. Architecturing and Configuring Distributed Applications with Olan. In *Proceedings of the International Conference on Distributed Systems Platforms and Open Distributed Processing (Middleware'98)*, The Lake District, UK, September 1998.

[9] Philippe Merle, editor. *CORBA 3.0 New Components Chapters*. OMG TC Document ptc/2001-11-03, November 2001.

[10] Enterprise JavaBeansTM Specification, Version 2.1, August 2002. Sun Microsystems, http://java.sun.com/products/ejb/.

[11] L. Bellissard, N. de Palma, A. Freyssinet, M. Herrmann, and S. Lacourte. An Agent Plateform for Reliable Asynchronous Distributed Programming. In *Symposium on Reliable Distributed Systems (SRDS'99)*, Lausanne, Switzerland, October 1999.

[12] T. Kalibera and P. Tuma. Distributed Component System Based On Architecture Description: the SOFA Experience. In *Proceedings of the 4th International Symposium on Distributed Objects and Applications (DOA'02)*, USA, October 2002.

[13] D. Kebbal and G. Bernard. Component Search Service and Deployment of Distributed Applications. In *Proceedings of the 3rd International Symposium on Distributed Objects and Applications (DOA'01)*, Roma, Italy, September 2001.

[14] M. Rutherford, K. Anderson, A. Carzaniga, D. Heimbigner, and A. Wolf. Reconfiguration in the Enterprise JavaBean Component Model. In *Proceedings of the 1st Working Conference on Component Deployment (CD'02)*, Germany, June 2002.

[15] R. Hall, D. Heimbigner, and A. Wolf. A Cooperative Approach to Support Software Deployment Using the Software Dock. In *Proceedings of the 21st International Conference on Software Engineering (ICSE'99)*, pages 174–183, USA, May 1999.

[16] F. Baude, D. Caromel, F. Huet, L. Mestre, and J. Vayssière. Interactive and Descriptor-based Deployment of Object-Oriented Grid Applications. In *Proceedings of the 11th International Symposium on High Performance Distributed Computing (HPDC'02)*, pages 93–102, Edinburgh, Scottland, July 2002.

Dynamic Deployment of IIOP-Enabled Components in the JBoss Server

Francisco Reverbel[1], Bill Burke[2], and Marc Fleury[2]

[1] Department of Computer Science, University of São Paulo
reverbel@ime.usp.br
[2] JBoss, Inc.
{bill,marc}@jboss.org

Abstract. JBoss is an extensible Java application server that affords remote access to EJB components via multiple protocols. Its IIOP module supports IIOP-enabled EJBs, which are accessible both to RMI/IIOP clients written in Java and to CORBA clients written in various languages. While other systems use compilation-based approaches to generate IIOP stubs and skeletons, JBoss employs reflective techniques to avoid extra compilation steps and support on-the-fly deployment. CORBA/IIOP is a dynamic feature of JBoss in two senses: (*i*) the IIOP module can be dynamically deployed into a running server, and (*ii*) IIOP-enabled EJBs are dynamically deployable components themselves. This paper presents the design of the IIOP module and describes the actions that module takes at EJB deployment time, including the creation of POAs, the instantiation of CORBA servants to implement IDL interfaces not known in advance, and the dynamic generation of IIOP stub classes made available to Java clients via HTTP.

1 Introduction

JBoss [10] is an extensible, reflective, and dynamically reconfigurable Java application server that supports two general kinds of software components: *application components*, which correspond to server-side parts of distributed applications, and *middleware components*, which provide middleware services to application components. Both kinds of components can be dynamically deployed into a running server. Users can deploy components either by interacting with the server through a (possibly remote) management client or simply by dropping deployment units in a well known directory of the server machine.

Nearly all the "application server functionality" of JBoss is modularly provided by a set of middleware components deployed on a minimal server. While middleware components employ a JBoss-specific extension of the JMX component model [17], application components follow Java 2 Enterprise Edition (J2EE) standards [19]. An important subset of application components is based on the Enterprise JavaBeans (EJB) architecture [18], a model for business components ("enterprise beans") whose methods can be invoked either by remote clients or by local clients.

W. Emmerich and A.L. Wolf (Eds.): CD 2004, LNCS 3083, pp. 65–80, 2004.

EJB-compliant application servers may support various protocols, but they must support IIOP as the interoperability protocol for remote method invocations on enterprise beans. RMI over IIOP affords interoperability between EJB components deployed in application servers provided by different vendors. It makes enterprise bean methods available both to RMI/IIOP clients written in Java and to CORBA clients written in various languages, including Java and C++. Even though IIOP-enabled EJBs are not equivalent to the CORBA components [14] defined by the OMG, they can actually be regarded as another kind of "CORBA component."

JBoss supports IIOP in a *dynamic* way. Here the word "dynamic" means two things: (*i*) IIOP support is a feature that can be dynamically added to a running server, and (*ii*) IIOP-enabled EJBs are dynamically deployable components themselves. At the root of the latter point there is a major difference between our "CORBA components" and existing Java implementations of the CORBA Component Model (CCM). In current CCM implementations [8, 15], component deployment involves an additional compilation step, as these systems use compilation-based approaches to generate IIOP stubs and skeletons. Our work, on the other hand, avoids extra compilation steps by employing reflective techniques. It allows IIOP-enabled EJBs to be deployed into a running server simply by dropping EJB-JAR files in the server's deployment directory. A change to a JBoss-specific deployment descriptor is all that is needed to convert a non-IIOP-enabled deployment unit (which contains neither IIOP stubs nor skeletons) into an IIOP-enabled one. There are no additional steps for stub or skeleton generation.

This paper is organized as follows: Section 2 contains background material, mostly extracted from [10], Section 3 presents the middleware components that support CORBA/IIOP, Section 4 describes the proxy factories that generate remote references to EJBs, Section 5 discusses design and implementation issues, Section 6 reviews related work, and Section 7 presents our concluding remarks.

2   JBoss Background

2.1   JMX

Java Management Extensions (JMX) [17] is an architecture for dynamic management of resources (applications, systems, or network devices) distributed across a network. It provides a lightweight environment in which components — as well as their class definitions — can be dynamically loaded and updated.

JMX components (*MBeans*) are Java objects that conform to certain conventions and expose a *management interface* to their clients. A Java virtual machine that contains JMX components must contain also an *MBean server*, which provides a local registry for MBeans and mediates any accesses to their management interfaces. At registration time, each MBean is assigned an *object name* that must be unique in the context of the MBean server. In-process clients use object names (rather than Java references) to refer to MBeans.

To invoke a management operation on an MBean, a local client (typically another MBean) issues a generic `invoke` call on the MBean server, passing the target MBean's object name as an argument. The client needs no information on the MBean's Java class, nor does it need information on the Java interfaces the MBean implements. This very simple arrangement favors adaptation: the absence of references to an MBean scattered across its clients facilitates the replacement of that MBean; the absence of client knowledge about its class and its Java interfaces enables dynamic changes both to the implementation and to the management interface of the MBean.

JBoss uses JMX as a realization of the microkernel architectural pattern [6], to provide a minimal kernel (the MBean server) that serves as software bus for extensions (MBeans), possibly developed by independent parties. The MBean server decouples components from their clients, allowing MBeans to adapt, and their management interfaces to evolve, while their clients are active.

2.2 Service Components

On top of JMX, JBoss introduces its own model for middleware components, centered on the concept of *service component*. The JBoss service component model extends and refines the JMX model to address some issues beyond the scope of JMX: service lifecycle, dependencies between services, deployment and redeployment of services, dynamic configuration and reconfiguration of services, and component packaging.

Service MBeans (also called *service components*) are JMX MBeans whose management interfaces include service lifecycle operations. *Deployable MBeans* (also called *deployable services*), a JBoss-specific extension to JMX, are service MBeans packaged according to EJB-like conventions, in deployment units called *service archives* (SARs). A service archive contains class files for one or more deployable services, plus a *service descriptor*, an XML file that conveys information needed at deployment time.

Service components plugged into a JMX-based "server spine" provide most of the "application server functionality" offered by JBoss. They implement every key feature of J2EE: naming service, transaction management, security service, servlet/JSP support, EJB support, asynchronous messaging, database connection pooling, and IIOP support. Service components also implement important features not specified by J2EE, such as clustering and fail-over.

2.3 Meta-level Architecture for Generalized EJBs

The conceptual definition of the EJB architecture [18] relies strongly on the abstract notion of an *EJB container*. In JBoss, a set of meta-level components works together to implement this conceptual abstraction. A *generalized EJB container* is a set of pluggable aspects that can be selected and changed by users. Extended EJB functionality is supported by a meta-level architecture whose central features are:

- usage of MBeans as meta-level components that support and manage base-level EJB components;
- a uniform model for reifying base-level method invocations;
- usage of dynamic proxies as the basis for a remote invocation model that supports multiple protocols;
- a variant of the interceptor pattern [16], used as an aspect-oriented programming [11] technique.

In this section we restrict ourselves to the case of EJB clients that do not use IIOP to interact with remote EJB components. Fig. 1 shows (in a non-IIOP scenario) the elements of the meta-level architecture implemented by JBoss. The base level consists of EJB components and their clients. Accordingly, we refer to EJB interfaces as base-level interfaces. From this perspective, MBeans belong to the meta level, and their management interfaces are meta-level interfaces.

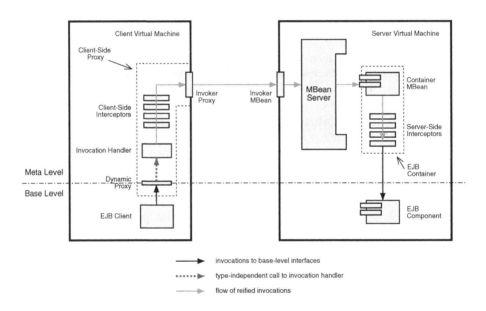

Fig. 1. Meta-level architecture for EJB: the case of a non-IIOP client

Interactions between base-level components follow a variant of the message reification model [9]. Inter-component method invocations performed at the base level are reified by special Invocation objects. Dynamic proxies receive all EJB invocations executed by non-IIOP clients (which may be EJBs themselves) and shift those invocations up to the meta level, by transparently converting them into Invocation objects.

The gray arrows in Fig. 1 show the flow of reified invocations. The invocation handler creates a reified invocation whenever a method call is issued on the client-side proxy. After traversing a chain of *client-side interceptors*, each reified invocation is sent by an *invoker proxy* to an *invoker MBean* at the server-side, where it is routed through the *container MBean* associated with the target EJB.

Figure 2 lists some of the fields of a reified invocation. The `objectName` field identifies a container MBean. The `method` and `args` fields specify a method call to be performed on the base-level component associated with that container. The `invocationContext` conveys information that is common to all invocations performed through the same (base-level) object reference. It always includes information on whether the invocation target in an `EJBHome` or an `EJBObject`, and may also specify the id of a particular `EJBObject` instance.

```
class Invocation {
    Object objectName;
    java.lang.reflect.Method method;
    Object[] args;
    InvocationContext invocationContext;
    ...
}
```

Fig. 2. Class that reifies method invocations

2.4   Remote Invocation Architecture for Non-IIOP Clients

Even though EJB clients expect typed and application-specific interfaces, EJB containers expose the generic management operation `invoke`, which takes an `Invocation` parameter. This operation plays the role of meta-level gateway to the EJBs deployed within a JBoss server. A flexible architecture supports remote invocations to EJB components by exposing the `invoke` operation through various protocols:

- An *invoker* makes the container's `invoke` operation accessible to remote clients through some request/response protocol, such as JRMP, HTTP or SOAP.
- Client-side stubs (or client-side proxies) are dynamic proxy instances that convert calls to the typed interfaces seen by clients into `invoke` calls on remote invokers.
- Each client-side proxy has a serializable invocation handler that performs remote calls on a given invoker, over the protocol supported by the invoker.
- Client-side proxies and their invocation handlers are instantiated by the server and dynamically sent out to clients as serialized objects.

The pattern just outlined is independent of the request/response protocol supported by the invoker. Client-side knowledge of this protocol is confined within the invocation handlers that clients dynamically retrieve from the server along with serialized proxies.

Invokers. An invoker is a service MBean that acts as a protocol-specific gateway to multiple EJB containers in the JBoss server. All invokers currently available in JBoss are deployable services implemented as standard MBeans. Each non-IIOP invoker exposes an `invoke` method to remote clients. This method takes an `Invocation` parameter and forwards the reified invocation to the container MBean specified by the invocation's `objectName` field.

Fig. 3 shows the remote invocation interface exposed by the JRMP invoker, which makes its `invoke` method available to RMI/JRMP clients. Other non-IIOP invokers implement either this interface or very similar ones.

```
interface Invoker extends javax.rmi.Remote {
    String getServerHostName();
    Object invoke(Invocation invocation);
}
```

Fig. 3. Generic invocation interface

Client-Side Proxies. In order to access an EJB component deployed into a JBoss server, a client must have a reference to a client-side proxy that represents the component. Local calls to application-specific methods are translated by the client-side proxy into `invoke` calls on a remote invoker object. To perform this translation, the proxy — or, more precisely, its invocation handler — must *know* the remote invoker. The exact meaning of "knowing the remote invoker" depends on the protocol over which the proxy interacts with the remote invoker. In the case of a client-side proxy associated with a JRMP invoker, that phrase means "holding an RMI/JRMP reference to the JRMP invoker." For client-side proxies associated with other invokers, the same phrase takes other meanings, such as "knowing the HTTP invoker's URL," or (in a clustered JBoss environment) "holding a collection of references to target invokers distributed across cluster nodes."

Invoker Proxies. Everything that is protocol-specific within a client-side proxy is encapsulated within an *invoker proxy*. Regardless of the protocol it supports, each invocation handler holds a local reference to an invoker proxy that implements the `Invoker` interface shown in Fig. 3. The invoker proxy interacts with a remote invoker, sending `Invocation`s and receiving results over a given protocol. Invoker proxies are created at the server side (as protocol-specific singletons) and sent out to clients along with serialized client-side proxies. They provide a good level of homogeneity to all client-side proxies.

3   The IIOP Module

Three deployable MBeans support CORBA and IIOP as a dynamically deployable feature: `CorbaORBService`, `CorbaNamingService`, and `IIOPInvoker`. They are packaged together as an "IIOP module", also known as JBoss/IIOP.

3.1   IIOP Engine

The `CorbaORBService` MBean is a thin wrapper around a third-party IIOP engine, which can be any Java ORB compliant with CORBA 2.3 or later. JacORB [4, 13], a free Java implementation of the CORBA standard, is the default IIOP engine included in the JBoss distribution. The IIOP engine is pluggable and may be replaced by users: attributes of the `CorbaORBService` MBean determine which ORB will be used. The values of these attributes are configurable via XML elements in the IIOP module's service descriptor.

3.2   CORBA Naming Service

IIOP-enabled EJBs are registered with the naming service made available by the `CorbaNamingService` MBean. Rather than allowing an external naming service to be plugged in via MBean attributes, this MBean provides an in-process CORBA naming service. It implements this service by reusing (through inheritance) code from the JacORB naming service. Users that want an external CORBA naming service have the option of replacing the `CorbaNamingService` MBean by a simpler one, which merely makes an external naming context available for EJB registration.

3.3   IIOP Invoker

The `IIOPInvoker` MBean differs from all other JBoss invokers in that it does not follow the pattern outlined in Section 2.4. For interoperability with CORBA clients written in other languages, IIOP is treated as a special case in JBoss. Even though we have implemented and tested an experimental IIOP invoker that strictly follows the "JBoss invoker pattern," this is *not* the `IIOPInvoker` included in JBoss distributions.

Non-Java clients expect application-specific interfaces to be exposed via IIOP, because they use IDL-generated stubs. In other words, they send out IIOP requests whose operation fields contain application-specific verbs. The invoker pattern, however, leads to an IIOP invoker that implements an IDL interface similar to the Java interface in Fig. 3. Such an invoker could not possibly interoperate with CORBA clients written in other languages, as it would expect IIOP requests with the verb `invoke` in their operation fields. Rather than implementing the invoker pattern, the `IIOPInvoker` included in JBoss follows the standard IIOP approach (albeit in a more dynamic way than most CORBA servers), and hence it does not suffer from language interoperability problems.

The IIOPInvoker maintains a collection of Portable Object Adapters (POAs) and a collection of CORBA servants. Fig. 4 shows how it fits into the JBoss meta-level architecture. The EJB client can be either an RMI/IIOP client written in Java, or a plain CORBA client, possibly written in another language. By performing a method invocation on an IIOP stub, the client causes an IIOP request to be sent out through the client-side ORB. The server-side ORB forwards the request to a POA, which issues an up-call to a CORBA servant. (Both the POA and the servant are logically contained in the IIOPInvoker.) The servant then converts the request into an Invocation object and routes the reified invocation through the container MBean associated with the target EJB.

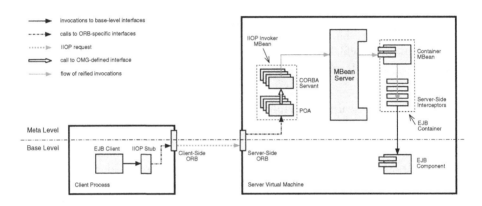

Fig. 4. Meta-level architecture for EJB: the case of an IIOP client

Note that the client/server interaction appears at different levels in the non-IIOP case (Fig. 1) and in the IIOP case (Fig. 4). The interaction takes place at the meta level in non-IIOP case, because non-IIOP invokers expose a meta-level interface (the Invoker interface) to remote clients. The IIOPInvoker, on the other hand, affords remote access to base-level EJB interfaces. More precisely, it gives remote clients access to IDL counterparts (per the Java to IDL mapping) of application-specific EJB interfaces. This is a CORBA/IIOP interoperability requirement.

4   Proxy Factories

An *EJB reference* is either a reference to an EJBObject or a reference to an EJBHome. EJB containers have the responsibility of creating such references, which in various situations they pass to EJB clients (e.g., when a client invokes a finder method on an EJBHome) or to EJB implementations (e.g., when a bean implementation invokes getEJBObject() on an EJBContext).

JBoss supports two general kinds of EJB references: (*i*) Java references to client-side stubs implemented as dynamic proxy instances, which are sent out to other virtual machines as serialized Java objects, and (*ii*) CORBA references, passed across process boundaries in the IOR format standardized by the OMG. In either case, a container MBean delegates to a *proxy factory* the task of creating EJB references.

Proxy factories implement the interface partly shown in Fig. 5. Three proxy factory classes currently implement that interface:

- `ProxyFactory`. Instances of this class create dynamic stubs (client-side stubs implemented as dynamic proxies) that talk to remote invokers over various protocols.
- `ProxyFactoryHA`. Instances of this class create dynamic stubs used in clustered JBoss environments. (The suffix "HA" stands for "high availability.")
- `IORFactory`. Instances of this class create CORBA references.

```
public interface EJBProxyFactory extends ContainerPlugin {
    ...
    Object getEJBHome();
    Object getStatelessSessionEJBObject();
    Object getStatefulSessionEJBObject(Object sessionId);
    Object getEntityEJBObject(Object primaryKey);
    Collection getEntityCollection(Collection prymaryKeys);
}
```

Fig. 5. Proxy factory interface

4.1 Relationship between Proxy Factories and Invokers

Each proxy factory is associated with an invoker MBean. Distinct `ProxyFactory` instances (or `ProxyFactoryHA` instances) may be bound to different invokers, e.g.:

- A `ProxyFactory` associated with the `JRMPInvoker` creates dynamic stubs that interact with the JBoss server via JRMP.
- A `ProxyFactory` associated with the `HTTPInvoker` creates dynamic stubs that interact with the JBoss server via HTTP.

`IORFactory` instances can only be bound to the `IIOPInvoker`; they are currently the only kind of proxy factory that can be associated with the `IIOPInvoker`.

4.2 Relationship between Proxy Factories and Containers

An EJB component deployed in JBoss has its own container, i.e., there is an one-to-one relationship between deployed EJB components and container MBeans.

Each container MBean owns a collection of proxy factories: it has a proxy factory instance for every protocol supported by its EJB component. Since these proxy factories are also associated with invoker MBeans, they define a many-to-many relationship between container MBeans and invoker MBeans.

Invoker MBeans are shared among containers (there is one invoker per protocol), but proxy factories are not. A proxy factory instance knows how to create dynamic stubs or IORs that correspond to the `EJBHome` or to an `EJBObject` implemented by a given container. Information on the identity of that container is included in every dynamic stub created by a `ProxyFactory`. The JNDI name of the EJB deployed into that container is embedded within the object key of every IOR created by an `IORFactory`.

4.3   Proxy Factory Configurations

At deployment time, the EJB deployer (an MBean that handles the deployment of EJB components) reads container configurations from XML files and creates containers. A *container configuration* has all the information the EJB deployer needs to create a container MBean, its plug-ins, and its interceptors. This includes information on the container's proxy factories, which are a special case of container plug-in. For each kind of client-side proxy that a container will export to EJB clients, the container configuration specifies a *proxy factory configuration*. XML elements in the proxy factory configuration specify the proxy factory class (a Java class) and the invoker MBean (that is, the protocol) to be used by the exported proxies, as well as additional parameters, which depend on the proxy factory class.

In the case of non-IIOP access to EJBs, XML elements in the proxy factory configuration fully specify the chain of client-side interceptors (see Fig. 1) to be included in every dynamic stub created by that factory. No similar elements exist in the configuration of a proxy factory for IIOP access to EJBs (an `IORFactory`), because interceptors instantiated at the server side would not make sense to non-Java clients. Serialized Java objects received from the server would be meaningless to CORBA clients written in other languages.

Global Configuration. JBoss has a global configuration file that includes default container configurations for the standard kinds of EJBs: stateless session beans, stateful session beans, entity beans, and message-driven beans. The global configuration file also contains alternative configurations for these kinds of EJBs. The default container configurations support remote access to EJBs by RMI/JRMP clients; alternative configurations support all other scenarios: remote access to EJBs by RMI/IIOP and CORBA clients, clustered session beans, etc. For each such scenario, the global configuration file has a proxy factory configuration, which container configurations may reference by name.

Local Configurations. A JBoss-specific deployment descriptor, optionally included with a given EJB, may refer to an alternative container configuration by its name, either to specify other protocol such as IIOP, or to use some non-standard feature such as clustering. Moreover, those deployment descriptors are not constrained to use container configurations defined in the global configuration file. A JBoss-specific descriptor may fully define a new container configuration, possibly specifying plug-in and interceptor classes included within the EJB deployment unit. More frequently, however, it will refer to a predefined container configuration and override some elements of that configuration.

The JBoss-specific deployment descriptor in an EJB may use a predefined container configuration and enhance it with additional proxy factory configurations, possibly also taken from the global configuration file. This way one can easily specify that an EJB should be simultaneously accessible via multiple protocols (e.g., RMI/JRMP, HTTP and IIOP).

5   IIOP Invoker and IOR Factory Internals

Recall that the EJB deployer creates an `IORFactory` whenever it deploys an IIOP-enabled EJB. All IIOP-related actions taken at EJB deployment time are performed within the initialization of the `IORFactory`. These actions include the instantiation of home and bean servants, the creation of POAs, the registration of the `EJBHome` in a JNDI context, and the creation of a specialized class loader that lazily generates class definitions for RMI/IIOP stub classes.

5.1   CORBA Servants

The `IIOPInvoker` has two CORBA servants per IIOP-enabled EJB deployed in JBoss: a *home servant*, which handles invocations on the `EJBHome`, and a *bean servant*, which handles invocations on all `EJBObject` instances of the IIOP-enabled EJB. What makes these servants interesting is that they must implement IDL interfaces not know in advance. A possible approach would instantiate EJB servants from classes created at deployment time. Another approach would rely on a dynamic (generic) server-side interface. To make deployment lighter, JBoss/IIOP follows the second approach.

CORBA standardizes two dynamic interfaces for server-side request dispatching: the dynamic skeleton interface (DSI), defined in IDL and mapped to various implementation languages, and the stream-based ORB API, specified only for the Java case. Both are equally powerful, but the DSI requires all operation parameters and results to be wrapped into CORBA `Anys`. To avoid this extra cost, JBoss/IIOP uses the stream-based API.

The CORBA servants depicted in Fig. 4 are stream-based dynamic skeletons that receive generic (type-independent) requests from POAs and convert these requests into `Invocation` objects, which they forward (through the MBean server) to container MBeans. Every servant knows the object name of the container MBean to which it should forward reified invocations. Moreover, each servant has marshalling knowledge specific to the IDL interface it implements.

Within a servant, marshalling knowledge takes the form of a map from IDL operation names to `SkeletonStrategy` objects. The `SkeletonStrategy` for a given operation knows how to read the sequence of operation parameters from an input stream, how to write into an output stream the return value of the operation, and how to write into an output stream any exception raised by the operation. It has an array of reader objects (instances of auxiliary classes such as `LongReader`, `StringReader`, `CorbaObjectReader`, . . .) for the operation parameters, an instance of a writer class (e.g, a `LongWriter`) for the operation result, and an `ExceptionWriter` for each exception that the operation may raise.

As a side note: dynamic deployment of IIOP-enabled components appears to be a new use case for dynamic server-side interfaces. The DSI was introduced in CORBA to allow the construction of interdomain bridges[3]. When Java ORBs started to use the DSI as a portability layer for IDL-generated skeletons, a more efficient portability layer — the stream-based ORB API — was defined. To the best of our knowledge, previous usage of dynamic server-side interfaces was restricted to these two scenarios (interdomain bridges and portability layer for IDL-generated skeletons).

5.2 POA Usage

JBoss/IIOP generates CORBA references with the following lifetimes: references to session bean instances are transient, references to entity bean instances and to `EJBHomes` are persistent. (This choice of reference lifetimes is quite natural, albeit not mandated by EJB specification. Moreover, it allows EJB handles and home handles to be implemented as thin wrappers around IORs.) Accordingly, JBoss/IIOP registers session bean servants with POAs that have the `TRANSIENT` liefespan policy, while it registers entity bean and home servants with POAs that have the `PERSISTENT` lifespan policy.

An XML element in the configuration of an IIOP proxy factory (`IORFactory`) specifies either *per-servant* or *shared* POAs. In the per-servant case, there are two POAs per deployed EJB: one for the home servant (a `PERSISTENT` POA), the other for the bean servant (either a `TRANSIENT` POA or a `PERSISTENT` POA, depending on the kind of EJB). This pair of POAs is created at deployment time. In the shared case, no POAs are created at deployment time. All deployed EJBs share a pair of POAs: a `PERSISTENT` POA dispatches requests to home and entity bean servants, a `TRANSIENT` POA dispatches requests to session bean servants.

The default `IORFactory` configuration specifies per-servant POAs, which are preferred because they make it possible to specify tagged components (such as codebase components for stub downloading) that should be added to specific IORs. The tagged components included in the IORs created by a given POA are determined by policy objects associated with that POA. The per-servant

---

[3] Such a bridge must implement CORBA objects that act as proxies for objects in another domain, with no compile-time knowledge of the interfaces of those CORBA objects.

configuration thus allows the specification of IOR components on a per-EJB basis.

5.3   Registration of EJBHomes

At deployment time, the EJBHome of an IIOP-enabled EJB is registered with the in-process CORBA naming service. It may also be optionally registered with JNP (Java Naming Provider), a JBoss-specific naming service that implements the JNDI APIs.

5.4   Lazy Generation of RMI/IIOP Stub Classes

An IORFactory can be optionally[4] associated with a *web class loader* that generates RMI/IIOP stub classes in a lazy way. The web class loader is an instance of WebCL, a subclass of URLClassLoader. Besides performing on-the-fly generation of stub classes, WebCL has a method getBytes, which returns a byte code array given a Class instance.

Recall that RMI/IIOP stub classes are named by appending the suffix "_Stub" to names of remote Java interfaces. When a WebCL instance is asked to load the class Foo_Stub, it performs Java introspection on interface Foo, applies the Java to IDL mapping on Foo, and uses code generation techniques to generate a byte code array with the class file for Foo_Stub, from which it obtains a Class instance. The WebCL instance keeps the byte code array in a hash map and returns this array whenever it is asked (via getBytes) for the byte code definition of the Foo_Stub class.

JBoss includes an in-process web server that allows remote clients to dynamically download class files via HTTP. A client downloads a class file by issuing an HTTP request for a resource whose name has two parts: (*i*) the id of a WebCL instance that can load the class, and (*ii*) the full name of the requested class file. When the web server receives such a request, it uses the WebCL both to obtain a Class object and to retrieve the class file given the Class object. RMI/IIOP stubs are therefore generated in a lazy way, as the web server receives requests from RMI/IIOP clients. If the server receives no download requests for the stub class associated with some EJB interface (perhaps because the EJB does not have any RMI/IIOP clients, but only CORBA clients), then no byte code generation is ever performed for that stub class.

In the default IORFactory configuration, every IORFactory has its own WebCL instance. (In other words, there is a web class loader per IIOP-enabled EJB.) Moreover, an IORFactory includes information on its web class loader in each IOR it creates. Such an IOR has a tagged component that specifies a codebase URL for RMI/IIOP stub downloading. The path component in this URL identifies the web class loader of the IORFactory that created the IOR.

---

[4] The usage of a web class loader is specified by an XML element in the proxy factory configuration.

6   Related Work

The JBoss meta-level architecture resembles FlexiNet [12], a Java middleware system that exploits reflective techniques in order to support flexible remote method invocation paths and multiple protocols, including IIOP. However, Flexi-Net does not define an application component model, nor does it address component deployment issues.

OpenCOM [7] is a lightweight component model upon which an adaptive ORB has been implemented. As an in-process model built atop a subset of Microsoft's COM, OpenCOM appears more suitable for very fine-grained components than the JBoss service component model. It supports dependence management, reconfiguration, and method call interception. Nevertheless, OpenCOM does not address deployment issues, nor does it support dynamic loading of component classes from remote locations.

Research prototypes have recently made significant advances at addressing dynamic deployment issues and supporting multiple protocols in component-based systems [1, 3, 5]. Unlike JBoss, these systems generally employ non-standard architectures and support component models not as well-established as EJB.

Very little has been published about the internal architecture of commercial J2EE servers. While JBoss employs reflective techniques, most commercial servers use compilation-based approaches. Nonetheless, the JBoss meta-level architecture appears to have important features in common with IONA's ART (Adaptive Runtime Technology) framework, which relies on the chain of responsibility pattern in order to support different transports, protocols, and interceptors, as well as different kinds of containers [20]. IONA uses ART as the basis for various middleware products, including a J2EE server.

Facilities for agile deployment of EJBs were absent from commercial J2EE servers until recently. In early J2EE products, the EJB deployment process even included a server restart. After JBoss introduced hot deployment of EJB components, this feature found its way into commercial servers, albeit with some restrictions. For example, BEA's WebLogic 8.1 supports hot deployment of EJBs, but does not recommend its usage in production environments [2]. Nearly all commercial offerings require vendor-specific EJB container or CORBA servant classes to be statically generated as part of the deployment process. In the case of IIOP-enabled EJBs, all other servers still require extra compilation steps for stub and skeleton generation. JBoss supports dynamic deployment of IIOP-enabled EJBs in a much stronger sense: a running server accepts IIOP-enabled deployment units that contain no JBoss-specific classes (such as EJB container or CORBA servant classes), no IIOP skeletons, and no IIOP stubs.

7   Concluding Remarks

Flexibility, developer friendliness, and ease of use are crucially important qualities in an application server. In fact, they have been frequently mentioned as reasons for the popularity of JBoss. The ability of deploying components on-the-fly has a very strong influence on those qualities. The absence of additional compilation steps, such as IDL translation, is also a significant positive factor for developer friendliness.

One of the main design goals of JBoss/IIOP was to support IIOP-enabled components without sacrificing the levels of flexibility, developer friendliness and ease of use that JBoss had already reached in the non-IIOP case. Toward this end, we have taken a reflective approach to CORBA/IIOP, and particularly to IIOP-enabled EJB components. This paper presented in detail the design and the implementation of a set of middleware components that strongly relies on reflection to meet the goal of making EJB deployment easy. Emphasis was placed on dynamic deployment issues, including the instantiation of CORBA servants for IDL interfaces not known in advance, the creation of POAs, and the lazy generation of RMI/IIOP stubs. Those issues were discussed in the context of a J2EE application server, but we believe that our techniques are equally applicable to CCM servers and to other highly dynamic component environments, in areas such as mobile computing and grid computing.

Acknowledgments

We thank Ole Husgaard, who implemented the mapping from RMI types to IIOP types used in JBoss/IIOP. We also thank Gerald Brose, for creating JacORB, and André Spiegel, for his work on valuetype support in JacORB.

The JBoss open-source server was designed and implemented by an international team led by Marc Fleury. At the time of this writing, the team has 95 members geographically dispersed across five continents. An up-to-date listing of team members is available at `http://sf.net/projects/jboss`.

References

[1] D. Balek and F. Plasil. Software connectors and their role in component deployment. In *Proceedings of DAIS'01*, Krakow, September 2001. Kluwer.

[2] BEA Systems. WebLogic Server 8.1 Documentation, 2003.

[3] I. Ben-Shaul, O. Holder, and B. Lavva. Dynamic adaptation and deployment of distributed components in Hadas. *IEEE Transactions on Software Engineering*, 27(9):769–787, 2001.

[4] G. Brose. JacORB: Implementation and design of a Java ORB. In *Proceedings of DAIS'97*, pages 143–154. Chapman & Hall, 1997.

[5] E. Bruneton, T. Coupaye, and J. Stefani. Recursive and dynamic software composition with sharing. In *Seventh International Workshop on Component-Oriented Programming (WCOP02)*, 2002.

[6] F. Buschmann, R. Meunier, H. Rohnert, P. Sommerlad, and M. Stal. *Pattern-Oriented Software Architecture: A System of Patterns*. Wiley, 1996.

[7] M. Clarke, G. S. Blair, G. Coulson, and N. Parlavantzas. An efficient component model for the construction of adaptive middleware. In *Middleware 2001 — IFIP/ACM International Conference on Distributed Systems Platforms*, volume 2218 of *LNCS*, pages 160–178. Springer-Verlag, 2001.

[8] EJCCM web site, 2003. http://www.cpi.com/ejccm/.

[9] J. Ferber. Computational reflection in class-based object-oriented languages. In *Proceedings of OOPSLA'89*, pages 317–326, 1989.

[10] M. Fleury and F. Reverbel. The JBoss extensible server. In *Middleware 2003 — ACM/IFIP/USENIX International Middleware Conference*, volume 2672 of *LNCS*, pages 344–373. Springer-Verlag, 2003.

[11] G. Kiczales *et al.* Aspect-oriented programming. In *Proceedings of ECOOP'97*, volume 1241 of *LNCS*, pages 220–242. Springer-Verlag, 1997.

[12] R. Hayton and ANSA Team. FlexiNet Architecture. ANSA Architecture Report, Citrix Systems Ltd., Cambridge, UK, February 1999. http://www.ansa.co.uk.

[13] JacORB Team. *JacORB 2.1 Programming Guide*, 2004. http://www.jacorb.org.

[14] Object Management Group. *CORBA Components, Version 3.0*, Jun 2002. OMG document formal/02-06-65.

[15] OpenCCM web site, 2003. http://www.objectweb.org/openccm/.

[16] D. Schmidt, M. Stal, H. Rohnert, and F. Buschmann. *Pattern-Oriented Software Architecture: Patterns for Concurrent and Networked Objects*. Wiley, 2000.

[17] Sun Microsystems. *Java Management Extensions — Instrumentation and Agent Specification, v1.1*, 2002.

[18] Sun Microsystems. *Enterprise JavaBeans Specification, Version 2.1*, 2003.

[19] Sun Microsystems. *Java 2 Platform Enterprise Edition Spec., v1.4*, 2003.

[20] S. Vinoski. Toward integration: Chain of responsibility. *IEEE Internet Computing*, 6(6):80–83, 2002.

A Policy-Driven Class Loader to Support Deployment in Extensible Frameworks

Richard S. Hall

Laboratoire LSR-IMAG, 220 rue de la Chimie
Domaine Universitaire, B.P. 53
38041 Grenoble Cedex 9, France
richard.hall@imag.fr

Abstract. The simplicity of dynamic code loading in Java has led to the increased popularity of extensible frameworks, where additional functionality is incorporated into a system at run time. These extensible frameworks take on many forms, such as component frameworks, plugin mechanisms, and programming environments. An interesting aspect of extensible frameworks is that they extend the software deployment life cycle down to the individual process or virtual machine level. This paper discusses how to generically support deployment for extensible frameworks and, in particular, presents a policy-driven class loader for simplifying the activation deployment process for Java-based extensible frameworks.

1 Introduction

The *software deployment life cycle* [7] is a set of inter-related activities performed after a software system is developed to make the system available for use by end users; refer to figure 1. Besides initial installation, the ultimate goal of the life cycle activities is the ongoing maintenance of the installed system. Typically, software deployment activities are viewed as occurring at two levels: the *site* and the *enterprise*. The site level is the nuts-and-bolts of software deployment, where file resources are copied into place and necessary platform state changes and/or registrations occur; the site is where the software system executes. The enterprise level is the more sophisticated process of performing deployment activities to multiple sites; this requires complex coordination to ensure properties such as atomicity and validity.

While these two levels are still completely valid and necessary, trends in recent years have extended the software deployment life cycle to a new, lower level. The dynamic class loading mechanism of Java [11] has fostered the development of *extensible frameworks*, such as those discussed in [18]. Extensible frameworks provide core functionality that is extended at run time via a module mechanism, where the term module is used in a very general sense to refer to components, plugins, or any similar modularization concept. The core functionality provided by an extensible framework may be very generic or it may be very specific. Component frameworks fall into the generic extensible framework category, such as Enterprise Java-Beans [17]. An example of a less generic extensible framework is Mozilla [12], a web browser whose functionality can be extended by plugins.

W. Emmerich and A.L. Wolf (Eds.): CD 2004, LNCS 3083, pp. 81-96, 2004.
© Springer-Verlag Berlin Heidelberg 2004

The software deployment life cycle is relevant to extensible frameworks because these frameworks perform some or all of the life cycle activities for their modules; in

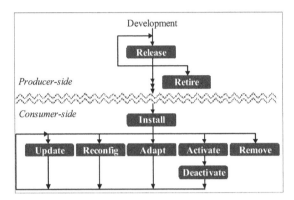

Fig. 1. Software deployment life cycle activities.

effect, the extensible frameworks are deployment frameworks for their associated modules. What makes extensible frameworks unique as deployment frameworks, when compared to traditional deployment frameworks like the Software Dock [7] or Tivoli Configuration Manager [9], is that all of the deployment activities are performed within a single process or more specifically, in the case of Java, within a single virtual machine. In addition, the likelihood that the deployment activities directly impact a running system is very high. In particular, the activation life cycle activity is central to extensible frameworks, since they form some portion of the execution environment for the dynamically loaded modules. Because of this, activation becomes closely tied to the dynamic code loading mechanics of the underlying execution environment; for example, class loading in the case of Java.

This paper focuses on providing generic, low-level support for deploying modules into Java-based extensible frameworks. While the concepts described in this introduction and the next section are relevant to extensible frameworks developed for any execution environment, the remainder of the paper focuses on the Java execution environment. First, the paper discusses the type of general deployment support that can be provided to extensible frameworks. After, a policy-driven class loader for Java is described in detail, followed by a usage scenario, related work, future work, and conclusions.

2   Generic Support for Deployment in Extensible Frameworks

Extensible frameworks perform most, if not all, of the software deployment life cycle activities; these activities are release, retire, install, update, reconfigure, adapt, activate, deactivate, and remove. The release activity is supported, at a minimum, by the definition of a packaging format for the unit of modularization associated with the extensible framework; this is generally an archive file plus meta-data. The release activity may be further supported by means of a module repository or resource discovery service that advertises and provides access to modules available for deployment.

Support for the install, update, reconfigure, adapt, and remove activities involve manipulating the release package archive; this may involve downloading, extracting, localizing, versioning, deleting, and other such activities. Activation is also supported by extensible frameworks, since a loaded module must execute to perform its function and this is generally accomplished by loading and instantiating classes or components. Activation is typically handled via a well-known interface or base class that a module implements or extends, respectively. Deactivation is typically handled using the same techniques as with activation, but it is not strictly necessary.

2.1 General Solution Approaches

Since all extensible frameworks perform some or all of the deployment life cycle activities, it is worthwhile to investigate the possibility of providing generic deployment infrastructure upon which extensible frameworks can be built. The benefits of such infrastructure are simplified development and robustness due to the re-use of common, tested code. There are two potential approaches to defining deployment infrastructure for extensible frameworks:

- *Prescriptive.* Precisely define how all aspects of deployment are to be handled, from packaging, installation, activation, code loading, etc.
- *Permissive.* Define very generic infrastructure that is malleable to many different definitions for all aspects of deployment.

The prescriptive approach requires that all extensible framework developers abandon proprietary deployment definitions and adopt the prescriptive definitions. This is nice for consistency and simplicity, but it is not always possible in practice. For example, some extensible frameworks are defined by industry-standard specifications and, as such, their approach to deployment cannot be altered by the framework developer. Another possibility is to map proprietary deployment definitions into the prescriptive ones. While this is possible, it can only be achieved if the prescriptive approach is sufficiently general to allow for such a mapping. This could result in two situations, a solution that is unwieldy if there is an attempt to include support for every possibility or, if the solution is made too generic, then it simply degenerates into the permissive approach.

Due to these reasons, the approach adopted for the work presented in this paper is the permissive approach. This results in the goal of defining deployment infrastructure that is generic enough to be re-used by any extensible framework, but still provides tangible benefits over completely proprietary development. This, then, raises the question of what types of deployment support are possible for extensible frameworks.

2.2 Potential Areas for Deployment Support

The possibility of providing high-level deployment support is not good, since high-level concepts are likely to depend on the solution domains of the individual extensible frameworks. In other words, high-level deployment concepts are more likely to be constrained by what the extensible framework is trying to achieve or by other interested parties. Because of this, it is more fruitful to consider support for common, low-level deployment tasks. Two particular low-level deployment-related tasks for extensible frameworks are:

- *File-based resource management.* This is necessary because modules are, at the simplest level, packaged as a file or, at the most complex level, a set of files with complex relationships.
- *Code loading mechanics.* This is necessary because modules must be dynamically loaded into the execution environment in order to perform their function.

File-based resource management is inherently related to the deployment life cycle activities of install, update, and remove. It is responsible for activities such as downloading, caching, accessing, and versioning the files associated with modules. Code loading mechanics is directly related to the deployment life cycle activities of activation and deactivation. Code loading bridges the gap between the file resources of the modules and the code loading mechanism of the execution environment. The remainder of this paper focuses on the latter task of code loading or, more appropriately, class loading for the Java execution environment. The paper introduces a generic, policy-driven Java class loader for extensible frameworks. The former task, file-based resource management, is the target of future work.

3   The Module Loader

The Java virtual machine locates and loads class definitions and resources at run time using an instance of the class, `ClassLoader`. Java uses a default class loading behavior that, among other things, searches a set of file system paths for available class definitions; this set of paths is called the class path. Java class loaders are arranged in a hierarchy, where each class loader instance has a parent class loader associated with it; the initial system class loader is at the root of the tree. This hierarchical relationship is the basis of the class loading delegation approach, where a request to load a class or resource is first passed to the parent class loader; only if the parent does not return a result may the child class loader respond. It is possible for applications to subclass `ClassLoader` and provide custom class search semantics for Java. The Module Loader uses this approach to create a generic, policy-driven class loader.

The Module Loader project started in response to the proliferation of custom class loaders for numerous Java-based extensible frameworks, such as plugin systems, application servers, and component frameworks. Invariably, these types of extensible frameworks extend one of Java's existing class loaders to provide custom class loading functionality for their associated units of modularization; this is necessary since extensible frameworks must perform activation of their modularization units and, in Java, class loading is central to this issue. The Module Loader is an attempt to unify custom class loaders for extensible frameworks by addressing the inherent weaknesses of the standard Java class loaders, which have led to the need for customized class loaders. One of the main weaknesses of standard Java class loaders is that they are static and do not provide support for modifying the search path to add or remove class definitions at run time. The default class loaders also do not provide explicit support for managing class versions and only allow hierarchical class loading delegation structures.

3.1 Main Concepts

Abstractly, Java class loading requires that classes, resources, and native libraries be retrieved from some sort of source, which is typically the file system, but is not limited to it. For example, it is possible to load classes and resources from a network or database. In the Module Loader, a *resource source* is a central concept. A resource source represents a place from which resources can be retrieved; it is an extension point for the Module Loader, allowing for the introduction of arbitrary sources for resources, such as the network or a database. The term *resource* is used here because at this level of Java class loading, there is no difference between retrieving bytes for a class or a resource; therefore, at this level the term may refer to either a class or resource. A resource source is represented as the following Java interface:

```
public interface ResourceSource
{
  public void open();
  public void close();
  public boolean hasResource(String name)
    throws IllegalStateException;
  public byte[] getBytes(String name)
    throws IllegalStateException;
}
```

Resource sources are grouped into *modules*; a module represents only a logical grouping of resource sources and does not prescribe a packaging or deployment unit format. Generally speaking, extensible frameworks will map their binary modularization units onto this module concept. The module concept is not strictly necessary, since it is possible to manage resource sources individually, but it adds convenience and does not restrict the possibility of individual resource source management. Each module has an associated class loader, which is used to load resources from the module's resource sources. The use of a separate class loader for each module is important, because in Java each class loader defines a unique namespace for classes; this means that if the same class file is loaded by two different class loaders, then it is considered a different class by the Java virtual machine. This distinction is very important, because it avoids naming clashes, allows the same or different versions of a class to be loaded at the same time, and provides a unit of management for groups of classes. Besides a class loader, a module also has a unique identifier and may have a set attributes associated with it.

A *module manager* maintains a set of modules; it is used to create, access, and destroy modules. The module manager also provides notifications to signal changes to the set of managed modules. It is possible to create multiple module managers, which results in multiple sets of independent modules. In this fashion, a module manager denotes a relationship among its corresponding modules, but it does not define the precise nature of this relationship. At such a generic level, only one common factor is evident: a mechanism is needed to search the modules for a specific, desired resource. Searching is the very essence of class loading in Java. The traditional manifestation of this search-related aspect of class loading is the CLASSPATH system variable for Java, which is used to direct the Java virtual machine when loading classes. This is similar to the PATH environment variable found in command shells for both UNIX and Windows, which is used to search for executable commands. To support this most basic concept of class loading, a module manager is associated with a *search policy*.

The search policy represents a "hook" that is used to precisely define how a specific resource is located among all the modules in the associated module manager. A module manager has a single search policy. The search policy is not used directly by the module manager, but is used by the module class loaders. The approach follows a delegation pattern, similar to the hierarchical class loading approach used by standard Java class loaders. When receiving a request for a class or resource, the specific module class loader receiving the request first delegates the request to the module manager's search policy. If the search policy returns a response or an error, then this response is returned as the final response to the request. On the other hand, if the search policy does not return a response, then the module class loader will search its associated resource sources and return the appropriate response if found or an error if not. A search policy is represented as the following Java interface:

```
public interface SearchPolicy
{
  public void setModuleManager(ModuleManager mgr)
    throws IllegalStateException;
  public Class findClass(Module module, String name)
    throws ClassNotFoundException;
  public URL findResource(Module module, String name);
}
```

The typical usage pattern for the Module Loader is to create an instance of the module manager, which requires a concrete search policy implementation. Next, using concrete resource source implementations, such as one that loads resources from an archive file or from the network, create any necessary modules. Then use the module manager to access a particular module and get its class loader. Finally, use the module class loader to load classes or resources using the normal class loader mechanisms, e.g., a method call to `loadClass()`. The main difference to standard class loaders at this level is that modules can be dynamically added and removed from the module manager. The implications of dynamically adding or removing modules is defined in the concrete search policy implementations; example search policies are discussed in the following subsection.

3.2 Example Search Policies

A search policy defines the actual semantics of how a resource is found in response to a specific load request; this separation of search semantics from the class loading infrastructure improves the organization and re-use of both concepts and code. This leads to the possibility of creating a standard library of search policy implementations, akin to class loading patterns, that can be used in many different types of extensible frameworks that currently require custom class loaders. In keeping with the policy-driven approach of the Module Loader, it is desirable that search policy implementations also separate policy decisions to allow for maximum flexibility. By doing so, extensible framework developers could simply select the search policy that most closely matches their desired class loading pattern and provide specific policy choices. The following subsections describe some example search policies implemented for the Module Loader; the first two examples are largely contrived for illustration purposes, but the third is reasonably sophisticated and is used in an actual extensible framework.

3.2.1 Self-Contained Search Policy

The simplest example of a search policy is the *self-contained search policy*. The self-contained search policy only looks at the resource sources of the module associated with the instigating module class loader. This means that each module class loader is completely independent of the other class loaders and that requests to load a resource are never delegated to another module class loader. This type of search policy is similar to those used for applets in a web browser, which creates boundaries around the individual applets.

3.2.2 Exhaustive Search Policy

Another simple policy is the *exhaustive search policy*. This policy sequentially searches all modules in the module manager when a resource load request is received. With the exhaustive policy, any class loader for any given module is effectively equivalent to any other module class loader. This is because all module class loaders delegate resource load requests to the other module class loaders in the same order; thus, a request sent to a module class loader will return the same resource loaded from the same class loader no matter which module class loader is used. The exhaustive policy is similar to the typical Java CLASSPATH class loading policy, with the exception that the class path can be dynamically modified by adding or removing modules in the module manager. This dynamic capability does not come without cost. For example, an application using this policy must explicitly define what happens when a module is removed.

3.2.3 Import Search Policy

The *import search policy* is a complex search policy example that deals with module dynamics. This policy enables resource sharing among modules based on import/export dependencies. The import search policy uses meta-data attached to modules via module attributes. There are three types of module meta-data used by the import search policy:

- *Export* – A set of versioned identifiers that define what the module is willing to share with other modules.
- *Import* – A set of versioned identifiers that define what the module requires from other modules.
- *Propagate* – A set of identifiers that define which of the module's imported identifiers are visible via its exports.

The term versioned identifier is purposefully vague, since the import search policy does not precisely define what a module may export or import. An example of a versioned identifier is a Java package name and version, such as "javax.servlet; 2.1.0", but other possibilities exist, such as component or library names and versions. The import search policy uses this meta-data to automatically *validate* modules by matching imports to available exports. A module is *valid* if there is a corresponding export available for each of its imports. Resources can only be loaded from modules that are valid. To maintain class loader consistency, the import search policy automatically attempts to validate a module before loading a resource with its class loader. If the module cannot be validated, the resource load request fails. The propagation meta-data also plays a role in validation.

```
package httpservice
import javax.servlet.*;
public interface HttpService {
  public void register(Servlet s);
}
```

Module *A* imports `javax.servlet` and exports `httpservice`, which exposes `javax.servlet.Servlet` in a method of one of its exported classes.

```
package httpclient;
import httpservice.*;
import javax.servlet.*;
public class HttpClient {
  ...
}
```

Module *B* imports httpservice and must also import javax.servlet since it is propagated by module *A*.

Fig. 2. Modules propagate their imports if the expose imported identifiers in their exports.

For a given module, the propagation meta-data describes which of its import identifiers are reachable via its export identifiers. Consider the following example that uses Java packages as identifiers. If, as in figure 2, a given module imports `javax.servlet` and then exports a package that contains a class with a method using a parameter type from `javax.servlet`, then the importing module propagates `javax.servlet` via this export. Not all imports are propagated, so this must be declared explicitly. Propagation knowledge is important when multiple copies, perhaps multiple versions, of the same import/export identifiers may exist in memory at the same time. In such a scenario, a transitive closure over propagation information is used to detect conflicts, since it is not possible for a single module to directly interact with more than one version of any imported class.

With the export, import, and propagate information, the import search policy performs the following generic algorithm, illustrated in figure 3, for maintaining module class loader consistency at run time when a module is modified, such as when a module is updated:

1. If an arbitrary module, *M*, is modified, then the class loader of *M* and the class loaders of any modules importing from *M* must be re-created.
2. If any identifiers propagated by *M* have changed, then importers of *M* must be re-validated and bound to the same propagated identifiers, assuming that the newly propagated identifiers are backwards compatible with the previous ones.
3. If the set of importers of *M*, called *S*, is re-validated and bound to new identifiers as a result of step 2, then all modules imported by the modules of *S* must also be re-validated and re-bound to any of the newly propagated identifiers if they propagate the same identifier.

The above algorithm deals with issues of class loader validity based on reachability of class definitions. It is possible to have multiple versions of a given class in memory at the same time, as long as the multiple definitions are not reachable by a single class loader during its lifetime. Thus, re-creating and re-binding a module class loader as the result of another module being modified is only necessary when a conflict occurs that would violate this constraint.

Re-creating a module class loader indicates that the old class loader and the classes loaded from it are no longer valid. The precise impact and response to this are left up to the extensible framework using the import search policy. The import search policy emits notifications signaling when modules are validated and invalidated. In response

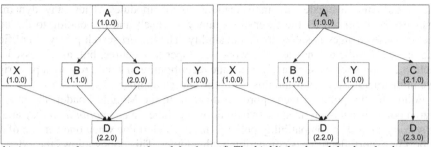

b) A scenario of interconnected module class loaders before module C is updated; no imports are propagated.

d) The highlighted module class loaders are re-created due to step #1 in the class loader consistency algorithm.

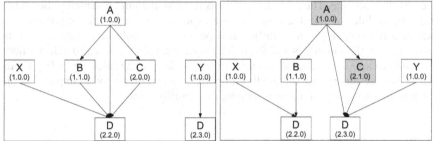

a) A scenario of interconnected module class loaders before module C is updated; C propagates D.

c) The highlighted module class loaders are re-created due to step #2 in the class loader consistency algorithm; in this scenario D must be backwards compatible.

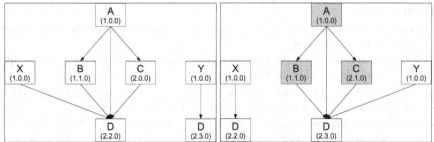

e) A scenario of interconnected module class loaders before module C is updated; both B and C propagate D.

f) The highlighted module class loaders are re-created due to step #3 in the class loader consistency algorithm; in this scenario D must be backwards compatible.

Fig. 3. Illustration of the import search policy's class loader consistency algorithm.

to module invalidation, the extensible framework should dispose of existing objects that were created using the invalidated class loader and re-create them using the new one. The extensible framework may define activation/deactivation routines for this process. Dynamic module modifications involve complex issues, but this area is the primary domain of extensible frameworks. The Module Loader is completely passive and it does not instigate any modifications to the modules. Thus, any dynamic changes are instigated by the extensible framework itself and responding to the impact of these changes is solely its responsibility. The import search policy simplifies this process for the extensible framework developer to a degree, but, as discussed in section 2, sophisticated support for run-time reconfiguration would require a prescriptive infrastructure approach and this is not the chosen approach.

Following the policy-driven approach inherent in the Module Loader, the import search policy is parameterized by two additional policies: a *compatibility policy* and a *selection policy*. The compatibility policy is used to determine when one version of an import or export identifier is compatible with another. This policy allows the extensible framework to define its own compatibility requirements. For example, the extensible framework can define a version numbering scheme that indicates when one identifier is backwards compatible with another and then implement a compatibility policy for this scheme. The selection policy is used by the import search policy when validating modules to select among multiple export candidates. Since any number of modules may export a given identifier, it is possible that multiple candidates will be available when the module is validated. The selection policy is used to select among the available candidates. An extensible framework can use the selection policy to implement precise algorithms for binding importers to exporters; for example, this approach could be used to implement scoping or visibility rules.

3.3 Other Technical Details

The search policy is the core aspect of the policy-driven approach of the Module Loader, but due to technical Java environment details an *URL creation policy* is also present. The URL creation policy is necessary because Java class loading is tied to URLs in two areas:

- *Security* – Permissions in Java are granted to classes based on the code source associated with the class.
- *Resource access* – Java applications can include required resources (e.g., image files, sound files, etc.) in their class packages.

In Java, class loading is a two-step process. First, the bytes associated with a class are loaded, then a special class loader method is called to "define" the class, which converts the bytes into an actual Java class object. It is during this "define" process that the code source is associated with a class. When a class is associated with a code source, it is possible to assign permissions to the class by granting permissions to the code source. Typically, permissions are granted to code sources using Java's security policy file. The Module Loader acquires the code source URL from the URL creation policy when it is constructing a class. By default, the Module Loader does not assign a code source URL.

With respect to resources, an application accesses its resources using the class loader. A resource request to the class loader returns an URL, which can then be used to open an input stream for loading the resource. The benefit of this approach is that applications can include and access required resources in a platform-neutral way. The default URL creation policy for the Module Loader creates URLs in the following manner:

```
module://<module-id>/<path-to-resource>/<resource-name>
```

The Module Loader registers a handler for the "`module:`" protocol, so whenever there is an attempt to create an input stream to such an URL, the Module Loader correctly interprets the host and path portions of the URL and creates the appropriate byte stream. The URL creation policy allows the extensible framework to control resource URL creation and protocol handling.

Another area that requires special support for Java class loading is native library handling. Section 3.1 introduced the concept of a resource source for retrieving both classes and resources, but native libraries are handled differently. While loading a class results in a class object and loading a resource results in an URL object, loading a native library results in a file path name pointing to the native library in the local file system. Due to this difference, the Module Loader introduced a *library source* concept that is attached to modules just like resource sources. This design decision requires additional thought, since it may be possible to unify these two sources at the expense of adding additional file handling capabilities to the Module Loader. If native libraries were made available from standard resource sources, then the Module Loader would have to "extract" native libraries from the resource sources and put them some place in the local file system and manage their existence. This is necessary because, for example, if the native library were packaged in an archive file, it is not possible for the Java virtual machine to load it directly from the archive.

The Module Loader includes the concrete search policy implementations and default implementations for all concepts necessary to start using it. In addition to everything already mentioned, a Java archive (JAR) file resource source implementation is provided for loading module classes and resources from JAR files. Other resource sources, such as one for a file system directory, a network server, or a database, are currently not included, but their implementations should not be difficult.

4 Usage Scenario

The Module Loader was created within the Oscar project [8], which is an open source implementation of the Open Services Gateway Initiative (OSGi) framework, but it was not specifically targeted for OSGi. Oscar, and the Module Loader, are part of a larger, European research project, called Open Source Middleware for Open Systems in Europe (OSMOSE). The goal of OSMOSE is twofold: to create generic, re-usable tools for building middleware systems and to use these tools to create open source implementations of the Java2 Enterprise Edition (J2EE), CORBA Component Model (CCM) [13], and OSGi [14] platforms. This section describes how the Module Loader was used in the Oscar implementation of OSGi.

4.1 OSGi Framework Overview

The OSGi Alliance is a non-profit corporation including many industrial partners for the express purpose of defining and promoting open standards for the delivery of managed services to networked environments. The initial focus of the OSGi Alliance was on the home services gateway market, but this focus has broadened to include any networked environment with a mixture of embedded devices and the need to deploy services to those devices, such as automobiles.

To that end, the OSGi Alliance created a specification for a service platform, which has at its core an extensible framework. The OSGi framework defines a unit of modularization, called a *bundle*, that is both a deployment unit and an activation unit. Physically, a bundle is a Java JAR file that contains a single component. The framework provides dynamic deployment mechanisms for bundles, including installation, removal, update, and activation. After a bundle is installed, it can be activated if all of its Java package dependencies are satisfied; package dependency meta-data is contained in the manifest of the bundle JAR file. Bundles can export/import Java packages to/from each other. The framework automatically manages the package dependencies among bundles.

After a bundle is activated it is able to provide service implementations or use the service implementations of other bundles within the framework. A service is a Java interface with externally specified semantics; this separation between interface and implementation allows for the creation of any number of implementations for a given service interface. When a bundle component implements a service interface, an instance of the corresponding service object is placed in the service registry provided by the framework so that other bundle components can discover it. All bundle interaction occurs via service interfaces.

4.2 Oscar and the Module Loader

Class loading is central to the OSGi framework since it is necessary to activate bundles and to enable interaction among bundles via common service interface definitions. Originally, class loading in Oscar was handled by a custom class loader that was specifically tailored to OSGi. Current versions of Oscar use the Module Loader for all class, resource, and native library loading.

Oscar maps the OSGi concept of a bundle directly onto the Module Loader's module concept, which requires resource sources for the bundle's JAR file and any embedded JAR files. It uses the import search policy, since this policy most closely resembles the OSGi class loading pattern. In using the import search policy, Oscar provides OSGi-specific compatibility and selection policies. The compatibility policy assumes that import/export identifiers are versioned Java packages and that all package version numbers are backwards compatible. The selection policy enforces that all modules importing a specific package, get that package from the same exporting module.

The latest OSGi specification, version 3, also allows bundles to dynamically import packages; this means that not all imported packages are known in advance. Dynamic imports are specified using a package name pattern that can include wildcards. To support dynamic package imports, Oscar subclasses the import search policy and adds functionality to dynamically import packages when the base import search policy fails to resolve a request. This is the most complicated aspect of using the Module Loader in Oscar because it performs run-time changes to the import meta-data of the underlying module. Changing meta-data at run time requires good knowledge of the import search policy; given that other extensible framework might require dynamic import/export meta-data modification, the creation of a *dynamic import search policy* as an extension of the existing import search policy is sensible for future work. If such a search policy was created, then Oscar could avoid this complicated task in its implementation.

Oscar is responsible for managing Java package dependencies among bundles. By using the import search policy, some of Oscars package management occurs automatically, because the import search policy directly supports validation of modules. The import search policy uses lazy module validation, which delays validating a module until there is a request to load a class or resource from the module. In this scenario, Oscar learns about dependency resolution via the import search policys notification mechanism. When a validation notification is sent, Oscar updates the state of the associated bundle. To manually resolve a bundles package dependencies, Oscar directly accesses a method provided by the import search policy to instigate the validation process on a specific module. During the validation process, whether automatic or manual, the import search policy automatically uses the compatibility and selection policies implemented by Oscar to precisely determine how to match imports to exports.

Using the Module Loader in this fashion gives the Oscar implementation the benefit of a clear separation between class loading policy and mechanism. This resulted in more understandable source code, since the specific policy implementations are explicitly separated from other functionality. It also simplifies experimenting with other policies, if desired, because policy code is easily accessible since it is not intermixed with application or class loading code.

5 Related Work

Due to the use of the term "module," immediate connections to other module approaches for Java arise. Projects such as Units [5], Keris [19], MJ [4] and [1] investigate adding module concepts to programming languages. In doing so, they are providing mechanisms for developers to structure their systems using program language constructs; this structure is then enforced at run time. The Module Loader is agnostic with respect to the actual unit of modularization, but since module systems such as MJ rely on class loading, it is possible for them to create or use Module Loader search policies for this purpose. MJ also defines a component registry that manages modules in the file system; this aspect is related to the generic file-based resource management introduced in section 2 and discussed further in the next section.

Java-based component frameworks and extensible frameworks are related to the Module Loader since they all must implement custom class loaders for dynamically loading extended functionality. The jBoss application server [10] is an implementation of the Enterprise JavaBeans (EJB) specification. The focus of EJB is on multi-tier, distributed enterprise applications, but class loading is at the heart of the application server, which uses it for loading and activating application logic and presentation components. The main extensible framework mentioned in this paper was OSGi, but many others exist, such as Eclipse [15] and NetBeans [2]. Both Eclipse and NetBeans are geared toward creating integrated development environments, but they are not limited to it. Their frameworks use a plugin mechanism a provide generic core services for such purposes as user interface construction (e.g., menus, windows) and file access.

All of the above types of frameworks, provide a generic foundation for building applications, but they do not provide a generic layer for building extensible frameworks. For example, creating an OSGi compliant framework using Eclipse or NetBeans would not be simple. It is these types of frameworks that the Module Loader targets in an effort to ease their implementation. Interestingly, the next release of Eclipse, version 3, will be built on top of the OSGi framework; the OSGi framework will serve as a dynamic plugin infrastructure for Eclipse.

The Module Loader was inspired by the dynamic class loading capabilities of the OSGi framework and the versioning capabilities of .NET assemblies [16]. In .NET, assemblies are the deployment unit for .NET components. Assemblies have manifests that contain meta-data describing their dependencies on other versioned assemblies, among other information. The .NET framework uses this meta-data to ensure that assemblies are bound to the correct versions of their required assemblies at run time. The default assembly loading policy in .NET is very similar to the import search policy of the Module Loader. Similarly, it is possible to have multiple versions of the same assembly in memory at the same time, with the .NET framework checking for conflicts. Assembly handling in .NET is not intended to be completely generic or policy driven, but it is possible to override default import-to-export matching via configuration files.

6 Future Work

The Module Loader is part of a larger effort to create generic tools and components for creating extensible frameworks. This paper presented some of the issues for supporting deployment for extensible frameworks and, more precisely, section 2 defines two areas of generic, low-level deployment support for extensible frameworks: file-based resource management and code loading. The Module Loader addresses the latter and a goal of future work is to address the former. Extensible frameworks have to manage the file-based resources associated with their units of modularization; for example, OSGi has a local cache where all deployed bundles are managed and MJ has a component registry where it stores its modules. The idea is to investigate whether it is worthwhile to develop a generic, file-based resource manager to simplify extensible framework development.

The details are still evolving, but initial thoughts for the file-based resource manager include a file repository that supports simple, policy-driven deployment processes for install, update, and removal of files. These deployment processes would be tailored to the lower level requirements of extensible frameworks versus the high-level deployment processes for sites or enterprises. The file-based resource manager should be independent of the Module Loader, allowing both to be used independently, but the two should be able to work together simply.

Currently, the main risk in the Module Loader work is determining whether there are other viable class loading policies to be created and getting feedback and/or experience on using available class loading policies. Two possibilities currently exist for gaining feedback and experience: OpenCCM [6] and Fractal [3]. OpenCCM is an open source implementation of the CORBA Component Model platform from the Computer Science Laboratory of Lille (LIFL). Fractal is a modular and extensible component model from France Telecom and the French National Institute for Research in Computer Science and Control (INRIA). Both of these projects and their corresponding organizations are part of the same OSMOSE project to which the Module Loader belongs. This experience could also be beneficial in determining the need for creating new search policies.

7 Conclusion

The simplicity of dynamic code loading in Java has led to the increased popularity of extensible frameworks, where additional functionality is incorporated into a system at run time. Extensible frameworks take on many forms, such as component frameworks, plugin mechanisms, and programming environments. An interesting aspect of extensible frameworks is that they extend the software deployment life cycle down to the individual process or virtual machine level. This broader scope of software deployment presents unique challenges for creating generic deployment support for these types of systems. Deployment processes in extensible frameworks generally impact a running system and are closely tied to activation and the execution environment.

This paper discussed how to generically support deployment in extensible frameworks and, in particular, presented a policy-driven class loader, called the Module Loader, for simplifying the activation deployment process for Java-based extensible frameworks. The Module Loader tries to separate policy decisions from class loading infrastructure. At a minimum, this results in better source code organization when developing extensible frameworks since specific class loading policy is clearly separated from other code. Further, the Module Loader unifies custom class loading concepts, which may lead to the creation of a library of standard class loading policies or patterns. The benefit of this is significant for both code re-use and for concept re-use, where it is possible to understand an extensible framework's code loading approach just by knowing the general policy it uses, similar to the benefit of design patterns.

References

1. L. Bauer, A.W. Appel, and E.W. Felten, "Mechanisms for Secure Modular Programming in Java," Software -- Practice and Experience, 2003.
2. T. Boudreau, J. Glick, S. Greene, V. Spurlin, and J.J. Woehr, "NetBeans: The Definitive Guide," OReilly and Associates, October 2002.
3. E. Bruneton, T. Coupaye, and J.B. Stefani, "The Fractal Component Model Specification, Version 2.0-2," http://fractal.objectweb.org/specification/index.html, September 2003.
4. J. Corwin, D.F. Bacon, D. Grove, and C. Murthy, "MJ: A Rational Module System for Java and its Applications," Proceedings of the 18th ACM SIGPLAN Conference on Object-Oriented Programming, Systems, Languages, and Applications, October 2003.
5. M. Flatt and M. Felleisen, "Units: Cool Modules for HOT Languages," Proceedings of the ACM SIGPLAN 98 Conference on Programmi ng Language Design and Implementation, June 1998.
6. A. Flissi, "Inside OpenCCM - Developer Guide, Version 1.0," http://openccm.objectweb.org/doc/0.6/Inside_OpenCCM_1.0.pdf, March 2003.

7. R.S. Hall, D. Heimbigner, and A.L. Wolf, "A Cooperative Approach to Support Software Deployment Using the Software Dock," Proceedings of the International Conference on Software Engineering, May 1999.

8. R.S. Hall and H. Cervantes, "An OSGi Implementation and Experience Report," Proceedings of IEEE Consumer Communications and Networking Conference, January 2004.

9. IBM Corp., "Introducing IBM Tivoli Configuration Manager," http://publib.boulder.ibm.com/tividd/td/ITCM/GC23-4703-00/en_US/PDF/GC23-4703-00.pdf, October 2002.

10. JBoss Group, "JBoss Application Server," http://www.jboss.org, January 2004.

11. S. Liang and G. Bracha, "Dynamic Class Loading in the Java Virtual Machine," Conference on Object-oriented Programming, Systems, Languages, and Applications (OOPSLA98), October 1998.

12. Mozilla.org, "Mozilla Web Browser," http://www.mozilla.org, January 2004.

13. Object Management Group, "CORBA Components Specification," Version 3.0, June 2002.

14. Open Services Gateway Initiative, "OSGi Service Platform Version 3," http://www.osgi.org, March 2003.

15. Object Technology International Inc., "Eclipse Platform Technical Overview," http://www.eclipse.org/whitepapers/eclipse-overview.pdf, February 2003.

16. D.S. Platt, "Introducing Microsoft .NET," Microsoft Press, Second Edition, 2002.

17. Sun Microsystems, "Enterprise JavaBeans Specification Version 2.0," http://java.sun.com/products/ejb/docs.html, August 2001.

18. C. Szyperski, "Independently Extensible Systems - Software Engineering Potential and Challenges," Proceedings of the 19th Australian Computer Science Conference, 1996.

19. M. Zenger, "Evolving Software with Extensible Modules," International Workshop on Unanticipated Software Evolution, May 2002.

MagicBeans: a Platform for Deploying Plugin Components

Robert Chatley, Susan Eisenbach, and Jeff Magee

Dept of Computing, Imperial College London,
180 Queensgate, London, SW7 2AZ, UK
{rbc,sue,jnm}@doc.ic.ac.uk

Abstract. Plugins are optional components which can be used to enable the dynamic construction of flexible and complex systems, passing as much of the configuration management effort as possible to the system rather than the user, allowing graceful upgrading of systems over time without stopping and restarting. Using plugins as a mechanism for evolving applications is appealing, but current implementations have limited functionality. In this paper we present a framework that supports the construction and evolution of applications with a plugin architecture.

1 Introduction

Almost all software will need to go through some form of evolution over the course of its lifetime to keep pace with changes in requirements and to fix bugs and problems with the software as they are discovered. Maintaining systems where components have been deployed is a challenging problem, especially if different configurations of components are deployed at different sites.

Traditionally, performing upgrades, fixes or reconfigurations of a software system has required either recompilation of the source code or at least stopping and restarting the system. High availability systems have high costs and risks associated with shutting them down for any period of time [18]. In other situations, although continuous availability may not be safety or business critical, it is simply inconvenient to interrupt the execution of a piece of software in order to perform an upgrade.

It is important to be able to cater for the evolution of systems in response to changes in requirements that were not known at the initial design time (unanticipated software evolution). There have been a number of attempts at solving these problems at the levels of evolving methods and classes [5,2], components [13] and services [19]. In this paper we consider an approach to software evolution at the architectural level, in terms of *plugin* components.

Oreizy *et al* [18] identify three types of architectural change that are desirable at runtime: component addition, component removal and component replacement. It is possible to engineer a generalised and flexible plugin architecture which will allow all of these changes to be made at runtime.

W. Emmerich and A.L. Wolf (Eds.): CD 2004, LNCS 3083, pp. 97–112, 2004.
© Springer-Verlag Berlin Heidelberg 2004

The benefits of building software out of a number of modules have long been recognised. Encapsulating certain functionality in modules and exposing an interface evolved into component oriented software development [3]. An important difference between plugin based architectures and other component based architectures is that plugins are optional rather than required components. The system should run equally well regardless of whether or not plugin components have been added. Plugins allow the possibility of easily adding components to a working system after it has been deployed, adding extra functionality as it is required. Plugins can be used to address the following issues:

- the need to extend the functionality of a system,
- the decomposition of large systems so that only the software required in a particular situation is loaded,
- the upgrading of long-running applications without restarting,
- incorporating extensions developed by third parties.

Plugin systems have previously been developed to address each of these different situations individually, but the architectures designed have generally been quite specifically targeted and therefore limited. Either there are constraints on what can be added, or creating extensions requires a lot of work on behalf of the developer, writing architectural definitions that describe how components can be combined [17]. In this paper we describe a more generalised and flexible plugin architecture, not requiring the connections between components to be explicitly stated.

In the remainder of this paper we describe the implementation of a platform for managing plugin-based applications, which we call MagicBeans. We highlight some technical issues of particular interest, and present a case study of the system in use. Finally we discuss related work and future directions.

2   The Software

We have implemented a generalised infrastructure for our plugin architecture, which we call MagicBeans. In this section we describe the requirements and details of the implementation. We also present an example application that runs on top of the MagicBeans platform. This application is a large piece of analysis software, which has been extended in various ways through plugin components.

2.1   Requirements

To enable the evolution of software systems through the addition, removal and coordination of plugin components at runtime, we require some kind of runtime framework to be built. We have a number of functional requirements for the system.

The framework should form a platform on top of which an application can run. The platform should launch the application, and from then on manage the

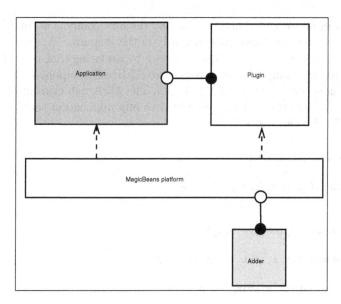

Fig. 1. Platform architecture managing a two component application

configuration of plugin components. It should work as automatically as possible, so that the right interfaces and classes from each component are detected and loaded, and components are matched and bound appropriately by the framework. It should be possible to plug components together in chains and other configurations. The configuration should be managed entirely by the platform.

Using the plugin platform should have minimal impact on the developer or the user (or system administrator). The developer should not be forced to design their software in a particular way, to make extensive calls to an API, or to write complex descriptions of their components in any form of architecture description language. There should be no particular installation procedure that needs to be gone through in order to add a component, simply allowing the platform to become aware of the new component's location should be enough.

The mechanism by which new components are introduced to the system should not be prescribed by the platform. It should be possible to adapt easily the framework to allow components to be added in new ways, for instance: located by a user, or discovered in the filesystem or network, etc.

2.2   Implementing Plugin Addition

MagicBeans is implemented in Java, and allows a system to be composed from a set of components, each of which is comprised of a set of Java classes and other resources (such as graphics files) stored in a Jar archive.

When a new plugin is added to the system, the platform searches through the classes and interfaces present in the new component's Jar file to determine what services are provided and required by the new component, and how it can be connected to the components currently in the system.

A class signifies that it provides a service by declaring that it implements an interface. In the example below, we show an AirBrush component that might be added as an extension to a paint program. The `AirBrush` class implements the `GraphicsTool` interface. It can be added to any application that can accept a `GraphicsTool` as a plugin.

```
interface GraphicsTool {

    void draw( int x, int y, Canvas c );
}

class AirBrush implements GraphicsTool {

    void draw( int x, int y, Canvas c ) {

        //implement drawing code here
    }
}
```

A component that can accept a plugin has a slightly more complex design. Here we show a paint program that can accept and use our `GraphicsTool` plugin. For a component to use the services provided by a plugin, it must obtain a reference to an object from the plugin. This is achieved through a notification mechanism. The mechanism is based on the Observer pattern [6]. Any object can register with the platform to be notified when a new binding is made which is relevant to it.

To register as an observer, an object calls the following (static) method in the `PluginManager` class:

```
PluginManager.getInstance().addObserver( this );
```

This only registers that an object is interested in new plugins, but does not specify the plugin type. An object signifies that it can accept a plugin of a certain type by declaring a method `pluginAdded(...)` that takes a parameter of that type, in this case `GraphicsTool`

When the AirBrush plugin is added, observing objects with a `pluginAdded()` method that can take a `GraphicsTool` as their parameter are notified. This is done by calling the `pluginAdded()` method, passing a reference to the new `GraphicsTool` object, through which methods can be called. It is normal to assign this reference to a field of the object or add it to a collection within `pluginAdded()` so that the reference is maintained. In the example below, the new tool is added to a list of all the available tools.

Classes can define multiple `pluginAdded()` methods with different parameter types, so that they can accept several different plugins of different types.

```
class PaintProgram {

    List tools;
    GraphicsTool current;

    PaintProgram() {

        PluginManager.getInstance().addObserver( this );
    }

    void pluginAdded( GraphicsTool gt ) {

        tools.add( gt );
    }

    void redrawScreen() {

        for ( Iterator i = tools.iterator() ; i.hasNext() ; ) {

            drawButton( (GraphicsTool)i.next() );
        }

        ...

        if ( current != null ) {current.draw( x, y, o_canvas );}

        ...

    }
}
```

For each component, the plugin manager iterates through all of the classes contained inside the Jar file, checking each for implemented interfaces (provisions) and **pluginAdded()** methods, and finding all the pairs that are compatible. For a class to be compatible with an interface, it must be a non-abstract subtype of that interface. The matching process is performed using Java's reflection [8], custom loading [14] and dynamic linking features, which allow classes to be inspected at runtime. If a match is found, a binding between the two components is added to the system. The class in question is instantiated (if it has not been already), and the notification process is triggered.

There are various mechanisms through which plugins could be introduced to the system, and which is chosen depends on the developer and the application. Possibilities include that the user initiates the loading of plugins by selecting them from a menu, or locating them in the filesystem; that the application monitors a certain filesystem location for new plugins; or that there is some sort of network discovery mechanism that triggers events, in the manner of Sun's Jini [12]. MagicBeans does not prescribe the use of any of these. It uses a known filesystem location as a bootstrap, but components that discover new plugins can be added to the platform in the form of plugin components themselves (the platform manages its own configuration as well as that of the target application) which implement the **Adder** interface. Figure 1 shows an example of the platform running, managing an application extended with one plugin, with an Adder component plugged in to the platform itself. Each Adder is run in its own thread, so different types can operate concurrently. Whenever an Adder becomes aware of a new plugin, it informs the platform and the platform carries out the binding process. We have written example applications that load plugins from a known filesystem location, and that allow the user to load plugins manually using a standard "open file" dialog box.

2.3   Plugin Removal

As well as adding new plugins to add to the functionality of a system over time, it may be desirable to remove components (to reclaim resources when certain functionality is no longer needed) or to upgrade components by replacing them with a newer version. Together these form the three types of evolution identified in [18].

Removal is not as straightforward as addition. In order to allow for the removal of components, we need to address the issue of how to revoke the bindings that were made when a component was added. The platform could remove any bindings involving the component concerned from its representation of what is bound to what, but when the component was added and bound, the classes implementing the relevant interfaces were instantiated, and references to them passed to the components to which they were connected. These components will retain these references and may continue to call methods on the objects after the platform has removed the bindings. It is not possible to force all of the objects in the system to release their references. If the motivation for removing the plugin was to release resources then this objective will not be met.

We can have the platform inform any components concerned when a plugin is about to be removed. This is done using the same observer notification mechanism as we use when a component is added, but calling a different method `pluginRemoved()`. Any references to the plugin or resources the component provides should then be released. For example:

```
class PaintProgram {

    ...

    void pluginRemoved( GraphicsTool gt ) {

        tools.remove( gt );
    }
}
```

When all of the notifications have been performed, the bindings can be removed. However, this technique relies on the cooperation of the plugins. We cannot force references to be released, only request that components release them. Components could be programmed simply to ignore notifications (or may not even register to be notified) and in this case will continue to retain their references after a binding is removed.

As a solution to this problem, in addition to using the notifiation mechanism, when classes providing services are initially instantiated, instead of providing another component with a reference directly to that object, the reference passed is to a proxy. All the references to the objects from the plugin are then under the control of the platform, as the platform maintains a reference to each proxy. When a component is removed, the reference from each proxy to the object that provides its implementation can be nullified, or pointed at a dummy implementation. In this way we can force that resources are released. In the event that at component does try to access a plugin that has been removed, we can throw a suitable exception.

In order to provide this level of indirection, we use Java's `Proxy` class (from the standard API) to create a proxy object for each binding created. The `Proxy` class allows us to create an object dynamically that implements a given interface (or interfaces), but which, when a method is called, delegates to a given `InvocationHandler` which actually implements the method or passes the call on to another object. Using this mechanism, the implementation of the method can be switched or removed at runtime simply by reassigning object references. This gives us exactly what we need. When a plugin is removed we can nullify the reference to the delegate. When a method is called we check for the presence of a delegate, and if it has been removed throw a suitable exception back to the caller.

Another major concern is deciding when it is safe to remove a component. For instance, it will be very difficult to replace a component if the system is currently executing a method from a class belonging to that component. This problem is solved by synchronising the methods in the proxy object, so that a component cannot be removed whilst another object is in the midst of executing a method supplied by this component.

2.4   Plugin Replacement

We can perform plugin replacement in order to effect an upgrade of a system. However, before removing the old component, checks must be made to ensure that the new version is compatible.

A safe criterion for compatability of components might be that the new one must provide at least the services that the one it is replacing provides, and must not require more from the rest of the system [22]. In this way we can compare two components in isolation to decide whether one is a suitable substitute for the other.

However, in the case of plugin systems, there are a few more subtleties to be considered. With plugin systems, components that are used by other components are not strictly *required* but optional extensions that may be accepted. Therefore, in comparing components for compatability we do not need to consider the case of what the components require, only what they provide. It is only this that is critical to the success of the upgrade.

Also, as we are performing upgrades at runtime, during system operation, we have more information than we would have if we just had the components in isolation. At any point the MagicBeans platform knows the current structure of the system, and so knows which of the interfaces that a plugin provides are actually being used (those for which a binding has been created during the addition process). We can therefore say that new component is safe to replace another if it provides at least the same services as those that are provided by the old one, and are currently being used.

For example, we might have a component Brush which contains classes that implement `GraphicsTool` and `Help`. We can use this plugin with a graphics application as was shown previously, which will use the `GraphicsTool` interface. We could also use it with an application that allowed help to be browsed, or an application that combined both of these features. However, let us consider the case where we are using the Brush with our simple paint application. In this case, only the `GraphicsTool` interface will be used.

We may now write or purchase a new tool, say a SuperBrush. We want to upgrade the system to use this instead of the Brush. The SuperBrush does not provide the `Help` interface, but its implementation of `GraphicsTool` is far superior. If we use our first criterion for deciding compatability, then we will not be able to upgrade from a Brush to a SuperBrush, as SuperBrush does not provide all the services that Brush does. However, if we use the second criterion, then in the context of the simple paint application, SuperBrush provides all the services that are being used from Brush, (*i.e.* just `GraphicsTool`) and so we can perform the upgrade.

Replacement could be done by first removing the old component, and subsequently adding the new one, using the mechanisms as described above. However, due to the presence of the proxy objects which allow us to manange the references between plugins, we can swap the object that implements a service, without having to notify the client that is using it. In this way it is possible to effect a seamless upgrade.

3   Technical Innovations

3.1   BackDatedObserver

There are some cases in which the notification system described above has limitations. If, on adding a new plugin, multiple bindings are formed, it may be the case that bindings are created before the objects that will observe the creation of these bindings have been initialised and registered as observers.

For example, consider the case where we have two components, each providing one service to and accepting one service from the other. If component A is already part of the system, and component B is added, a binding may be formed connecting B's requirement with A's provision. Currently no observers from B have registered, and so none are informed of the new binding.

A second binding is then formed between B's provision and A's requirement. At this point, a class from B is instantiated. A reference to this object is passed to any observers in A. During the creation of the object from B, the constructor is run, and the object registers as an observer with the PluginManager. As the registration is too late, although the PluginManager matched two pairs of interfaces to create bindings, the situation that results is that A holds a reference to B, but not the other way around.

To solve this problem, we introduce the notion of a BackDatedObserver. This is an observer which, on registering, has the opportunity to catch up on previous events that occurred before it registered, but which are relevant to it. In the last example, having the observers register as BackDatedObservers would mean that the observer from B would be passed a reference to the object from A as soon as it registers, and it would be possible to call methods in both directions.

Implementing this variation on the traditional observer pattern requires that the participant that performs the notification keeps a history of past events, so that it can forward them to new observers when they register.

3.2 Distinguishing Components

In order to be able to tell which observers need to be notified about which new bindings, it is necessary to maintain a record of which objects come from which components. That is to say, which component contains the class from which the object was created. This could be done by calling a special factory method that would create objects and update the relevant data structures. However, such a scheme would impinge greatly on the natural style of programming. It would be necessary for the programmer to write something like:

```
A myA = (A)ObjectFactory.create( ''A'' );
```

instead of the usual

```
A myA = new A();
```

There are a number of problems with this. Firstly, it is a lot more cumbersome to write. Secondly, it removes static type safety. Thirdly, we cannot force programmers to use this mechanism, and no information will be recorded about any objects created in the normal style.

In a language that allows operator overloading (for example C++), we could implement a new operator that performs the appropriate record keeping, allowing object creation using the normal syntax. However, operator overloading is not available in Java.

The solution to this problem that has been adopted utilises the fact that in Java every object created holds a reference to its class, and every class in turn to its class loader. By associating a separate class loader with each plugin component, we can group objects into components on the basis of their class loaders. In fact, we made the class Component, which manages all of the information relevant to a particular plugin, a subclass of java.lang.ClassLoader, so that for any object, calling

```
getClass().getClassLoader()
```

will return a reference to its `Component`.

3.3   Multi-methods

As all of the objects that come from plugin components may be of types that are unknown to the MagicBeans platform, objects are created using reflection, and the references that are used to point to them have the static type `Object`, which is the ultimate superclass of all classes in Java.

If the PluginManager were to attempt to call one of the `pluginAdded()` methods in a component, it would pass a parameter with static type `Object` and the Java runtime would require that the method being called took a parameter of type `Object` even if the dynamic type of the parameter was something more specific.

In fact, during the compilation of the plugin component, the Java compiler will complain that there is no method `pluginAdded( Object o )`. If the developer adds this method, this is the one that will be called at runtime, regardless of the dynamic type of the parameter passed. The reason for this is that methods in Java are only dispatched dynamically on the type of the receiver, not that of the parameters [7].

This causes a problem as we wish to use `pluginAdded()` methods with different parameter types to specify the types of plugin that a component can accept.

In the implementation of MagicBeans we have overcome this problem by using reflection to dispatch certain methods dynamically on the parameter types as well as the receiver. This is often called "double-dispatch" or "multi-methods" [4].

We created a class `MultiMethod` which has a static method `dispatch()` which takes as parameters the intended receiver, the name of the method and the parameter.

```
MultiMethod.dispatch( receiver , ''pluginAdded'' , parameter );
```

Reflection is used to search through the methods of the given receiver to find one with the given name and a formal parameter type that matches that of the parameter passed as closely as possible. This method is then invoked, again using the reflection mechanism. Double dispatch is only used when calling the `pluginAdded()` and `pluginRemoved()` methods, not for any subsequent calls between components. This means that the performance penalty incurred by calling methods in this way is kept to a minimum.

4   Case Study: Extensible LTSA

The Labelled Transition System Analyser (LTSA) [10] is a Java application that allows systems to be modelled as labelled transition systems. These models can be checked for various properties, making sure that either nothing bad happens (safety) or that eventually something good happens (liveness). The core functionality of LTSA is to take textual input in the form of the FSP process calculus, to compile this into state models which can be displayed graphically and animated, and to check properties of these models.

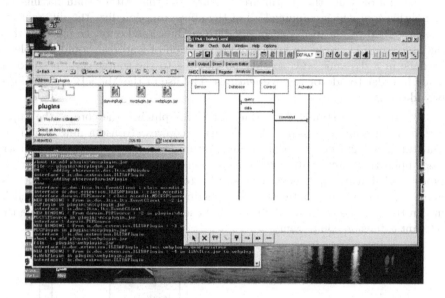

Fig. 2. LTSA tool running with plugins

On top of this core functionality, various extensions have been built, notably to allow more illustrative animations of the behaviour of models; to allow FSP to be synthesised from graphical Message Sequence Charts (MSCs) representing scenarios [23] so that properties of these scenarios can be analysed; to harness the sructural information given by the Darwin architecture definition language (ADL) in generating models; and to provide a facility for interacting with behaviour models by means of clicking items on web pages served over the internet to a web browser [21]. The various extensions have been implemented as plugins using MagicBeans. Figure 2 shows the LTSA tool running with three plugins connected. The console windows shows the output from MagicBeans as it loaded and bound the plugin components. The MSC and ADL plugins interact directly if both are present. Figure 3 shows the different classes and interfaces in the different components of LTSA. The grey boxes represent components which contain classes and interfaces. These are all loaded and managed by the MagicBeans platform (not pictured). The dashed arrows signify implementation of an interface, so the class MSCSpec implements the FSPSource interface. These interface implementations form the basis for the bindings between the components. For example, the ADL Editor can use an FSPSource, and an implementation of this is provided by the MSCPlugin component, so when both of these plugins are present, a binding is formed between them.

More extensions for LTSA are currently in development and the use of the plugin framework has made it very easy to for different parties to develop new functionality and integrate it with the tool.

The aim of using the plugin architecture was that rather than having one monolithic tool which combined all of the above functionality, the different extensions could be encapsulated in separate modules, and only the modules that the user required would be loaded. This selection of features should be able to be done in a dynamic way, so that no changes to the source code need to be made in order to add or remove features. The use of the MagicBeans platform provides this.

By providing a standard interface for LTSA plugins, the core of the application can use any extensions that the user requires. To use a new plugin, all that the user has to do is to drop the relevant Jar file into a certain directory. The application interrogates each plugin to find out whether it provides certain types of GUI features (menus, tool bar buttons etc) that should be added to main application's user interface. The plugins then respond to the user clicking on the buttons or menus by executing code from handler classes inside the relevant extension component.

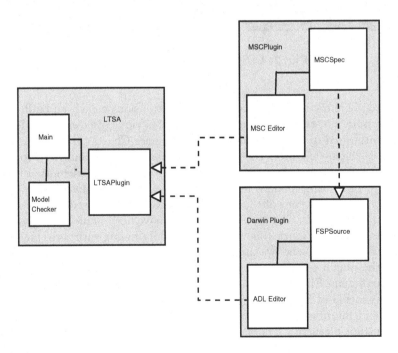

Fig. 3. Class diagram showing classes in different plugins

5   Related Work

5.1   JavaBeans

JavaBeans [11] is Sun's original component technology for Java. Beans are formed by packaging classes and other resources into Jar files, but the focus is on combining and customising Beans to create an application using a graphical builder tool. They are commonly used for combining user interface components to create a complete GUI. The technology that we have presented here differs from this approach in that we intend the coordination of components to form applications to be as transparent as possible, and to be performed in a way that is reactive to the other components that have already been deployed in the system.

5.2   OSGi and Gravity

The Open Services Gateway initiative (OSGi) [20] Service Platform is a specification for a framework that supports the dynamic composition of services. An implementation of this specification can be integrated into applications to provide a plugin or extension mechanism. OSGi compliant applications work by managing "bundles" that are registered with a platform. Clients can query the OSGi registry for components that provide a certain service.

Gravity is an application that uses Oscar [9], an implementation of OSGi, to allow applications to be built dynamically from components that may vary in their availability. In order to use a bundle with Gravity, the component needs to contain an XML description of its provided and required services, which is not the case with MagicBeans.

5.3   Java Applets

Java applets [1] allow modules of code to be dynamically downloaded and run inside a web browser. The dynamic linking and loading of classes that is possible with Java allows extra code, extending the available functionality, to be loaded at any time.

A Java program can be made into an applet by making the main class extend `java.applet.Applet` and following a few conventions. The name of this main class and the location from where the code is to be loaded are included in the HTML of a web page. A Java enabled browser can then load and instantiate this class.

The applet concept has proved useful in the relatively constrained environment of a web browser, but it does not provide a generalised mechanism for creating extensible applications. As all applets must extend the provided Applet class, it is not possible to have an applet which has any other class as its parent (as Java has single inheritance).

5.4 Lightweight Application Development

In [15] Mayer *et al* present the plugin concept as a design pattern (in the style of [6]) and give an example implementation in Java. The architecture described in the design pattern is similar to that used by MagicBeans. It includes a plugin manager that loads classes and identifies those that implement an interface known to the main application.

Their work does allow for one application to be extended with multiple plugins, possibly with differing interfaces, but makes no mention of adding plugins to other plugins.

The plugin mechanism is described in terms of finding classes to add to the system, where we work in terms of components. Although our components do contain sets of classes (along with other resources such as graphics), it is the component as a whole that is added to provide the extension to the system.

5.5 ActiveX

ActiveX is a technology developed by Microsoft in the 1990's. ActiveX controls are reusable software components that can add specialised functionality to web sites, desktop applications, and development tools [16]. They are primarily designed for creating user-interface elements that can be added to container applications. There is no standard mechanism for establishing peer-to-peer connections between ActiveX components, only between the container and the control. This means that the configurations that can be created are a lot less flexible than what can be achieved using the MagicBeans framework.

5.6 Eclipse

The Eclipse Platform [17] is designed for building integrated development environments. It is built on a mechanism for discovering, integrating and running modules which it calls plugins.

Any plugin is free to define new extension points and to provide new APIs for other plugins to use. Plugins can extend the functionality of other plugins as well as extending the kernel. This provides flexibility to create more complex configurations.

Each plugin has to include a manifest file (XML) providing a detailed description of its interconnections to other plugins. The developer needs to know the names of the extension points present in other plugins in order to create a connection with them. With the MagicBeans technology, the actual Java interfaces implemented by classes in plugins are interrogated using reflection, and this information is used to organise and connect components.

On start-up, the Eclipse Platform Runtime discovers the set of available plugins, reads their manifests and builds an in-memory plugin registry. Plugins cannot be added after start-up. This is a limitation as it is often desirable to add functionality to a running program without having to stop and restart it. Version 3.0 of Eclipse will address this by using an OSGi implementation to manage plugins.

6 Conclusions

We have presented a system of plugin components that allows flexible applications to be constructed by deploying sets of components that are combined to form a system. Functionality can be added to an application over time, as it is required or becomes available, by deploying a new component alongside those that are already in use by the system. Components that are no longer needed can be removed, allowing resources to be reclaimed, and components can be replaced when later versions become available.

We described MagicBeans, a platform supporting self-assembling systems of plugin components, written in Java. The platform allows applications to be constructed and reconfigured dynamically at runtime. It allows the architecture of an application to be altered by adding, removing or replacing components, without halting execution or having to restart the system.

We showed how to write a program that uses the MagicBeans framework to allow components to be be added and removed dynamically, demonstrating that the extra code that a developer needs to write to take advantage of the system is minimal. We also discussed some of the technical challenges involved in implementing the platform.

Future work in this area could address the problems of coordinating components deployed across a distributed environment, or look at the possibility of expressing some sort of structural constraints or goals for the system, so that when components are assembled, not only are interfaces matched, but a certain structure, say a ring, is maintained. This could involve inserting components between components that are already connected, which is not something that our system currently allows.

7 Acknowledgments

We would like to acknowledge our colleagues in the Distributed Software Engineering group and the SLURP group at Imperial College London for their helpful discussions. We would also like to acknowledge the support of the European Union under grant STATUS (IST-2001-32298).

References

1. Applets. Technical report, Sun Microsystems, Inc., java.sun.com/applets/, 1995-2003.
2. G. Bierman, M. Hicks, P. Sewell, and G. Stoyle. Formalising dynamic software updating. In *Second International Workshop on Unanticipated Software Evolution at ETAPS '03*, 2003.
3. C. Szyperski. *Component Software: Beyond Object-Oriented Programming.* Addison-Wesley Pub Co, 1997.
4. C. Clifton, G. T. Leavens, C. Chambers, and T. Millstein. MultiJava: Modular open classes and symmetric multiple dispatch for Java. In *OOPSLA 2000 Conference on Object-Oriented Programming, Systems, Languages, and Applications, Minneapolis, Minnesota*, volume 35(10), pages 130–145, 2000.

5. M. Dmitriev. HotSwap Client Tool. Technical report, Sun Microsystems, Inc., www.experimentalstuff.com/Technologies/ HotSwapTool/index.html, 2002-2003.

6. E. Gamma, R. Helm, R. Johnson, John Vlissides. *Design Patterns: Elements of Reusable Object-Oriented Software.* Addison-Wesley Pub Co, 1995.

7. J. Gosling, B. Joy, G. Steele, and G. Bracha. *The Java Language Specification.* Addison Wesley, 2 edition, June 2000.

8. D. Green. The Reflection API. Technical report, Sun Microsystems, Inc., http://java.sun.com/docs/books/tutorial/reflect/, 1997-2001.

9. R. S. Hall. Oscar. Technical report, ungoverned.org, oscar-osgi.sourceforge.net, 2003.

10. J. Magee and J. Kramer. *Concurrency – State Models and Java Programs.* John Wiley & Sons, 1999.

11. Javabeans. The Only Component Architecture for Java Technology. Technical report, Sun Microsystems, Inc., java.sun.com/products/javabeans/, 1997.

12. JINI. DJ - Discovery and Join. Technical report, Sun Microsystems, Inc., wwws.sun.com/software/jini/specs/jini1.2html/discovery-spec.html, 1997-2001.

13. J. Kramer and J. Magee. The evolving philosophers problem: Dynamic change management. *IEEE TSE*, 16(11):1293–1306, November 1990.

14. S. Liang and G. Bracha. Dynamic class loading in the Java virtual machine. In *Conference on Object-oriented programming, systems, languages, and applications (OOPSLA'98)*, pages 36–44, 1998.

15. J. Mayer, I. Melzer, and F. Schweiggert. Lightweight plug-in-based application development, 2002.

16. Microsoft Corporation. How to Write and Use ActiveX Controls for Windows CE 2.1. Technical report, Microsoft Developer Network, http://msdn.microsoft.com/library/default.asp?url=/library/en-us/dnce21/html/activexce.asp, 1999.

17. Object Technology International, Inc. Eclipse Platform Technical Overview. Technical report, IBM, www.eclipse.org/whitepapers/eclipse-overview.pdf, July 2001.

18. P. Oriezy, N. Medvidovic, and R. Taylor. Architecture-based runtime software evolution. In *ICSE '98*, 1998.

19. M. Oriol. Luckyj: an asynchronous evolution platform for component-based applications. In *Second International Workshop on Unanticipated Software Evolution at ETAPS '03*, 2003.

20. OSGi. Open Services Gateway initiative specification. Technical report, OSGi, http://www.osgi.org, 2001.

21. R. Chatley, J. Kramer, J. Magee and S. Uchitel. Model-based Simulation of Web Applications for Usability Assessment. In *Bridging the Gaps Between Software Engineering and Human-Computer Interaction*, May 2003.

22. S. Eisenbach, C. Sadler and S. Shaikh. Evolution of Distributed Java Programs. In *IFIP/ACM Working Conference on Component Deployment*, volume 2370 of *LNCS*. Springer-Verlag, June 2002.

23. S. Uchitel, R. Chatley, J. Kramer and J. Magee. LTSA-MSC: Tool Support for Behaviour Model Elaboration Using Implied Scenarios. In *Proc. of TACAS 2003*. LNCS, April 2003.

Dynamic Deployment of Executing and Simulating Software Components

Alexander Egyed

Teknowledge Corporation
4640 Admiralty Way, Suite 1010
Marina Del Rey, CA 90292, USA
aegyed@ieee.org

Abstract. Physical boundaries have caused software systems to become less monolithic and more distributed. The trend is progressing to a point where software systems will consist of numerous, loosely-coupled, heterogeneous software components. Increased software dynamism will allow these components to be composed, interchanged, upgraded, or even moved without shutting down the system itself. This form of dynamism is already well-supported through new programming constructs and support libraries (i.e., late binding, introspection); however, we are currently ill-equipped to analyze and simulate those kinds of systems. This paper demonstrates that software dynamism requires not only new modeling constructs but also new simulation environments. While in the past, simulation merely mimicked some real-world behavior, we argue that in the future it will become necessary to intertwine the model world with the real world. This will be essential but not limited to cases where (1) one has incomplete access to models (i.e., proprietary COTS components), (2) it is too expensive to model (i.e., Internet as a connector between software components), or (3) one has not complete faith in models (i.e., legacy components). This paper presents our approach to the concurrent execution and simulation of deployed software components. It will also discuss key differences to "traditional" simulation, emulation, and other similar concepts that are being used to integrate the model world with the real world.

1 Dynamism in Today's World

Today, systems are dynamic entities. A modern CPU can reduce its processor power to conserve energy when its energy supply (i.e., battery) is low. A cell phone adapts to different geographical zones (environments) it is taken into. Examples like these show that systems adapt dynamically to their environment or that systems adapt to dynamic environments. There are many reasons why such dynamic behavior is beneficial but the primary reason is that systems continue to operate even if their surroundings vary or are not as expected.

Although it is as much software as it is hardware that gives systems their flexibilities, it is still not often possible to take "pieces of software systems" during run-time and manipulate them. We believe that this will change in the future. Existing technology, such as late binding between software components, already makes it possible to

W. Emmerich and A.L. Wolf (Eds.): CD 2004, LNCS 3083, pp. 113-128, 2004.
© Springer-Verlag Berlin Heidelberg 2004

compose software components into systems dynamically. This technology also makes it possible to replace, upgrade, or move software components dynamically without requiring the overall software system to shut down.

The key benefit of component dynamism is increased flexibility in constructing and maintaining software systems. The benefits range from better reuse of legacy and commercial-off-the-shelf (COTS) components, easier upgrading of older versions of components, simpler replacement of faulty components, added flexibility in distributing components, ability to move components between processing devices (wearable software), and increased generality of component interfaces.

These are not new abilities. Distributed systems, for example, long had many of these flexibilities relying on network protocols. What has changed today is the proliferation of many new component composition technologies, such as remote method invocation [18], COM [21], CORBA [13], or Beans [17] that provide similar flexibilities with different cost-benefit trade-offs.

1.1 Modeling and Simulating Dynamism

Modeling is a form of handling the complexity of software development. To date, we have available a rich set of modeling techniques to cover development aspects such as requirements engineering, software architecting, designing, risk management, testing, and others. The chief benefit of modeling is to support the early evaluation of functional and non-functional properties of software systems. However, short of programming, only the simulation of those models can ensure certain desired qualities and functionalities.

Though we believe that software components will remain complex entities, it is foreseeable that software components in general will become more independent of one another and more configurable to support much needed flexibilities., This poses new challenges to the modeling and simulation of software components and it raises the issue how to represent a system's environment(s).

To increase component flexibility (composability, replaceability, etc.) it is not sufficient to build software components with better user interfaces and export/import features. Instead, the increasing number of uses of a software component have to be taken in consideration while designing it. During execution, for example, components have to be able to reconfigure themselves into different modes of operation (e.g., self healing [20]) corresponding to environmental changes (temporary absence of another component). During design, the designers may spend considerable time and effort in understanding the many environments a component may find itself in. Potentially more effort may be spent in understanding a component's environment than in understanding that component's internals.

This paper emphasizes the modeling and simulation of dynamic software systems. We will briefly discuss some of the new modeling constructs that are required to model dynamic systems but we will concentrate primarily on the execution (simulation) of software models, which is particularly affected by software dynamism. While both static analysis (e.g., model checking) and dynamic analysis (e.g., execution/simulation) are essential for software modeling, it is simulation we believe to be the most weakly prepared. In a world where a component's environment is becoming more complex, modeling that environment will become more so expensive. Even worse, models may not be available in cases where COTS or legacy software is being used. This paper shows that the lack or incompleteness of models does not prevent the simulation of the overall system. We will present a dynamic simulation environment that can link real software components with simulated software components so that the simulated components interact with real components in absence of their models. Note that we use the terms *component* and *system* interchangeably. A system is a collection of software components but a system can be a component.

2 Intertwining of Model World and Real World

Design-time validation is effective on systems that are modeled formally and completely. If such systems incorporate un-verified components (e.g., COTS software, legacy software, or other third-party software) or operate on un-verified environments (e.g., hardware, network, middleware, operating system) then these un-verified elements add potentially unknown constraints [5]. These unknown constraints are uncertainties that limit our ability to reason precisely in their presence.

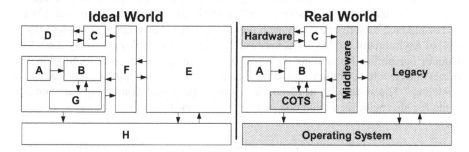

Figure 1. Ideal World where all components are defined (left); Real World with some model descriptions missing (right)

Figure 1 depicts two different perspectives on a seemingly identical, hypothetical system. Both perspectives depict the system's architecture in form of their components and interactions. The left perspective assumes that all components are well-defined (i.e., complete models). Simulating this idealized architecture is simple because of complete knowledge. The right perspective differs only in the use of unverified components. There, some components are well-defined (e.g., component A) but the reuse of existing knowledge introduces undefined components (e.g., COTS). It is typical that model definitions are unavailable for unverified components (e.g., hardware, COTS software, middleware, legacy code, and operating system). This is problematic during reuse because it limits early analysis and simulation. Several choices are available for dealing with this limitation:
  1) Disallow the use of unverified components/environments
  2) Model unverified components/environments explicitly

3) Ignore the effects of unverified components/environments or make default assumptions about their effects (e.g., ignore the middleware)

4) Prototype, emulate unverified components/environments

The first choice is clearly impractical. It has become highly desirable to reuse existing software into software systems as it can significantly reduce development cost and effort, while maintaining overall software product quality. The second choice is ideal but it is also very costly and time consuming; especially in cases where the environment is more complex than the modeled part of a software system. It is done occasionally in special-purpose domains (e.g., safety critical systems) but it may not be feasible always to create explicit, precise models of unverified components/environments (e.g., due to the proprietary). The third choice is the most practical approach for many situations. Typically, it does not matter (and should not matter) what kind of middleware connects two or more software components. The effects of the middleware are then ignored or trivialized. However ignoring its effects bears risks (e.g., time delays imposed by middleware in real-time systems). Similarly, making default assumptions may trivialize the effects of components/environments (e.g., if the middleware communication is based on a UDP network then there is no guarantee that messages arrive in the same order as transmitted; if a RF network is used then there is not even a guarantee that messages arrive at all).

Simulation requires a sufficiently complete model of the software system and all relevant environmental aspects that affect it. In dynamic systems, the problem is an increasing lack of software component models (e.g., COTS component, legacy) and a lack of environment models (e.g., hardware, operating system). In the very least, this reduces our ability to simulate dynamic systems. In extreme cases, simulation becomes impossible. In Figure 2, we refer to a pure modeling approach as "idealized modeling." The simulation of idealized models is the simulation of software components together with the simulation of their environment (see bottom, right of the table).

	Real Environment	Simulated Environment
Real Component	construction	emulation testing support
Simulated Component	???	idealized modeling

prototyping

Figure 2. Integrating Real and Simulating Components and Environment

If complete models are not available then several choices exist. It is possible to execute real software components (e.g., deployable component implementations) in context of some emulated environment. This is a technique used during testing to "artificially engineer" test scenarios that are normally hard to enact (e.g., simulate test scenario that are too costly or too dangerous to do in reality). This testing support is often referred to as simulation (see upper, right of Figure 2) but this form of simulation is limited to specialized environmental conditions. Indeed, developers tend to create different specialized models of the same environment to support distinct test scenarios. These specialized environments are typically *not* adequate to represent an environment generically.

Prototyping is another common form of testing dynamic software systems. The middle, left of Figure 2 indicates that prototyping tests real, albeit simplified, software components in context of a real environment (e.g., environment of a deployed component implementation). In principle, prototyping is not very different from implementation although its simplified realization of the software component and its early availability in the software lifecycle gives it the flair of simulation. However, there are key reasons why prototyping is not a substitute for simulation.

1) prototyping language is a programming language
2) abstract modeling concepts are not present in a prototype
3) hard to translate model to programming language
4) harder to re-interpret prototype changes in terms of model changes (consistency problem between prototype and model)
5) hard to observe prototype behavior from a model's point of view
6) prototypes emphasize the interaction among to-be-developed components and their environment ignoring key architectural decisions
7) temptation to keep prototype and throw away model

3 Dynamic Simulation

Many forms of dynamic behavior can be modeled today. Even simulation support exists that can mimic such dynamic behavior. However, dynamic systems exhibit many forms of predicable and unpredictable behavior that are imposed from the "outside" (the environment). The previous section discussed some of these outside influences and concluded that they often cannot be modeled. Ignoring dynamic behavior imposed through the environment may be valid in some cases but bears a risk. That is, in a world where environmental conditions drive component behavior, it becomes increasingly important to understand a component's environment – the ways components can be composted, moved, interchanged, or upgraded. This is especially important for modeling and simulation because a *component's environment may become more complex to model and to simulate than the component itself*.

Unmodeled dynamic behavior imposed by the environment diminishes our ability to simulate dynamic software systems. Not only can it be very expensive to model unavailable components, environments, and infrastructures but once available there is no guarantee of adequacy or correctness. Moreover, the very nature of modeling implies course grain descriptions. Details needed for fully realistic simulation may not be captured in models. This poses the challenge on *how to simulate dynamic systems adequately*? This section introduces dynamic simulation and discusses how the real world is made to interact with the simulated world to substitute models that are unavailable, inadequate, or potentially incorrect.

In dynamic simulation, simulating components may interact with real, executing components. This may serve many purposes such as simulating a component interacting with a real component (e.g., COTS) or simulating a component interacting with another simulating component through a real, intermediary component (e.g., middleware). Dynamic simulation falls into the lower left area of Figure 2.

Being able to intertwine the execution and simulation of real components and simulating components provides significant flexibility to analyzing dynamic software systems. Such flexibility cannot be accomplished without crossing the border between the simulated world and the read world somehow and somewhere. This is a problem because a simulator typically cannot interact in arbitrary ways with the real world and neither can a real component interact with a simulation.

Thus, if a simulating component sends an event to a real component then the simulator must be aware that the recipient of the event is a real component. The simulator must then pass on the event to some mediator that understands both the simulating world and the real world. The mediator will receive events and forward them to the recipients. The mediator will also acts as a recipient of events from the real world to forward them to the simulated world.

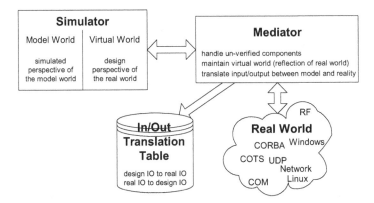

Figure 3. Dynamic Simulation Concept

Figure 3 depicts dynamic simulation schematically. It shows the Mediator as proxy between the Simulator and the Real World (a virtual simulating component) to facilitate interaction between both worlds. The translation table defines how to translate real interactions into simulated interactions and vice versa. More than one simulator may interact with the real world.

While dynamic simulation is simple in principle, there are several key challenges to master. The following introduces an example system to support the subsequent discussion on the key challenges of dynamic simulation in Section 5.

4   Video-on-Demand Case Study

We illustrate the modeling of software dynamism and the dynamic simulation using a video-on-demand software system developed by Dohyung Kim [2]. The video-on-demand system, or VOD system, consists of a movie player, a movie list server, and a commercial data file server. The details of the software system are proprietary but we can discuss some of its modeling aspects.

Figure 4 depicts a course grain, architecture-level overview of the VOD system. The player itself is a client component that is installable and executable on distributed nodes. The movie player consists of a display component for showing the movie (MovieDisplay) and a streamer component for downloading and decoding movie data in real-time (VODPlayer). The movie list server is essentially a database server that provides movie lists and information on where to find those movies. The movie list server handles requests from new players (VODServer) and it instantiates separate handler for every player (ClientHandler). Movies are kept on a file system.

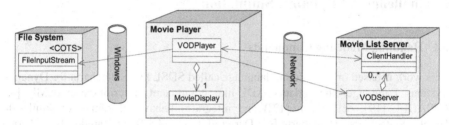

Figure 4. Component Model of Video-On-Demand System (VOD)

The VODPlayer initiates interaction with the VODServer. Upon construction of the ClientHandler, the VODPlayer then interacts with the ClientHandler. The player starts downloading movie data only when a movie is selected. Movie data is downloaded from a file system.

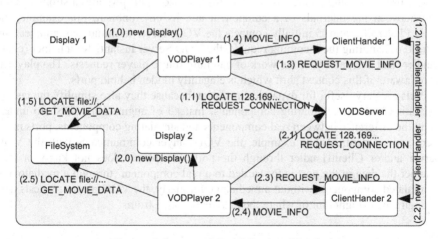

Figure 5. Instance Model During Simulation

The normal operational mode of the VOD system requires the movie list server and the file system to be operational for the player to function. Many players may be executing concurrently on different devices. Figure 5 depicts one possible configuration of two player instances interacting with the movie list server (VODServer) and the file system. The figure shows two instances of the VOD Player, both interacting with the same VOD Server. Two instances of the ClientHandler exist (created by VODServer) to interact with the two instances of the VODPlayer (i.e., one for each player). The role of the client handler is to return details about movies and whole movie lists upon request. Once movie data is available, the player downloads and displays the movie. A possible sequence of events is indicated through the numbers. The example is somewhat simplified from the original for brevity. See also [3] for a more detailed description of the VOD system with architectural models.

5   Challenges of Dynamic Simulation

5.1   Handling Modeling Commands

This work is based on a modeling language called SDSL [3], Statecharts for Dynamic Systems Language, that adapts ADL-like component descriptions (ACME [4], C2SADEL [19], or Darwin [12]) and integrates behavioral semantics similar to Harel's Statecharts (Statecharts [6], Darwin/LTSA [11,12], or Rapide [10]). A rich language was built to express internal component behavior and interactions among components. Unlike Statecharts, SDSL can model advanced dynamic constructs like remote method invocation, late binding, introspection, instance localization. The dynamic instantiation and destruction of components is also supported. It is not necessary here to understand the SDSL in detail. Please refer to [3] for details.

A component maintains references to other components through ports. Ports are a widely used modeling concept (e.g., [14,16]) because a port provides a strong separation between the internals of a component and its environment. For example, the VOD Player in Figure 5 initially contacts the VOD Server to initiate communication. Instead of handling the incoming request, the VOD Server instantiates a helper (client handler) and delegates to it the work of handling future player requests. The player is never aware of this context shift which is elegantly hidden behind ports.

Ports are very useful for dynamic simulation because they also simplify the task of separating real and simulating components. Instead of augmenting SDSL to understand the difference between real components and simulating components, ports make them appear identical. For example, the VOD player communicates with the VOD Server and/or ClientHandler through the port. The player does not know or care whether the data in the port is forwarded to a real component (through a mediator) or a simulated component (without a mediator). Similarly, the VOD player requests data through the port ignorant of where the data really came from.

5.2   When to Use Mediators

A real component is hardwired to interact in a specific way (or set of ways) with other components. Unfortunately, a simulating component in a dynamic system has two choices. If a simulating component interacts with another simulating component then it needs to follow a different interaction strategy than if a simulated component interacts with a real component. In the first case, a mediator is required whereas in the second case not. This problem is analogous of local versus remote calls in container-based systems (e.g., COM, CORBA) with distributed components.

An easy solution to this problem is to create a modeling language that lets the designer decide the interaction strategy. This could be accomplished by, say, creating two different commands for sending an event or by using a with/without mediator flag (i.e., parameter). Unfortunately, this has the disadvantage that the model description of a component is affected by how it is being simulated. This seems unreasonable in that the use of the mediator during simulation should not affect any functional or non-functional property of any component (i.e., no model change).

Perhaps a better way of determining whether to use mediators is through their existence and availability. Flags could be added to mediators to indicate this. If a mediator is available then it will be used; otherwise not. This solution is much better but has one significant drawback. The decision of whether to use mediators is made statically. It is thus not possible to customize the use of mediators for individual instances. For example, if Player 1 (Figure 5) is simulated on a different machine than, say, the Movie List Server and Player 2 is simulated on the same machine then Player 1 requires a mediator to interact with the server while Player 2 does not.

If the use of mediators differs among instances of the same component then simulation needs to make a decision dynamically. We offer five strategies:

1) Simulation (no mediation) first: the component always interacts with another component without a mediator. Only if the simulator fails to interact with the component then a mediator is used (if available).
2) Mediation first: reverse of above
3) Simulation only: do not use mediation even if available
4) Mediation only: do not use simulation even if available
5) Decision hardwired: resolution strategy is hardwired into the mediator in form of an algorithm that is executed during the instantiation of a component

A designer may define the strategy on a model, on individual components, or even on individual ports within components. For example, the whole model can be defined *simulation first* except for component X, which is defined *mediation only*. Strategies 3) and 4) are useful if all instances should be treated equally. Strategy 5) can individualize the behavior of instances.

5.3 Maintaining Dependencies between Real Instances and Simulated Ones

While the previous discussion pointed out how information is sent and received through ports, it did not answer how to maintain correct associations between simulating components and their real interfaces for correct communication. Recall the discussion about mediators and the dual role they play to facilitate the interaction between the simulating world and the real world.

During dynamic simulation, components get instantiated in three different ways. A real component, for which no model exists, is instantiated in the real world only. Similarly, a model component, for which no implementation exists, is instantiated in the simulated (model) world only. However, a model component that interacts with a real component (its environment) requires a model description and an implementation of its real interface. Only it is capable of communicating with both the simulating world and the real world. The others are limited to interacting with components of their respective worlds only.

The model description of a component captures the internal functionality of the simulating component and how it interacts with its ports. If the model component has a real interface then it mediates the component's ports (only those ports that are meant to communicate with real components) and translates data/command contents (provided through the simulation) into real data/commands (and vice versa). The top of Figure 6 shows the result of instantiating the player and the movie list server (normal boxes). Both have real interfaces (boxes with double side bars) attached to ports (circles) underneath them to indicate that they talk to both the real world (the network between them) and the simulated world. The player also instantiates a display component that interacts only with the simulating player in the model world.

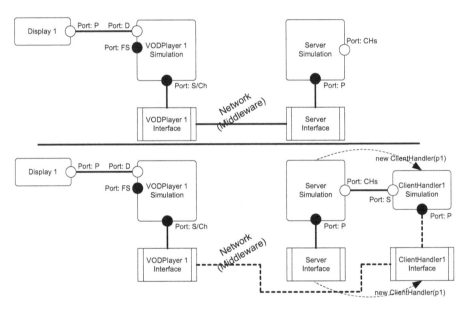

Figure 6. Parallel Construction of Model Components and Implemented Interfaces causes a Dependency Problem

Since there are many simulating (model) components that interact with real components, it is vital to maintain correct associations between simulating components and their interfaces to the real world. Otherwise, the routing of data/commands between ports and interfaces is erroneous. In Figure 6 (top), this was indicated through lines connecting real interfaces with ports of simulating components. During startup it is typically easy to maintain correct associations because the instantiation of a model component coincides with the creation of its real interface. Once created, simulated data/commands placed into ports are picked up by listeners, translated into real data/commands, and executed by the interface.

This solution works nicely for as long as the simulating components do not instantiate other simulating components that also interact with real components and engage in some form of data exchange that is relevant to the real world. As an example, consider the player/server communication once more (bottom Figure 6). After the player contacts the movie list server, the server creates a client handler to handle this and future requests from the player. ClientHandler, much like Server, is a model component that interacts with the player through the real world. Therefore, a real interface for the client handler must be instantiated together with the instantiation of the simulating client handler. Herein lays the problem. A reference to the port of the player is passed from the server to the client handler. The real interface of the client handler thus requires the real reference (a socket variable) that is defined only in the real interface of the server. How is it possible to pass this reference (the socket) along with the simulated instantiation of the client handler?

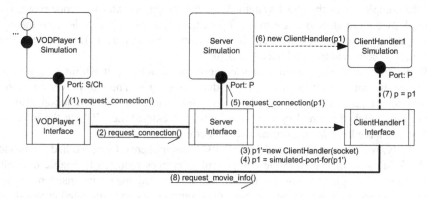

Figure 7. Maintaining the Dependency between Simulation and Reality

Obviously, the real interface of the server must create the real port of the client handler (called ClientHandler1 Interface) in order to pass along the real socket variable. Also, the simulated server must instantiate the simulated client handler to pass along the simulated socket variable. Yet, the mediator must establish an association between these separately created elements. This problem is further complicated in that requests for connection may or may not be routed through mediators (recall Section 5.2) and that the model description of player, server, and client handler should be identical in both cases.

Our solution is to have the interface of the server create the interface for the client handler, create a simulated port for the new interface, and pass the port as part of the simulated instantiation of the client handler. Figure 7 depicts the order of events for this solution. When the server interface receives a request_connection from a player, it creates a real port as well as a simulated port. The simulated server is then notified of the request connection event with the parameter being the simulated port of the player (i.e., the simulated port is a references to the real port). The server then instantiates the client handler, passes along the simulated port, and substitutes its port to the player with the one passed along. This solution is consistent with the implementation where the client handler receives the real port as part of its construction.

6 Discussion and Validation

We applied our simulation language SDSL and its dynamic simulator SDS on four major case studies to date. Three case studies involved third party components and one was developed in-house. All our case studies were based on real software systems, which were used to evaluate how well the simulation mimiced them. Our case studies used a wide range of dynamism technologies such as COM, late binding, remote method invocations, and networks. The largest SDSL model we created to date is the VOD system with about 40 states and 50 transitions.

The cost of building SDSL models is proportional to the required level of detail. SDSL models can be very generic but also very specific. The effort of building the VOD system was about 7 person hours. The effort of building the mediators and translators was about 14 person hours. The latter is surprisingly little given the size and the complexity of the VOD system. We attribute this to extensive code reuse. For example, we were able to reuse over 70% of the server interface code from the real server and 64% of the player interface code from the real player. In total, less than 130 lines of code had to be added or modified.

Depending on the complexity of a component, simulating it within a real-world environment can be significantly cheaper than building it. The real player has about 4000 lines of code, its simulation less than 300. Naturally, the simulation also requires the model. If the real system would not have existed then 70% of the interface code could have been reused during code generation.

Initially, we constructed a model of all VOD components. Once we had the model of the VOD system, we built the component interfaces required to enable dynamic simulation. Through dynamic simulation we discovered major inconsistencies between the model and the system because real components and simulated components did not interoperate. It took only little effort to detect, locate, and fix those flaws to a point where we have strong confidence in the model's correctness.

We also used our simulator as a test environment for real software components. For instance, we had the simulator instantiate a large number of simulated players (almost) instantaneously to see how the real servers handle the load. Or, we had the simulated server send bogus answers or scrambled text to see how the players react. This form of stress testing required no additional coding but would have been much more costly if we had done it purely in the real world. Moreover, we could define those hypothetical test scenarios in form of SDSL models and we could test them directly on real components. We find that this is a very efficient way of testing model scenarios.

We found that SDSL and its simulator make models more active participants during design (simulation), coding (dynamic simulation and code generation), and testing (scenario testing). During design, simulation helps finding flaws quickly. During coding, dynamic simulation and code generation enable rapid application development. And during testing, model test scenarios can be validated directly on real components. As a result, we intertwined programming and modeling to a point where it is hard to distinguish them. In fact, in another case study we adopted a simulated COM component as a real component because it satisfied all our requirements [20]. We saw no need of implementing that component. It must be noted that these extended features of dynamic simulation overlap with prototyping, emulation, and testing.

Despite all advantages, dynamic simulation also has downsides. Traditional simulation mimics the real-world in a reproducible way. Thus, re-running a specific simulation scenario produces the exact same results every time. Unfortunately, dynamic simulation opens simulation to the unpredictability of the real world. With a real network between two simulated components no two simulations will be exactly alike. Simulating scenarios during dynamic simulation is thus comparable to testing during coding. Although we found that dynamic simulation is often good enough, we do not believe that it can replace closed-world simulation or static analysis.

7 Related Work

There are only few behavioral modeling languages available that can handle dynamism in some form. Harel-Gery [7] combined class diagrams with statechart diagrams to enable design time dynamism and their tool, Rhapsody [8], incorporates design-time dynamism constructs. This approach does not integrate the model world and the real world during simulation.

Rhapsody's integration with object models makes it a suitable candidate to model dynamism in the context of UML (i.e., construction, destruction). However, modeling constructs, such as ports, are not supported. This limits the dynamic behavior of Rhapsody to direct method invocations (i.e., procedure calls). Even in cases where architectural languages (ADLs) and their advanced concepts have been mapped successfully to UML (e.g., C2 [19] to object model mapping) [1] this mapping also changed the meaning of those objects (that is a main reason why stereotypes were used). For instance, in C2 one component is not aware of components next to it and thus cannot refer to it directly by name. An object model representing a C2 component model thus cannot make use of Rhapsody's statechart simulation capabilities.

Two ADLs that have stressed the ability to describe dynamism require some mention. First, the event-based model of Rapide [10] has been used to describe architectural components and the events they are exchanging. Its tool suite can then be used to analyze event patterns to identify potential problems (e.g., an invalid causality relationship). Again, although we are unaware of any other efforts to provide runtime (model) dynamism, Rapide only supports some forms of design-time dynamism like the creation of components dynamically. The use of Rapide for dynamic modeling purposes is additionally hampered by its tight links to the rest of Rapide; this is much the same criticism as we have for Rhapsody as well.

A second ADL used to describe dynamic effects is Darwin [12]. The language is certainly of a kindred spirit in that it specifies what services are provided and what services are needed for each component. The language is unique for proscribing structural dynamism, by emphasis on lazy binding of (potentially unbounded) recursive structures and, as with both Rhapsody and Rapide, direct dynamic instantiation. Darwin is not event-based, and is incapable of modeling change to as fine a grain size as statecharts.

The ability of SDSL to integrate real-world components and simulated components allows for rapid application development to some degree. Nonetheless, we do not see our approach as another form of prototyping. Prototyping is characterized by quick and dirty programming without adequate design. SDSL models, unlike prototypes are not intended to be thrown away. They can be analyzed statically and dynamically in closed environments. They can also be used for code generation and testing. SDSL models thus have extensive use outside the realm of prototyping.

Dynamic simulation also has some overlap with code generators. Code generators transform model descriptions into code. Models and code can then be executed and analyzed separately. Dynamic simulation also separates models from code through mediators but it does not necessarily distinguish the analysis of code and model as separate activities. Our approach does not have to handle problematic versioning issues during code generation (i.e., overwriting changes) however, it causes its own set of problems that were discussed previously.

8 Conclusion

Simulators play a vital role in validating component dynamism. They enable the rapid testing of dynamic software systems with minimal coding. Simulation allows the safe exploration of a proposed solution in an environment that shields from physical harm and monetary harm [15]. We know from previous studies that simulation is a very cost effective and economical way of building and validating software systems [9].

This work proposed dynamic simulation as a complement to validation and testing under situations where it is uneconomical or infeasible to model un-verified components. Dynamic simulation combines the simulation of modeled components with the execution of deployed, un-verified components within un-verified environments. It only requires the modeling of newly developed components and uses existing components and infrastructure. It is complementary to other forms of static and dynamic analyses and can be used for prototyping or testing. Careful attention was given on how to separate models from code during dynamic simulation. We use mediators and translators to ensure that neither model nor code needed to be tailored towards dynamic simulation scenarios.

Still, the concept of dynamic simulation is not revolutionary. It borrows heavily from prototyping, emulation, and even testing. Nonetheless, this paper contributed strategies on how to handle problems associated with the dynamic behavior of software components and on how to maintain dependencies between the model world and the real world correctly. To the best of our knowledge, these issues have not been explored in the past for these domains.

Dynamic simulation also has disadvantages. Its main downside is that it opens modeling to some of the unpredictability of the real world. This is not always problematic but it limits the usefulness of dynamic simulation in some cases. Future work is needed to further validate our approach to determine the trade-offs between closed and dynamic simulation and the cost of building mediators. It is also intended to investigate whether component simulation can be done concurrently with their real counterparts to reason about state and consistency. Furthermore, it is future work to generalize the current tool support for dynamic simulation. To date, mediators have to be created manually. We believe that this could be automated partially.

References

1. Abi-Antoun, M. and Medvidovic, N.: "Enabling the Refinement of a Software Architecture into a Design," *Proceedings of the 2nd International Conference on the Unified Modeling Language (UML)*, October 1999.

2. Dohyung, K.: "Java MPEG Player," *http://peace.snu.ac.kr/dhkim/java/MPEG/*, 1999.

3. Egyed, A. and Wile, D.: "Statechart Simulator for Modeling Architectural Dynamics," *Proceedings of the 2nd Working International Conference on Software Architecture (WICSA)*, August 2001, pp.87-96.

4. Garlan, D., Monroe, R., and Wile, D.: "ACME: An Architecture Description Interchange Language," *Proceedings of CASCON'97*, November 1997.

5. Grundy, J. C. and Ding, G.: "Automatic Validation of Deployed J2EE Components Using Aspects," *Proceedings of the 17th International Conference on Automated Software Engineering (ASE)*, Edinburgh, Scottland, UK, September 2002.

6. Harel D.: Statecharts: A Visual Formalism for Complex Systems. *Science of Computer Programming* 8, 1987.

7. Harel, D. and Gery, E.: "Executable Object Modeling with Statecharts," *Proceedings of the 18th International Conference on Software Engineering*, March 1996, pp.246-257.

8. iLogix: Rhapsody at http://www.ilogix.com/.

9. Jackson, D. and Rinard, M.: "Software Analysis: A Roadmap," *Proceedings of the 20th International Conference on Software Engineering (ICSE)*, Limerick, Ireland, June 2000, pp.133-145.

10. Luckham D. C. and J. Vera J.: An Event-Based Architecture Definition Language. *IEEE Transactions on Software Engineering*, 1995.

11. Magee, J.: "Behavioral Analysis of Software Architecture using LTSA," *Proceedings of the 21st International Conference on Software Engineering*, Los Angeles, CA, May 1999.

12. Magee, J. and Kramer, J.: "Dynamic Structure in Software Architectures," *Proceedings of the 4th ACM SIGSOFT Symposium on the Foundations of Software Engineering*, October 1996.

13. Object Management Group: The Common Object Request Broker: Architecture and Specification. 1995.

14. Perry D. E. and Wolf A. L.: Foundations for the Study of Software Architectures. *ACM SIGSOFT Software Engineering Notes*, 1992.

15. Sanders, P.: "Study on the Effectiveness of Modeling and Simulation in the Weapon System Acquisition Process," *Report, Test Systems Engineering and Evaluation, Office of the Under Secretary of Defense (Acqusition & Technology)*, 1996.

16. Shaw, M., Garlan, D.: Software Architecture: Perspectives on an Emerging Discipline. Prentice Hall, 1996.

17. Sun Microsystems: Java Beans Specification a*t*
    http://java.sun.com/beans/docs/beans.101.pdf.

18. Sun Microsystems: Java Remote Method Invocation - Distributed Computing for Java. 2001.(UnPub)

19. Taylor R. N., Medvidovic N., Anderson K. N., Whitehead E. J. Jr., Robbins J. E., Nies K. A., Oreizy P., and Dubrow D. L.: A Component- and Message-Based Architectural Style for GUI Software. *IEEE Transactions on Software Engineering* 22(6), 1996, 390-406.

20. Wile, D. and Egyed, A.: "An Architectural Style for Self Healing Systems," *under submission to WICSA 2004.*

21. Williams S. and Kindel C.: The Component Object Model: A Technical Overview. *Dr. Dobb's Journal*, 1994.

Towards a Dynamic Resource Contractualisation for Software Components

Nicolas Le Sommer

Valoria Laboratory
University of South Brittany, France
Nicolas.Le-Sommer@univ-ubs.fr

Abstract. In this paper we present a framework defining the architecture of systems providing software components with means to contractualise their resource access conditions with their deployment environment dynamically. We also present the JAMUS platform, a prototype we have developed in order to show how our framework can be used to support the dynamic definition and enforcement of contracts binding components and their deployment environment regarding resource access conditions.

1 Introduction

Software components are emerging as fundamental architectural elements in the software industry. It can actually be expected that, in a near future, the development of application programs shall be reduced to the selection and the assembly of pre-existing off-the-shelf components. However, this prediction will not be confirmed unless software components can themselves be considered as reliable, effective, and flexible elements. It is our conviction that, to achieve this goal, attention should be paid to the functional properties as well as to the non-functional properties of components.

The current software component models (EJB [12], CORBA [1], Fractal [5], etc.) allow developers to specify within descriptors some kinds of non-functional properties of software components, such as persistence or security. On the one hand, these models do not allow developers to specify the non-functional properties pertaining to the resources components need to use at runtime. Yet, all software components are not equivalent regarding resource utilisation: some components can run perfectly with sparse resources and without any guarantee about the availability of these resources, whereas other components require guarantees regarding resource availability in order to provide their users with a certain level of quality of service (e.g. distributed multimedia components: video on demand, online music). In such a context, it is our opinion that components should be able to describe their resource requirements in terms of access permissions, quotas and availability constraints. Additionally, deployment environments should be able to take these requirements into account. Because of the heterogeneity of the equipments on which components are likely to be deployed nowadays (e.g.

W. Emmerich and A.L. Wolf (Eds.): CD 2004, LNCS 3083, pp. 129–143, 2004.
© Springer-Verlag Berlin Heidelberg 2004

mobile phones, PDAs, laptops, workstations), we believe that software components should also be able to adapt their behaviour to their execution context (i.e. to the resources that can be offered to them).

In this paper, we present a generic, modular and extensible framework we have designed to reach the goals we have just mentioned. This framework defines the overall structure of systems that enable software components to dynamically contractualise their resource access conditions with their deployment environment. In this paper, we also present the RAJE environment and the JAMUS platform we have developed in order to demonstrate how our framework can be used. RAJE (Resource-Aware Java Environment) is an extensible Java environment that provides facilities to handle resources using objects. JAMUS (Java Accommodation of Mobile Untrusted Software) is an open platform dedicated to hosting potentially untrusted components. In JAMUS, emphasis is put on providing a safe and guaranteed runtime environment for hosted components, as well as guaranteed QoS as far as resource availability is concerned.

The remainder of this paper is organised as followed. Section 2 presents the framework we have designed to support dynamic resource contractualisation. Section 3 presents the RAJE environment and the JAMUS platform. Section 4 gives some performance results of the JAMUS platform. Related work is presented in section 5. Section 6 concludes this paper.

2   Framework

To solve the problems we have underlined in the previous section, we propose to define and to capture within contracts the behavioural dependencies binding components and their deployment environment regarding resource access conditions.

Contracts can be used by components to provide their deployment environment with indication about the context in which they want run. Contracts can also be used by deployment environments to inform components about the resource access conditions assigned to them (i.e. information about their execution context).

Resources offered by the environments on which components are liable to be deployed (e.g. PDAs, laptops, workstations) can be radically different. It is thus necessary to build a generic, modular and extensible system supporting resource contractualisation. To achieve this goal, instead of designing a ready-to-use system, we have designed a framework defining the structure of such a system. A system supporting dynamic resource contractualisation can thus be defined by specialising our framework (i.e. by providing implementations of the functionalities of our framework). To build their system, developers can either use the pre-defined implementations we provide, or define their own implementations. A system designed in this way is thus perfectly suited to the developers needs. Our framework, whose architecture is presented in Figure 1, is structured as a set of distinct functionalities organised in two levels. The first (and lower) level of the framework defines a set of functionalities necessary to monitor and manage resources. The second (and higher) level defines functionalities to support the definition, the evaluation and the monitoring of contracts. It is worth mentioning that the functionalities defined by the first level can be used to build systems supporting resource contractualisation, but also to build adaptive components or secure open environments (since such components and environments need to be able to monitor resource utilisation at runtime).

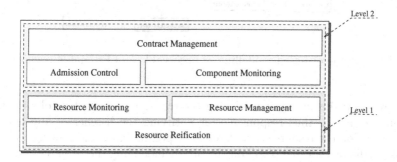

Fig. 1. The framework architecture

2.1   First Level's Functionalities

Resource Reification. In order to ease resource reification, our framework provides a set of interfaces reflecting a resource taxonomy. This taxonomy makes it possible to classify resources depending on whether they are *observable, listenable, lockable, shareable, reservable* or *limitable*. These interfaces are used to define the operations that should be provided by the resource objects (i.e. by the reified resources). For instance, on an operating system that offers mechanisms to observe and reserve the CPU resource, then the object modelling this resource should implement the *Observable* and the *Reservable* interfaces. This implementation makes it possible to observe and to reserve the CPU resource by invoking appropriate methods on the CPU object. Figure 2 presents two of the interfaces reflecting our taxonomy (*Observable* and *Listenable* interfaces).

Resource monitoring.   Resource contractualisation requires that resource monitoring functionalities are available in order to decide whether contracts submitted by components can be satisfied, considering resources available in the environment. Similarly, resource monitoring functionalities are necessary to check whether resources used by components at runtime conform with the contract components subscribed with their deployment environment. Our framework defines two kinds of resource monitoring: an event-based monitoring scheme and a polling-based monitoring scheme. The event-based monitoring, which is illustrated in Figure 3(a), is provided by listenable resources. It consists in registering an object listener (an object implementing the *ResourceListener* interface of the

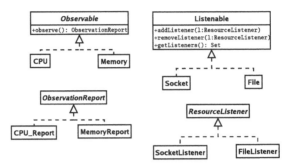

Fig. 2. Object-based modelling of observable and listenable resources.

framework) with the object modelling the resource that must be observed. The resource object is thus responsible for notifying the listener of any operation that occurs on the resource considered. The polling-based monitoring consists in invoking the method *observe()* on the object modelling the resource considered. This method returns an observation report describing the state of the resource (see Figure 2). This kind of resource monitoring is illustrated in Figure 3(b). A discussion about the relevance of these two complementary types of resource monitoring can be found in [10].

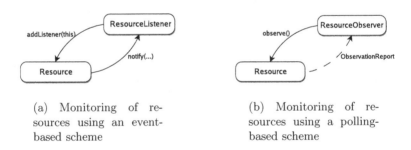

(a) Monitoring of resources using an event-based scheme

(b) Monitoring of resources using a polling-based scheme

Fig. 3. Resource monitoring schemes

Resource management. The framework we have designed provides resource management functionalities such as resource access control, resource access priority and resource reservation. Such functionalities are necessary since the resource contractualisation can lead deployment environments to manage resources dynamically in order to ensure resource availability for certain components. In the next section, we show how resource access functionalities of our framework can be used to ensure that component do not use other resources than those they require explicitly.

2.2   Second Level's Functionalities

Admission control. The second level of our framework defines an admission control functionality that can be used to design deployment environments capable of evaluating dynamically whether resources access conditions required by components can be satisfied. Several implementations of this functionality can be defined. For example, a reservation-based implementation should declare a component acceptable only if the resources it requires can be reserved. An example of the utilisation of this functionality is given in the next section.

Component monitoring. Our framework defines a component monitoring functionality that enables dynamic instantiation of monitors capable of observing the resources used at runtime by a specific component, and capable of comparing their observation with the directives they received at creation time. These monitors can also apply sanctions against components if they do not behave as expected. For example, resource access can be denied by throwing exceptions or by locking resource access. This functionality can be used by the deployment environment to check whether components use resources as specified in their contracts. In the next section, we show how this functionality works in the JAMUS platform.

Contract management. This functionality enables to reify contracts as objects, so that both components and deployment environments can define, negotiate, renegotiate and verify contracts dynamically. Components must thus implement this functionality in order to contractualise resource access conditions with their deployment environment. Contracts can be used by components to provide their environment with indications about the context in which they want to run (i.e. about the resource access conditions they require). Components designed as reflexive entities can also use contracts as abstractions of their execution context, and perform their behavioural adaptation according to the contracts they subscribed with their environment. The contract management functionality must also be implemented by deployment environments, so that components can contract their resource access conditions dynamically. This functionality relies on the concepts of contract, amendment, contracting party and resource utilisation profile.

In our framework, contracts are defined as a set of so-called resource utilisation profiles. A resource utilisation profile basically aggregates four objects, which implement the *ResourcePattern, ResourcePermission, ResourceQuota* and *ResourceAvailabilityConstraints* interfaces respectively (see Figure 4). By including a given type of *ResourcePattern* in a *ResourceUtilisationProfile* one indicates that this profile is only relevant for those resources whose characteristics match the pattern, and that the *ResourcePermission, ResourceQuota* and *ResourceAvailabilityConstraint* objects defined in this profile only pertain to this particular set of resources. By including a *ResourceAvailabilityConstraint* object in a resource utilisation profile, we make it possible for components to provide their deployment environment with information about their resource availability requirements. Components can thus indicate that they require reservation of a particular resource –or set of resources–, or on the contrary that they do not have any specific requirement regarding this resources –or set of resources–, and thus that resources can be assigned to them under a best-effort scheme. Based on this *ResourceAvailabilityConstraint* object, components can thus indicate which resources are necessary to their execution and which resources they might use at runtime.

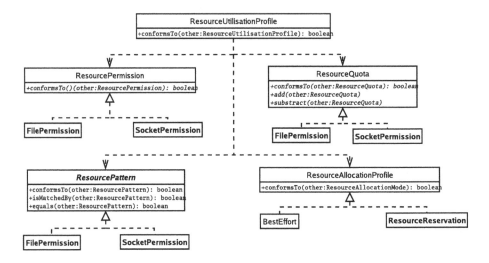

Fig. 4. Object-based modelling of resource utilisation profiles

For the sake of illustration, let us consider a component called *GetMusic*, whose role is to download a compressed audio file from a remote Internet site, and to convert the audio data thus obtained into a non-compressed format, before storing the result in the local file system (in directory /opt/music). In this particular case, the requirements of the program could for example be specified as shown below:

– Network requirements: 1 TCP socket-based connection is required to the remote site *www.music.com*; expected data transfers through this socket: 1 Mbytes in send mode, 15 Mbytes in receive mode. No particular resource availability requirements: resource allocation can be performed based on best-effort scheme;
– Filesystem requirements: read and write access to directory /opt/music ; expected file access profile: 20 Mbytes in read and write modes with guarantees about the availability of these resources, or 5 Mbytes in read and write modes with availability guarantees and 15 Mbytes in read and write modes without resource availability guarantees;

Our demonstrator component exhibits alternative resource requirements that reflect the different behaviour it is likely to adopt dynamically.

```
int MB = 1024*1024;
int KB = 1024;
ResourceUtilisationProfile R1,R2, R3, R4;
// Selective requirement for connections to the specified Web server: 15 MB received, 1 MB sent.
R1 = new ResourceUtilisationProfile(new SocketPattern("http://www.music.com"),
                          new SocketPermission(SocketPermission.ALL),
                          new SocketQuota(15*MB, 1*MB), new BestEffort());
// Selective requirement concerning access to directory /opt/music : 20 MByte read, 20 MB written.
R2 = new ResourceUtilisationProfile(new FilePattern("/opt/music"),
                          new FilePermission(FilePermission.WRITE_ONLY),
                          new FileQuota(20*MB, 20*MB), new ResourceReservation());
// Selective requirement concerning access to directory /opt/music : 5 MByte read, 5 MB written.
R3 = new ResourceUtilisationProfile(new FilePattern("/opt/music"),
                          new FilePermission(FilePermission.WRITE_ONLY),
                          new FileQuota(5*MB, 5*MB), new ResourceReservation());

// Selective requirement concerning access to directory /opt/music : 15 MByte read, 15 MB written.
R4 = new ResourceUtilisationProfile(new FilePattern("/opt/music"),
                          new FilePermission(FilePermission.WRITE_ONLY),
                          new FileQuota(15*MB, 15*MB), new BestEffort());
Definition of two different contracts
ResourceOrientedContract contract1 = new ResourceOrientedContract ({R1,R2});
ResourceOrientedContract contract2 = new ResourceOrientedContract (R1,R3,R4});
```

Fig. 5. Example of contracts pertaining to resources

The piece of code given in Figure 5 shows how our demonstrator component *GetMusic* can define two different contract objects modelling its different resource requirements. Each resource requirements expressed by our component is defined by a specific profile.

Contracts can be dynamically renegotiated with amendments. Amendments allow both contracting parties (i.e. components and their deployment environment) to add, remove or modify resource utilisation profiles within the contract that binds them.

Using amendments, software components can require new resource access conditions at runtime. Similarly, deployment environments can use amendments in order to set new restrictions on the resources they offer. Figure 6 gives an example of an amendment that could be submitted by our component *GetMusic* to its deployment environment.

Our framework models the notion of contracting party as an *Contracting-Party* interface (see Figure 7). This interface must be implemented by compo-

```
// Definition of an amendment for contract contract1 : connection to a new web site
ResourceUtilisationProfile R5 = new ResourceUtilisationProfile(new
SocketPattern("http://www.mp3.com"),
                                          new SocketPermission(SocketPermission.ALL),
                                          new SocketQuota(50*MB, 10*MB)
                                          new BestEffort());
// Addition of a new resource utilisation profile in the contract contract1
AmendmentClause ac1 = new AmendmentClause(R5,AmendmentClause.ADD);
Amendment a1 = new Amendment (contract1,{ac1});
....
```

Fig. 6. Example of amendment

nents and deployment environments in order to propose contracts and amendments to their respective contract partner.

ContractingParty
+submitContract(c:Contract): SubmissionReport
+subscribeContract(c:Contact): SubmissionReport
+submitAmendment(a:Amendment): SubmissionReport
+subscribeAmendment(a:Amendment): SubmissionReport
+terminateContract(c:Contract)

Fig. 7. Object-based modelling of contracting party

Contract submission and contract subscription have been differentiated in our model in order to allow component to request that the platform examines several alternative contracts (corresponding to different sets of resource requirements), before the component eventually decides which of these contracts it actually wishes to subscribe with the platform.

3   The Raje Environment and the Jamus Platform

Using the framework presented in the previous section and the pre-defined implementations of this framework's functionalities, we have developed two prototypes: the environment RAJE (Resource-Aware Java Environment) and the platform JAMUS. These two prototypes, which are defined by specialisation of the first level and of the second level of the framework respectively, are presented in the remainder of this section.

3.1   Overview

The environment RAJE, whose architecture is presented in Figure 8, relies on a modified version of the [1] virtual machine Kaffe (version 1.0.7), which run on

---
[1] http://www.kaffe.org

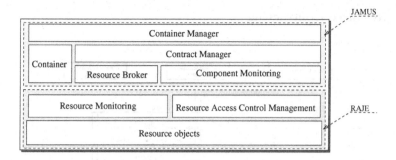

Fig. 8. Architecture of the RAJE environment and the JAMUS platform

standard Linux operating systems. RAJE does not currently implement all of the functionalities provided by the first level of our framework. Indeed, RAJE does not currently include the resource reservation functionality since standard Linux operating systems do not support themselves resource reservation. RAJE is thus an open and extensible Java environment that supports the reification and the access control of any kind of resource using objects in Java. It allows the accounting of the memory and CPU time consumed by each Java thread. Some classes of the standard Java API (such as *Socket*, *DatagramSocket*, *File*, and *Thread*) were augmented so that any access to the resources they model can be monitored at runtime. New classes were defined in order to model system resources, such as the CPU, system memory, and system swap.

The platform JAMUS is built on top of RAJE (see Figure 8). It is dedicated to hosting potentially unstrusted mobile software components. All of the functionalities defined by the second level of our framework are implemented in JAMUS. Its resource broker is designed to maintain a data structure reflecting the state of the resources and to perform resource management (i.e. resource reservation and resource release) by updating this structure. The broker also provides an implementation of the admission control functionality of the framework that relies on this data structure. Since the JAMUS platform is dedicated to hosting non-trusted components, it implements the component monitoring functionality of the framework in order to ensure that components do not use other resources than those they have contracted. The platform's contract manager implements the contract management functionality of the framework, so that components can contract dynamically their resource access conditions with the platform. The contract manager relies on the resource broker to evaluate the contract submitted by the components, and on the component monitoring system to check whether contracts are respected by components at runtime. Furthermore, each component hosted in the JAMUS platform runs in a dedicated container in order to remain isolated from other components. The container manager of the JAMUS platform is responsible to load components in their container, and to create and configure within containers component monitoring mechanisms according to the contract components subscribed with the platform. The different elements that make component monitoring possible are described in Section 3.3.

3.2   Resource Contracting

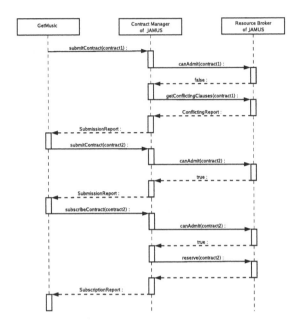

Fig. 9. Example of a contract negotiation between a component and the JAMUS platform

Any component that applies for being deployed on the JAMUS platform is expected to spontaneously initiate a contract negotiation with the platform. Components that neglect this negotiation step receive a set of default resources defined by the administrator of the platform. As mentioned previously in this paper, contract negotiation is performed as a two-step process. In the first step, several alternative contracts can be submitted to the platform. In the second step, one of the contracts the resource broker has approved (assuming there is at least one) must be selected by the candidate component, and subscribed with the platform. It is important to notice that the resources for which components require reservation are not reserved when a component submits a contract, as contract *submission* and contract *subscription* are considered as different services in the platform. When a candidate component *submits* a contract, the resource broker simply checks whether this contract can be accepted or not, based on the current status of resources on the platform.

For the sake of illustration, let us consider the two alternative contracts described in Figure 5. These contracts could be considered for our demonstrator component *GetMusic*. Figure 9 shows a possible sequence of interactions between the component and the platform's contract manager. In this example the first contract submitted by the component is rejected by the broker. Such a negative reply might be justified by the detection of a conflict between one of the component's requirements and the resources available on the platform. Whenever a contract is rejected by the resource broker, the candidate component receives in return a detailed report that specifies which profiles in the contract could not be accepted by the platform. This kind of information is expected to be useful to candidate components that are capable of choosing between several behavioural scenarios, or to components that can adjust their demand about resources based on information returned by the platform.

In Figure 9, once component *GetMusic* has seen its first contract rejected, it can still submit the second contract it defined, as shown in Figure 9. Assume that this time, the contract thus submitted is marked as acceptable by the resource broker. The component can then try to subscribe this contract. However, since the platform may be carrying out several negotiations concurrently with as many candidate components, the status of resources may change between the time a submitted contract is declared acceptable by the resource broker, and the time this contract is actually subscribed. Consequently, whenever a component subscribes a contract, the terms of this contract are examined again by the resource broker, if only to check that they are still valid. If so, then the resources required by the candidate component are reserved for this component.

As mentioned in the previous section, resource-oriented contracts can be renegotiated as and when needed, by negotiating and subscribing amendments. The principles underlying the negotiation and the subscription of amendments are similar to those of contracts. Again, resource reservation is not achieved when a component submits an amendment but when it subscribes an amendment.

3.3 Resource Monitoring

Every application program hosted by the JAMUS platform runs under the control of a dedicated component monitor. This monitor uses the resource utilisation profiles contained in the contract subscribed by the program in order to instantiate so-called resource monitors. The mission of a component monitor is to observe the utilisation of the resource –or collection of resources– considered in a given profile, and to ensure that this utilisation conforms to the access permissions and quotas defined in this profile.

JAMUS provides a specific implementation of a resource monitor for each basic resource type considered currently in RAJE. Each resource monitor admits a resource utilisation profile as a creation parameter. The role of a resource monitor is to supervise the utilisation of the resource –or collection of resources– considered in this profile, and to ensure that this utilisation conforms to the access permissions and quotas defined in the profile.

As an example, let us assume that our demonstrator component *GetMusic* has been admitted to run on the JAMUS platform, and that it is bound to behave according to the contract *contract2* it subscribed with the platform (see Figure 5). Before starting the execution of the component, the container manager of the platform creates within the component's container a resource register dedicated to maintaining references to all the resources the component creates at

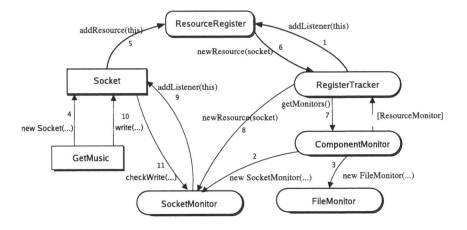

Fig. 10. Monitoring of a component

runtime. It also creates a resource tracker that registers itself with the resource register as a listener (action 1 in Figure 10) and whose role is to bind appropriate resource monitors to the resources the component creates dynamically. Finally, the container manager creates a component monitor that is responsible for creating resource monitors from the contract it received as a construction parameter. Since contract *contract2* is composed of two profiles pertaining to two different resources, the component's monitor must create two dedicated resource monitors (actions 2 and 3 in Figure 10). The first of these resource monitors is a *SocketMonitor,* whose role is to monitor the use of any socket the component may create at runtime, so as to ensure that the utilisation of each socket conforms to the conditions expressed in the first profile of *contract2.* The second resource monitor is similarly created in order to enforce the second and the third profiles of the contract. When the component *GetMusic* creates a socket object (action 4), the socket notifies the resource register of this creation (action 5). It is worth mentioning that in RAJE resource objects are all designed in a such a way that they register themselves spontaneously with a resource register at creation time. The resource register then informs the resource tracker of the creation of a new resource (action 6). The resource tracker invokes the component monitor in order to obtain the list of resource monitors instantiated in the container, and to select from this list the monitor that must monitor the socket. Once the appropriate resource monitor (the *SocketMonitor*) has been selected, the resource tracker notifies this monitor of the creation of the socket object. To monitor the socket, the *SocketMonitor* can register itself as a listener of this resource for instance (action 9) . Afterwards, when the component writes data to the socket, the socket monitor is automatically notified of this operation, and can thus react by throwing an exception if is needed.

When a resource monitor detects a contract violation, it reports this violation to the component monitor, which in turn applies the sanction defined in the platform's configuration. In the current implementation of the platform, several kinds of sanctions are applicable to faulty programs. These sanctions range from a simple warning addressed to a faulty program (using an event-based model), up to the immediate termination of this program.

4   Performance Results

When designing a deployment platform such as JAMUS, one can legitimately worry about the overhead imposed by dynamic contract negotiation and monitoring in this platform.

In order to evaluate how these mechanisms can impact on the performances of the application programs launched on the platform, we have recently begun an evaluation process. This process consists in running a series of demanding programs (that is, programs that use resources extensively), while measuring their performances in different conditions.

For example we launched an FTP server (written in pure Java code) in JAMUS, and we measured the network throughput observed while downloading large files from this server. This experiment was conducted using two workstations (2.4 GHz Pentium 4 processor, 512 MB RAM) connected by a point-to-point Fast Ethernet link (100 Mbps, Full Duplex). The throughput observed during file transfers was measured when running the FTP server with two standard JVMs (IBM's and Kaffe), and with JAMUS (which relies on a modified version of Kaffe). Moreover, in the latter case the FTP server was launched with a varying number of requirements, so that at runtime its behaviour was observed by a varying number of resource monitors (typically one monitor for filesystem access, and one or several monitors for network access).

JVM	Throughput (Mbps)
Kaffe (version 1.0.7)	89.5 *(100 %)*
IBM JVM (version 1.4.1)	89.3 *(99.8 %)*
JAMUS (no monitor)	88.9 *(99.3 %)*
JAMUS (2 monitors)	86.3 *(96.4 %)*
JAMUS (3 monitors)	84.6 *(94.5 %)*
JAMUS (5 monitors)	81.9 *(91.5 %)*

Table 1. Performances observed with an FTP server running either in a standard JVM or in JAMUS (with a varying number of monitors).

The throughputs we observed during this experiments are reported in Table 1. In this table the throughput observed with the standard JVM Kaffe is used as a reference value. We consider that these results are quite satisfactory. Obviously the monitoring infrastructure implemented in JAMUS significantly alters the performances of the application programs launched in this platform. Yet, in our opinion the degradation of performances observed while running the FTP server (which is a quite demanding program as far as filesystem and network resources are concerned) remains acceptable. Besides, it is worth mentioning that the source code pertaining to resource consumption accounting in RAJE, and to contract monitoring in JAMUS, was primarily developed so as to be readable and flexible. Parts of this code could probably be written differently, though, in order to reduce the overhead imposed on the programs launched on the platform.

5   Related Work

5.1   Related to Our Contract-Based Framework

Contracts of quality of service pertain traditionaly on the quality of the results returned by methods of an object –or of a component– [4, 11, 7]. We think that it is not relevant to consider the resource requirements necessary to run a specific method, but that it is rather suitable to consider the resources requirements of the component in a global way. It should thus be easier to estimate resource requirements of application programs from those of its components.

5.2   Related to Jamus

The Java Runtime Environment (JRE) implements the so-called sandbox security model. In the first versions of the JRE, this security model gave local code –considered as safe code– full access to system resources, while code downloaded from the Internet (for example under the form of an applet) was considered as untrusted, and was therefore only granted access to a limited subset of resources [8]. With the Java 2 platform this restrictive security model was abandoned for a new model that relies on the concept of protection domain [9, 8]. A protection domain is a runtime environment whose security policy can be specified as a set of permissions.

The security models implemented in the JRE rely on stateless mechanisms. Access to a specific resource cannot be conditioned by whether the very same resource was accessed previously, or by how much of this resource was consumed previously. Hence, quantitative constraints (amount of CPU, I/O quotas, etc.) cannot be set on the resources accessed from protection domains.

Environments such as JRes [6], GVM [3] , and KaffeOS [2] partially solve the above-mentioned problem. They include mechanisms that permit to count and to limit the amounts of resources used by an active entity (a thread in JRes, a process in GVM and KaffeOS). However, resource accounting in these environments is only achieved at coarse grain. For example it is possible to count the number of bytes sent and received by a thread (or by a process) through the network, but it is not possible to count the number of bytes exchanged with a given remote host, or with a specific remote port number. Yet, we consider that such fine-grain accounting would be an advantage when deploying untrusted programs, as it would permit the definition and the enforcement of very precise security policies.

6   Conclusion

In this paper, we have presented a framework defining the structure of resource contracting systems. The framework is designed in generic, modular and extensible manners in order to be used in various applications domains, to support the future evolution of environments and components in the future and also to allow developers to choose the functionalities that must be implemented in their systems.

Based on this framework we have implemented an environment called RAJE that provides facilities to perform resource monitoring and resource access control in Java, and a deployment platform called JAMUS that supports dynamic resource contracting and monitoring. It is our conviction that many application domains and systems could benefit of —or take inspiration from— the models and mechanisms we develop in this framework and these prototypes.

References

[1] CORBA Component Model Specification v1.2 - Public Draft. Object Management Group. http://www.omg.org.

[2] Godmar Back, Wilson C. Hsieh, and Jay Lepreau. Processes in KaffeOS: Isolation, Resource Management, and Sharing in Java. In *The 4th Symposium on Operating Systems Design and Implementation*, October 2000.

[3] Godmar Back, Patrick Tullmann, Legh Stoller, Wilson C. Hsieh, and Jay Lepreau. Techniques for the Design of Java Operating Systems. In *USENIX Annual Technical Conference*, June 2000.

[4] Antoine Beugnard, Jean-Marc Jzquel, Nol Plouzeau, and Damien Watkins. Making components contract-aware. In IEEE, editor, *Computer*, page 38 44. IEEE, June 1999.

[5] Eric Bruneton, Thierry Coupaye, and Jean-Bernard Stefani. *The Fractal Component Model*, September 2003. http://fractal.objectweb.org/.

[6] Grzegorz Czajkowski and Thorsten von Eicken. JRes: a Resource Accounting Interface for Java. In *ACM OOPSLA Conference*, 1998.

[7] Svend Frolund and Jari Koistinen. Quality os Service Aware Distributed Object Systems. In *5th Usenix Conference on Object-Oriented Technologies and Systems (COOTS)*, 1999.

[8] Li Gong. Java Security: Present and Near Future. *IEEE Micro*, -:14–19, May 1997.

[9] Li Gong and Roland Schemers. Implementing Protection Domains in the Java Development Kit 1.2. In *Internet Society Symposium on Network and Distributed System Scurity*, March 1998.

[10] Nicolas Le Sommer and Frdric Guidec. Towards resource consumption accounting and control in Java: a practical experience. In *Workshop on Resource Management for Safe Language ECOOP 2002*.

[11] Stephane Lorcy, Nol Plouzeau, and Jean-Marc Jzquel. A Framework Managing Quality of Service Contracts in Distributed Applications . In IEEE Computer Society, editor, *TOOLS Proceedings*, 1998.

[12] Sun Mircosystems. Entreprise Java Beans Specification 2.1 Final Release, 2003.

Keeping Control of Reusable Components

Susan Eisenbach[1], Dilek Kayhan[1], and Chris Sadler[2]

[1] Department of Computing
Imperial College
London, UK SW7 2BZ
[sue, dk02]@imperial.ac.uk
[2] School of Computing Science
Middlesex University
London, UK NW4 4BT
c.sadler@mdx.ac.uk

Abstract. Development and deployment via components offers the possibility of prolific software reuse. However, to achieve this potential in a component-rich environment, it is necessary to recognize that component deployment (and subsequent composition) is closer to a continual process than a one-off operation. This is due to the requirement that newly-evolved components need to replace their ancestors in a timely and efficient manner at the client deployment sites. Modern runtime systems which employ dynamic link-loading mechanisms can permit such *dynamic evolution*. We review the capabilities of several alternative runtime environments to establish some requirements for dynamic evolution. Then we describe a tool designed to support developers and administrators in the migration of component updates within the Microsoft .NET framework.

1 Introduction

In simple terms, the primary aim of software reuse is to allow for specialist developers to make their software available to more general (applications) developers in multiple and diverse contexts. To achieve this it is necessary to package each software artefact such that it is *composable* — it is capable of interoperating with other artefacts; and *deployable* — it can be installed independently in a runtime environment where it can be composed, on-the-fly, with other artefacts. These requirements bring the 'reusable software artefact' very close to the conventional definition of a software component [30] and in this paper we shall take reuse as the raison d'etre of the software component.

The component model of software envisions an application as a collection of collaborating components emanating from different developers, probably from different vendors. Over time it is to be expected that each component will undergo evolutionary adaptation (or maintenance). In a regime where applications are statically linked (the interoperability requirements of all components are fully resolved at build-time) evolutionary adaptation implies that the functionality and performance of the application may depend crucially on precisely when

W. Emmerich and A.L. Wolf (Eds.): CD 2004, LNCS 3083, pp. 144–158, 2004.

the build-time occurred. However, in a regime where applications are dynamically linked, they may be able to benefit from evolutionary adaptations which their components have undergone subsequent to their own build-time. This phenomenon can be characterised as *dynamic evolution.*

Nobody who has written software for use by other developers and who has had to maintain that software for any period or for any reasonably-sized client population would argue that the promise of dynamic evolution is not a better alternative than anything else on offer. Nevertheless, experience of those regimes which implement dynamic linking mechanisms shows that it has not been easy to live up to that promise.

In section 2 we review these (dynamic linking) mechanisms as implemented in a number of modern runtime systems before considering how dynamic evolution can be assured. Section 3 describes the development of SNAP, our prototype tool for system administrators and .NET application developers. In sections 4 and 5 related and future work have been outlined.

2   Dynamic Evolution

2.1   The Component Object Model

Dynamic evolution imposes a responsibility on the runtime system to locate required components in a timely fashion, whether they be memory-resident or in need of prior loading. To enable efficient loading and linking, systems (like COM [24]) have adopted a *registry* mechanism. The Registry is a data structure which stores essential information (for example, component locations) needed to facilitate rapid component interoperation. To improve efficiency, each component (or *dynamic link library* — DLL) has at least two entries in the Registry, one indexed by its *class identifier* (CLSID), and the other by its *programmatic identifier* (ProgID). There is an access method DllRegisterServer() to create entries in the Registry. Microsoft encourages third party developers to utilise this method to ensure that their installation will be successful, viz.

> "Most setup programs call DllRegisterServer as part of the installation process." [24]

Version control is implemented in COM by allowing ProgID entries for components to include a version number field (so that it is theoretically possible to register multiple versions of a component). However, there is some evidence that this is not taken very seriously, since the Registry also supports a version-independent *Current Version* (CurVer), and —

> "In most cases the client doesn't care which version of the component it connects to (so) a component usually has a ProgID that is version independent (that) maps to the latest version installed on the system." [24]

This way of managing components can give rise to a number of problems. In the first place it can be difficult to maintain the integrity of the registry:

correctly formulating multiple entries for a single entity is never straightforward and any 'uninstallation' that is done relies on the an *explicit* activation of DllUnregisterServer(). Arbitrarily deleting DLLs will also compromise the integrity of the Registry.

Secondly, as we have seen, most client applications routinely register their own DLLs (that is, the versions of the components they were built against) upon installation, and routinely load the CurVer version of the component whenever they are launched. Thus the only active version of the component will be overwritten practically every time a new client is installed. If it is truly the latest version (in absolute historical terms, rather than just the most recently registered) then there may be older applications which suffer an *upgrade problem* [12]. Most component developers can help users to avoid this by maintaining backwards compatibility, at least for a few generations. Equally, the *latest* version could be an historically earlier version that the application just happened to be built against. In this case, previously-built clients may experience the *downgrade* problem [12]. Component developers can only protect users here by maintaining *forward* compatibility, which is a bit like being able to foretell the future. In either case, the user risks entering the gates of DLL Hell [2, 23, 22, 11].

Even though the COM architecture does not dictate that distinct versions of a component cannot be implemented, it does not make it very easy to impose a rigorous version control system which will support dynamic evolution. Each client can either be loaded alongside the version it was built against (and never evolve) or can be loaded alongside the CurVer version and take pot-luck on DLL Hell. So CurVer is one of the causes of DLL Hell. It is unlikely that any single version of a well-utilised component can satisfy all clients. Instead, for each individual client, there is likely to be a 'latest' version which satisfies its service requirements and which may or may not be the most recently produced (or installed) version. It is difficult to see how this kind of information can be compactly and reliably stored in a Registry.

There seem to be two things about COM which make dynamic evolution turn into DLL Hell. The first is the separation of the component from its *metadata* as recorded in the Registry. Since client applications build and link with reference to the Registry, the build *history* of each client — the record of the actual versions of the components it was built against — becomes lost as the Registry is updated. The second is the relative difficulty of maintaining multiple versions of a component in such a way that differing client requirements can be simultaneously satisfied.

2.2   The Java Virtual Machine

A different approach to dynamic linking has been used in the Java Virtual Machine (JVM). Here the compiler embeds 'fully qualified' path references to service components directly into the object code. Instead of using a registry therefore, each application and each component carries information about the compile-time location of its dependencies. At runtime the classloader recursively loads the full class hierarchy in order to enable *late binding*. If evolved versions occupy the same (or hierarchically lower) locations in the classpath, dynamic evolution will occur automatically. However, all the clients of the superclass will access the same (*current*) version of the class or method, and we are right back in DLL Hell, unless the user is somehow prepared to define distinct classpaths for each application.

This cumbersome solution is unlikely to be feasible, so we designed DeJaVue, a distributed tool [26] which allows a Java library developer to export a custom classloader to clients. Applications which invoke this classloader at runtime can immediately benefit from compatible server-side component updates at the cost of a little network traffic when the application is launched. The server maintains a repository of all versions of each component and, using information about the last version downloaded to that client, it will automatically update the client with the most recent version that is *binary* compatible, even though more recent (but *incompatible*) generations may exist in the repository.

At this point it might be worth digressing to consider binary compatibility [17, 8]. When one component is composed with another, some of the services it exports are imported by its clients. When the first component evolves, it will be composable with its client provided that none of the services required by the client have been removed or changed. In this case, the original and the evolved component are said to be binary compatible *relative* to that particular client. They will be *absolutely* binary compatible if they are binary compatible relative to all possible clients of the original service components. Most interesting evolution involves either expanding the export interface so that new clients can be accommodated, or modifying the behaviour of the services. The first kind of evolution should not make any difference to the effect of services on existing clients. However, the second kind does and leads to the distinction between *syntactic* binary compatibility (where components will link without error but the composed behaviour may be different) and *semantic* binary compatibility where the behaviour remains the same [30]. Throughout this paper we are only concerned with syntactic binary compatibility.

In the current implementation of DeJaVue [3], if the user site has two or more applications that utilise the same library, then each application needs to maintain its own copy of each component, so some of the benefits of reuse are lost. In addition, any application that utilised components from several libraries would require a separate classloader for each one, which makes application startup rather slow. Finally, any library developer who had a substantial client base would need to devote quite a lot of computing resources at the server-side to satisfying the update requirements of each client application every time it was launched. Although this might provide a solution for specialist Java library providers with reasonably limited clientele, a more general solution to the problem requires an approach focussed exclusively on the client side - but one which can bypass the problems of the COM registry.

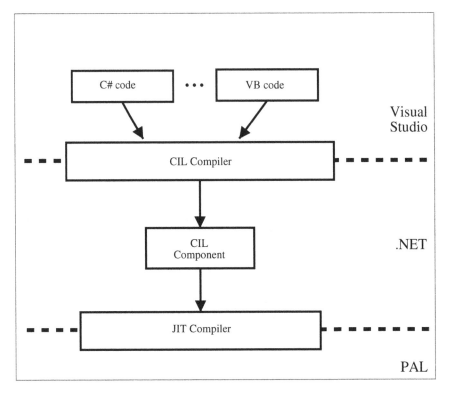

Fig. 1. .NET Framework Code Pathway

2.3   Microsoft .NET Framework

.NET is a framework devised by Microsoft to promote the development of component-based applications and to enable their efficient and effective deployment [23, 10]. The core component of .NET is the Common Language Runtime (CLR) which is actually a runtime environment. The CLR accommodates the interoperation of components rendered into the Common Intermediate Language (CIL). Rather than interpreting these statements for a virtual machine (as in the Java virtual machine setup) the CLR uses a Just-in-Time (JIT) compiler to generate momentary native code for the local platform. Having a *common* intermediate language means that applications can compose components written in different source languages (see Fig. 1) whilst the Platform Adaptation Layer (PAL), together with the Framework Class Library, makes .NET applications potentially highly portable across Windows platforms.

A number of the .NET design goals [29] are particularly relevant to dynamic evolution:

1. "Resolve intertype dependencies at runtime using a flexible binding mechanism." This is what makes it *dynamic*.

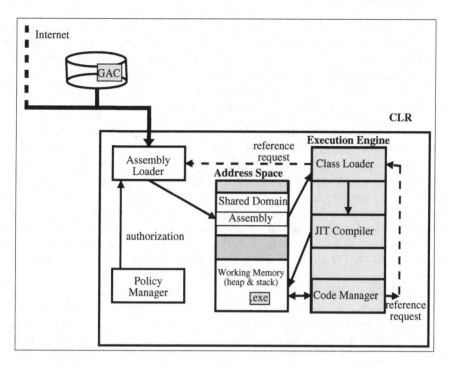

Fig. 2. CLR Loading

2. "Design runtime services to ... gracefully accommodate new inventions and future changes." This is what is meant by *evolution*.
3. "Package types into portable, self-describing units." 'Portable' means that the packages are effectively components, as defined earlier, and in .NET are referred to as *assemblies*. The 'self-describing' means that the CLR need not depend on a registry to compose components at runtime. Instead, each assembly incorporates a *manifest* which lists the resources provided by the assembly and the nature and locations of any resources it depends on from external assemblies.
4. "Ensure isolation at runtime, yet share resources." This implies a DeJaVue-type repository that can hold multiple versions of a component and a runtime system that can correctly select and use the different versions appropriate for each application. In .NET this repository is known as the Global Assembly Cache (GAC) and the runtime capability is referred to as 'side-by-side' operation. The runtime address space is divided into Application Domains (*appdomains*). At runtime an Assembly Loader loads assemblies from secondary storage (or a URL) into the appropriate appdomain on demand. Assemblies loaded from the GAC are loaded into the Shared Domain where they are accessible to any running application. Other domains exist for system services and application-specific classes. Security checks are performed during the loading process.

5. "Execute code under the control of a privileged execution engine ... ". The CLR execution engine in Fig. 2 performs 'managed execution' of code produced by the JIT compiler. When an executing object references an unloaded class, the ClassLoader loads the class from the appdomain for compilation. If the reference is to an unloaded assembly, the request is passed to the Assembly Loader. Code verification is performed during JIT compilation.

A .NET assembly that is capable of entering the GAC and participating in side-by-side operations must be identified by a *strong-name*. A strong-name incorporates a name; a four-part version number divided into <major>, <minor>, <build> and <revision> parts; a 'culture' and a public key ID originating from the assembly author. Any two assemblies are regarded as distinct if there is a variation in any one of these. Thus even if two providers simultaneously update the same assembly with the same version number increment, the public key information still allows the system to distinguish between them. Assemblies which are not in the GAC (and hence are not intended for side-by-side operation) need not be strong-named.

The CLR can handle the runtime code so flexibly and effectively (as illustrated in Fig. 2) because of the use it makes of the descriptive metadata embedded in each assembly. Thus the Assembly Loader uses dependency metadata from one assembly to locate and authenticate a required assembly for loading. It also uses the target assembly's own metadata to bind its services to the appdomain. Likewise the ClassLoader uses assembly metadata to construct type descriptors and method tables for the runtime layout and for type-checking within the JIT compilation process.

Compared with other runtime systems we have studied, .NET appears to have a lot to offer for dynamic evolution. The reflective potential of the available assembly metadata allows us to escape the registry difficulties of COM; strong-names provide the necessary multiple versioning missing from the JVM model; the GAC gives a client-side DeJaVue-style repository; and JIT-compilation makes binding as late as possible[18]. So .NET looks like a good candidate for rational component management.

3   Rational Component Management

The strong-name assemblies in the GAC, which are so uniquely specified, are equally uniquely referenced in the metadata of dependent (client) assemblies. Thus, every time a client runs, it will only ever request the exact service assembly it was built against. Any improvements arising in future versions will by default be lost to the client until its next rebuild. This is deliberate:

> "Historically, platform vendors forced users to upgrade to the latest version shipped. Software developers ... were responsible for resolving any resulting incompatibilities" [21]

and the result was DLL Hell!

Instead, the default behaviour can be overridden because the Assembly Loader consults a sequence of XML 'policy' files which can be used to redirect the load operation. So

"the .NET Framework team (puts) complete control in the hands of system administrators and developers who use the framework ..." [21].

Thus one policy file is the Application Configuration file and another is the Machine Configuration file, and these give some (manual) control to the client-side system administrator. On the developer side, there is a Publisher Policy file. Taken together, these files can no doubt provide a dynamic evolutionary pathway for any application provided that all parties with write-access to the policy files have full information about component dependencies and versions (that is, they know the information in the metadata and will act on it).

We wanted to provide this functionality in a way which could be more systematic and reliable than requiring a system administrator to update some files every time a component was updated. We planned to update the metadata embedded in the client assemblies, in situ, following component evolution. This proved to be very difficult for two reasons. Firstly, we wanted to use the Reflection API to extract and manipulate the strong-name assembly metadata and so loaded the assembly into an appdomain, where it immediately became 'locked'. Unloading it required that the entire appdomain be unloaded. This implies that finding the most recent component for a particular application might require aborting and restarting the application numerous times and this seemed too much to ask the average user. Secondly, writing revised metadata back into the components, as we had planned, looks, from .NET's point of view, very much like the kind of virus attack that the CLR defences have been constructed to defeat, so we gave up.

Instead, for experimental purposes we built a GAC simulation and redirected the Assembly Loader to access that [12]. In addition, for ease of access and analysis, we extracted the assembly metadata and held it in separate XML files. This completely violates many of the .NET principles and it was never intended to be used in a 'production' environment. However it did allow us to develop and test an abstract model of suitable GAC operations and to establish the requirements for our current tool — SNAP (the Strong-Named Assembly Propagator).

The aim of SNAP was to exploit the evolutionary facilities offered by .NET to provide software support to application developers who wanted to migrate the benefits of service component updates to their own products. A major decision was to abandon the idea that updating should occur at application load-time (as with DeJaVue) when the appdomain locking occurs. Instead we envisaged a separate maintenance phase in which the user directs the tool to update the GAC and/or the policy files.

Before stating the requirements this imposes on the tool, it will be useful to list some terms and concepts derived from the theoretical model [12]:

Component A *Component* is a uniquely (strong-) named entity which requires a set of *import* services, provides a set of *export* services and maintains a set

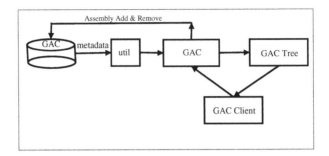

Fig. 3. GAC Administration via SNAP

of *required* components (which collectively export those services which the component imports).

Cache A *Cache* is a set of components.

Coherent A cache is *coherent* if every service required by each component in the cache can be provided by one or more other components in the cache.

Add A component can be *added* to a coherent cache provided it is not already there and providing that adding it does not compromise the coherence property of the cache (*i.e.*, it cannot require any service which is not, a priori, provided).

Remove A component can be *removed* from a coherent cache provided that this does not compromise the coherence of the cache (*i.e.*, there must be other components that provide the services provided by the target component).

Where a sequence of 'physical' components (components actually stored in the cache) represents the temporal evolution of a single 'logical' component (a component designed to export a specific set of services), it is *assumed* that the ordering of the sequence can be deduced by examining component (strong-)names.[3]

3.1 Tool Requirements

A tool to manage GAC assemblies in the way envisaged should:

1. encapsulate the contents of the GAC;
2. be able to discover the types, methods and fields *exported* by any assembly in the GAC;
3. be able to discover the types, methods and fields *imported* by any assembly in the GAC;
4. be able to provide the names of assemblies *required* by any assembly on the grounds that they export types and services that it imports;
5. establish dependencies between assemblies in the GAC utilising the capabilities in 2 — 4;

---

[3] This should be possible if the 4-part .NET version number is used consistently. For our work we assumed a simple linear sequence.

6. establish and maintain the *coherence* of the GAC utilising the capabilities in 2 — 5.
7. determine whether a later version of an assembly is (absolutely) binary compatible with an earlier version;
8. for a given version of an assembly, determine which of a sequence of subsequent versions is the most recent binary compatible version;
9. allow a system administrator to view the dependency tree of assemblies in the GAC;
10. allow a system administrator to *add* an assembly to the GAC provided this does not compromise coherence. The GAC is not a flat file-system, so this requirement involves creating an appropriately-named path to a folder containing the relevant .dll file together with an .ini file holding a copy of some of the manifest.
11. allow a system administrator to remove an assembly from the GAC. It is not possible to apply a simple 'coherence' test here since the target assembly may be explicitly referenced in the *required* metadata of another GAC assembly. If this is true, the *remove* function will not be applied. If the target is explicitly referenced in an external application, it would be necessary to rebuild the application before it could be coherently removed.
12. allow an application developer to configure an application so that it utilises the most recent (relative) binary compatible version of any available assembly. This requirement involves creating and/or maintaining an XML Application Configuration file. Note that this operation obviates the need to rebuild the application mentioned in 11.

3.2   System Design and Use

In the spirit of the .NET framework, it was decided to implement the tool as a set of cooperating components. In order to avoid the appdomain locking problem referred to in the previous section, it is necessary to extract the GAC assembly metadata without loading the assembly. This function is performed by an assembly called util which parses the byte-streams of each DLL in the GAC and constructs a table recording each assembly's strong-name, its required assemblies and a list of its strong-named clients.

This table is accessed by an assembly called GAC whose role is to fulfil the first requirement, namely to encapsulate the GAC. GAC exports methods which allow other components to gather assembly data and to Add and Remove assemblies from the GAC.

GACClient is the user-interface for system administrators, through which they can view the GAC and intra-assembly dependencies, via GACTree; and Add and Remove assemblies via GAC. Fig. 3 illustrates the component configuration for the fulfillment of requirements 9-11.

Fig. 4 shows the system administrator's tool (labelled Configure in SNAP). All the assemblies in the GAC are listed and the listing can be expanded to show each assembly's dependencies. The dependencies are colour-coded to distinguish between the required assemblies (red on the screen) and client assemblies (green

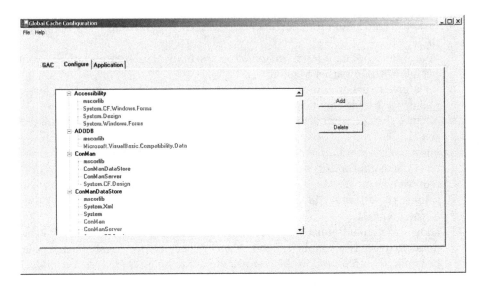

Fig. 4. GAC Configuration

on the screen). The Add button opens a browser so that the target assembly can be selected for insertion into the GAC. The requirements are that the assembly be strong-named — in particular that it has been 'signed'; and that any (strong-named) assemblies it depends on are already present in the GAC. Otherwise the Add operation will not succeed.

For the Delete operation, an assembly must be selected before the Delete button is pressed. Only the top-level (parent) components can be removed — it is not possible using the tool to remove entries from the dependency lists[4]. The operation will only succeed if the assembly has no dependants in the GAC.

The requirement for the Application Developer (requirement 12) involves the comparison of different versions of an assembly to discover whether the later one is binary compatible with the earlier one *relative* to the application in question. In order to do this it is necessary to establish whether the types, fields and methods imported by the application are the same as those exported for each version.

This information was extracted using reflection. The export metadata is easily available via the 'Managed' Reflection API; however when it comes to import metadata, the Managed Reflection API does not reveal the token values needed to compare with the corresponding exports. Therefore, the 'Unmanaged' Reflection API was used to examine the assembly header files, and a Wrapper assembly devised to bring this unmanaged component into the managed fold. The comparison is done in the BinaryCompatibilityChecker assembly (Fig 5), starting with the application imports and recursing through the entire dependency tree. Any

---

[4] This would horribly violate the coherence of the GAC.

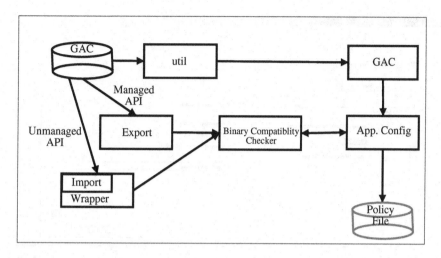

Fig. 5. Application Configuration Client

redirections detected are recorded in an XML file created in the application source directory.

Fig. 6 depicts the Application Configuration tool in SNAP. The Browse button allows the user to select an application for analysis. The left window then displays a dependency tree showing all the GAC-resident assemblies. Selecting one these results in the display of its strong-name on the right-hand-side together with a window showing all available versions found in the GAC. Selecting any one of these will, via the Configure tab, result in the binary compatibility check being performed and, if this is successful, the selected assembly will be linked with the application via an entry in the application configuration file.

4   Related Work

Following the formal treatment of static linking [4], formal approaches to dynamic linking have been undertaken [14, 1, 25]. In addition, there have been proposals for modelling software evolution, utilising Requirements/Assurances Contacts [9], Reuse Contracts [28] and 'smart' composition [20]. In [12] the modelling of the GAC was accomplished using the Alloy specification language [6].

Recent work has turned to devising classification systems to assist in understanding and organising evolutionary actions and outcomes. Thus [5] identifies twelve types of maintenance activity, differentiated in terms of the purpose of the change — for example adaptive, preventative or corrective maintenance. By contrast [13] and [27] examine software source modifications from the point of view of when and how they propagate to the client module. Focussing exclusively on runtime changes, [16] have derived a very useful classification that distinguishes between the technical and motivational aspects of maintenance. The motivational facet of a change (identified as a bug fix, altered functionality

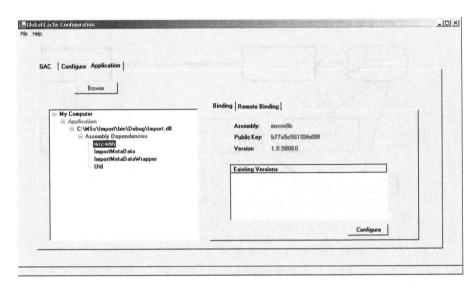

Fig. 6. Application Configuration Client

or re-factoring) come into play when semantic compatibility is under consideration. The technical side of a change can be a code change, a state change and a
restriction to the timing of the change. State changes and timing restrictions are
in the domain of 'hot-swapping' [7, 15] and have not been considered as part of
the current study. However, the twenty nine different categories of code-change
identified here cover the complete range of syntactic binary compatible (and incompatible) changes which SNAP has been designed to differentiate between. In
an attempt to classify software change support tools [19] have proposed a taxonomy based on considerations of when (for example, compile-time), where (the
scale and impact of the change), what (the nature of the change) and how (the
mechanism). They have applied the taxonomy to categorize a number a number
of change support tools (for example a re-factoring browser).

5   Conclusions

Dynamic linking permits dynamic evolution — but the design and implementation of the runtime system can make a very big difference to how easy or practical
it is to achieve. With extensive metadata and a repository capable of containing
multiple versions of a component the .NET CLR is a good candidate. We have
developed a tool, SNAP, to help to manage the GAC and the propagation of
modifications between components.

A useful and practical development for SNAP would be to extend support
to remote component providers and to try to make the assurance of the GAC's
integrity a normal part of any deployment. Handing your GAC over to the tender
mercies of any setup program downloaded from the Internet should be avoided. It

would also be useful to consider ways to embrace semantic binary compatibility perhaps utilising the Publisher Policy file to convey the publisher's intentions. This is a difficult area but not one that has been left untouched by researchers.

Acknowledgements

We would like to thank Sophia Drossopoulou and the rest of the SLURP for useful insights in our numerous discussions about dynamic linking. SNAP was influenced by work done by Vladimir Jurisic and Vassu Joseph on the earlier Dejavue.NET tool and by was influenced by Shakil Shaikh and Miles Barr's Java program evolution tool DeJaVue.

References

[1] Davide Ancona, Sonia Fagorzo, and Elena Zucca. A Calculus for Dynamic Linking. In *ICTCS 2003 Proceedings*, volume 2841 of *LNCS*, pages 284–301. Springer Verlag, 2003.

[2] R. Anderson. The end of dll hell. In *MSDN Magazine*, http://msdn.microsoft.com/, January 2000.

[3] M. Barr and S. Eisenbach. Safe Upgrading without Restarting. In *IEEE Conference on Software Maintenance ICSM'2003*. IEEE, Sept 2003.

[4] Luca Cardelli. Program Fragments, Linking, and Modularization. In *POPL'97 Proceedings*, January 1997.

[5] N. Chapin, J. Hale, K. Khan, J. Ramil, and W. Than. Types of Software Evolution and Software Maintenance. *Journal of Software Maintenance and Evolution*, 13(1):3–30, Jan. 2001.

[6] D. Jackson, I. Schechter, and I. Shlyakhter. *Alcoa: the Alloy Constraint Analyzer*, pages 730–733. ACM Press, Limerick, Ireland, May 2000.

[7] Misha Dmitriev. The Java HotSpot^{TM} Virtual Machine. http://java.sun.com/products/hotspot/, August 2002.

[8] S. Drossopoulou, D. Wragg, and S. Eisenbach. What is Java Binary Compatibility? In *Proc. of OOPSLA*, pages 341–358, 1998.

[9] Dominic Duggan. Sharing in Typed Module Assembly Language. In *Preliminary Proceedings of the Third Workshop on Types in Compilation (TIC 2000)*. Carnegie Mellon, CMU-CS-00-161, 2000.

[10] F. Redmond (ed.). Microsoft .NET Framework. In *MSDN*, http://msdn.microsoft.com/ netframework/, January 2004.

[11] S. Eisenbach, V. Jurisic, and C. Sadler. Feeling the way through DLL Hell. In *The First Workshop on Unanticipated Software Evolution USE'2002*. http://joint.org/use2002/proceedings.html, June 2002.

[12] S. Eisenbach, V. Jurisic, and C. Sadler. Managing the Evolution of .NET Programs. In *6th IFIP International Conference on Formal Methods for Open Object-based Distributed Systems, FMOODS'2003*, volume 2884 of *LNCS*, pages 185–198. Springer-Verlag, Nov. 2003.

[13] S. Eisenbach and C. Sadler. Changing Java Programs. In *IEEE Conference in Software Maintenance*, November 2001.

[14] Kathleen Fisher, John Reppy, and Jon Riecke. A Calculus for Compiling and Linking Classes. In *ESOP Proceedings*, March 2000.

[15] Jens Gustavsson. Jdrums. www.ida.liu.se/ jengu/jdrums/, 2004.

[16] Jens Gustavsson and Uwe Assmann. A Classification of Runtime Software Changes. In *The First Workshop on Unanticipated Software Evolution USE'2002.* http://joint.org/use2002/proceedings.html, June 2002.

[17] G. Steele J. Gosling, B. Joy and G. Bracha. *The Java Language Specification*, pages 251–273. Addison Wesley, 2 edition, June 2000.

[18] E. Meijer and C. Szyperski. What's In A Name: .NET as a Component Framework (Invited Paper). In *First OOPSLA Workshop on Language Mechanisms for Programming Software Components*, pages 22–28. http://www.ccs.neu.edu/home/lorenz/oopsla2001/, Oct. 2001.

[19] Tom Mens, Jim Buckley, Awais Rashid, and Matthias Zenger. Towards a taxonomy of software evolution. In *Proc. of OOPSLA*, 2003.

[20] M. Mezini and K. J. Lieberherr. Adaptive Plug-and-Play Components for Evolutionary Software Development. In *Proc. of OOPSLA*, pages 97–116, 1998.

[21] Microsoft. Versioning, Compatibility and Side-by-Side Execution in the .NET Framework. In *MSDN Flash Newsletter*, http://msdn.microsoft.com/netframework/technologyinfo, 2003.

[22] M. Pietrek. Avoiding DLL Hell: Introducing Application Metadata in the Microsoft .NET Framework. In *MSDN Magazine*, http://msdn.microsoft.com/, October 2000.

[23] S. Pratschner. Simplifying Deployment and Solving DLL Hell with the .NET Framework. In *MSDN Magazine*, http://msdn.microsoft.com/, November 2001.

[24] D. Rogerson. *Inside COM*. Microsoft Press, 1997.

[25] S. Drossopoulou, G. Lagorio and S.Eisenbach. Flexible Models for Dynamic Linking. In *Proc. of the European Symposium on Programming*. Springer-Verlag, March 2003.

[26] S. Eisenbach, C. Sadler and S. Shaikh. Evolution of Distributed Java Programs. In *IFIP/ACM Working Conference on Component Deployment*, volume 2370 of *LNCS*. Springer-Verlag, June 2002.

[27] P. Sewell. Modules, Abstract Types, and Distributed Versioning. In *Proc. of Principles of Programming Languages*. ACM Press, January 2001.

[28] P. Steyaert, C. Lucas, K. Mens, and T. D'Hondt. Reuse Contracts: Managing the Evolution of Reusable Assets. In *Proc. of OOPSLA*, 1996.

[29] D. Stutz, T. Neward, and G. Shilling. *Shared Source CLI Essentials*. O'Reilly Press, 2003.

[30] C. Szyperski. *Component Software – Beyond Object Oriented Programming*. Addison-Wesley / ACM Press, 2 edition, 2002.

Eureka – A Resource Discovery Service for Component Deployment

Karl Pauls[1] and Richard S. Hall[2]

[1]Institut für Informatik
Freie Universität Berlin
Takustraße 9
14195 Berlin, Germany
pauls@inf.fu-berlin.de

[2]Laboratoire LSR-IMAG, 220 rue de la Chimie
Domaine Universitaire, B.P. 53
38041 Grenoble Cedex 9, France
richard.hall@imag.fr

Abstract. Component orientation is a current trend for creating modern applications. The concept of a component is broad and includes plugins and other units of modularization. Typically, components exhibit dependencies on other components or resources; any such dependencies are requirements needed for the component to function. As a consequence, deploying a component requires deploying the transitive closure of all dependencies. This paper describes a project, called Eureka, that simplifies this process by creating a resource discovery service to locate required component resources when deploying a component. The target environment is the Open Services Gateway Initiative framework, but the concepts and issues are applicable to general component resource discovery. The approach is based on Rendezvous from Apple Computer, Inc.

1   Introduction

Component orientation is a current trend for creating modern applications. The concept of a component is broad and includes plugins and other units of modularization. In general, component models and systems employing component-oriented approaches all define a concept similar to a component, e.g., an independently deployable binary unit of composition [21]. The ability to compose a component is related to the component model's ability to express dependencies on other components or resources. Dependencies describe prerequisites for a component that are needed for it to function. Component dependencies may exist at the deployment unit level, such as a dependency on a resource like a library, or they may exist at the instance level, such as a dependency on a service provided by another component instance. Such dependencies present a challenge when deploying and disseminating components.

In the simplest case, if components are completely independent from each other, then deployment is relatively easy, since it only involves copying the deployment unit. On the other hand, if components have dependencies on other components or

W. Emmerich and A.L. Wolf (Eds.): CD 2004, LNCS 3083, pp. 159–174, 2004.
© Springer-Verlag Berlin Heidelberg 2004

resources, then deployment is more complicated. In practice, if a component has dependencies, then the component cannot be used until the transitive closure of all its dependencies are satisfied. This raises the issue of how to locate the resources required to resolve the dependencies. If one considers components as providing and requiring services, then this issue shares much in common with service discovery. Consequently, it is interesting to investigate whether the ideas from the service discovery domain are useful for component discovery and deployment.

To this end, this paper describes the Eureka resource discovery system. Eureka provides the ability to programmatically discover components that provide or depend on specific resources, such as libraries or component services. Additionally, keyword-based searching is also possible for end-user directed searches. Eureka uses the Rendezvous [2] approach from Apple Computer, Inc. to create a peer-to-peer resource discovery service for components. Eureka targets the Open Services Gateway Initiative (OSGi) framework [15], but the concepts and implementation issues are applicable to resource discovery for most component frameworks. This paper discusses component resource discovery issues in the next section, then Eureka is presented in detail; this is followed by usage scenarios and related work. The paper finishes with future work and conclusions.

2   Resource Discovery Issues for Components

The usage of the term "component" in this paper is intended to be vague. In general, the meaning of component for this paper is an independently deployable binary unit of composition. Components may provide both service interfaces and resources to other bundles. A composition of components results from the dependencies of one component on the services and/or resources provided by another. Two levels of dependencies exist: *deployment* and *instance*. Deployment-level dependencies are on provided resources, such as libraries (e.g., Java packages), whereas instance-level dependencies are on component service interfaces. To resolve these dependencies, components that require services or resources must be matched to components that provide them. This leads to complications when deploying components, because the transitive closure of all dependencies is necessary for a component to function. A resource discovery service for components could alleviate deployment issues.

While it is possible to resolve the transitive closure of dependencies in advance of execution, instance-level dependencies allow for the possibility of dynamically extensible systems, which is common today in applications that support dynamically loadable plugins, for example. To support extensible systems, a resource discovery service should not only provide support prior to run time, but during run time so that extensible systems can integrate new components dynamically. Further, both programmatic and interactive discovery processes should be possible. The examples in this paper specifically focus on run-time integration of both programmatically and interactively directed discovery.

Additionally, when locating components a resource discovery service should support at least two different ways to search for components: by what a component provides and by what it requires. Locating components by what they provide is necessary for deployment-level dependencies, while locating components by what they require is more applicable to instance-level dependencies. For example, consider a text editor application that uses an editor component. Suppose that the end user wants to see if a spell checker component is available for integration into the application. This can be accomplished by querying the resource discovery service for all components that require the service interfaces provided by the editor component. The resulting list of components will depend on the editor component's provided services and one of these might be a component that implements a spell checker service if one is available. If the end user finds the desired component, the underlying application may use the resource discovery service to install it and to resolve the subsequent transitive closure of its deployment dependencies.

2.1 Distributed System Architectures

The resource discovery service discussed in this paper is intended to be network-based. Consequently, this subsection discusses the two leading distributed system architectures, specifically *client/server* and *peer-to-peer*. Both of these approaches have advantages and disadvantages. In the client/server approach, resources and information are kept at a specific server that is responsible for a specific set of resources. Clients contact the specific server that is responsible for the desired resource using a well-known name or address, typically an URL or IP address. The client/server approach has proven its usefulness, but servers represent single points of failure and suffer from the risk of Denial-of-Service (DoS) attacks. Additionally, clients must be aware of all servers that are responsible for all resources that are of interest; if a server responsible for a resource is not known, then it is impossible for the client to find the resource. In response to some of these shortcomings, the peer-to-peer approach has gained popularity recently. Peer-to-peer computing treats clients as servers and vice versa, which allows workload to be shifted from a dedicated server onto the network of clients. By effectively increasing the number of available servers, the provided service no longer has a single point of failure and is less vulnerable to DoS attacks.

Another benefit of the peer-to-peer approach is that clients do not need to know which specific server is responsible for a specific resource, they only need to know an entry point into the peer network. This is because searches in a peer-to-peer network are propagated from peer node to peer node and answers are returned from all reachable nodes. This leads to an obvious downside of the peer-to-peer approach, querying for resources is expensive since it creates a lot of network traffic. Also, it is often the case that resources are heavily duplicated in peer-to-peer networks, especially in networks where membership is highly dynamic, and this duplication consumes more resources. As a consequence of dynamic membership and attempts to limit network bandwidth consumption, peer-to-peer networks do not normally guarantee that a query will discover all resources, even if they are available in the network. Sometimes the outcome of a search is dependent on the position of the peer in the network. Even though querying available servers is easier in the peer-to-peer approach, finding an entry point to the network is still difficult and generally requires a well-known server for this purpose.

An argument can be made for using neither a client/server nor a peer-to-peer approach. Instead, a modified client/server approach might make more sense for component resource discovery. As Napster [12] has shown, a single server with a resource registry can efficiently handle queries and just refer clients to other clients that provide the actual resources. A modified client/server approach uses less bandwidth, since queries are more efficient. Further, since it is likely that the number of providers of components is much smaller than the number of consumers, having every client double as a server is not necessary. The downsides are that the system has a single point of failure, that the server must carry a heavy load, and that multi-server cooperation is difficult.

2.2   Using Service Discovery Techniques for Component Discovery

The distributed system architecture discussion in the previous subsection, especially the discussion of the peer-to-peer and Napster approaches, implicitly makes an analogy between component discovery and file sharing. Ultimately, a component is a file or a collection of files, which leads to this analogy, but perhaps a different analogy would lead to a different solution. Conceptually, components can be viewed as service providers, which makes it interesting to investigate technological solutions that target service discovery in networks, rather than file sharing mechanisms.

Apple Computer, Inc. has recently focused attention on network service discovery. Apple realized that the Domain Name System (DNS) [11] address resolution protocol and its associated server infrastructure provided a convenient, well-tested, and ubiquitous infrastructure for advertising and querying for network services. However, to use the DNS infrastructure for discovering network services, an approach was needed to generalize DNS from publishing domain names and querying for IP addresses to publishing and querying for network services, such as printers. To facilitate this, Apple defined DNS-based Service Discovery (DNS-SD) [4] that describes a convention for naming and structuring DNS resource records for discovering a list of named instances of services using standard DNS queries. The DNS infrastructure and DNS-SD create an effective approach for service discovery in wide-area networks, but there is also a need to discover services in local, ad-hoc networks where DNS servers are not present. For this, Apple defined Multicast DNS (mDNS) [5], which defines a way to perform DNS queries over IP Multicast in a local-link network without a DNS server. The combination of DNS-SD and mDNS forms the basis of Apple's Rendezvous technology.

Rendezvous, also known as Zero Configuration networking, is an open protocol that enables automatic discovery of computers, devices, and services in ad-hoc, IP-based networks. Due to mDNS, Rendezvous does not require a DNS server in the local-link network, nor does it require devices to have statically configured IP addresses. Participants in the Rendezvous protocol must be able to dynamically allocate an IP address without the aide of a Dynamic Host Configuration Protocol (DHCP) server, translate between device names and IP addresses without a DNS server, and advertise or locate services without a directory server. To do this, a participant first chooses an arbitrary link-local address (i.e., IPv4 address range 169.254.0.0/16) using a protocol to avoid address clashes. After a participant has chosen a link-local address, it is free to choose an arbitrary name in the .local domain, which is the domain that signifies the local link. Participants can then publish services under their local-link domain name using DNS resource records in the fashion specified by DNS-SD. Finally, participants may query for available services in the local-link domain using standard DNS queries via mDNS. In response to an mDNS query and depending on the type of query, participants advertising a given

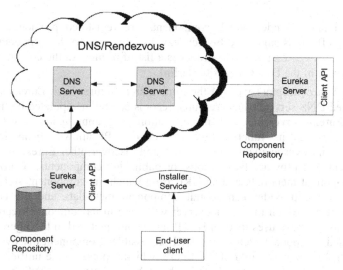

Fig. 1. The architecture of Eureka.

service will respond with its local-link name or address. When Rendezvous is combined with the standard DNS infrastructure, it provides an effective mechanism for service discovery in both local-link and wide-area networks

The DNS/Rendezvous infrastructure also has features that fit well with the requirements of a resource discovery service. For example, clients of a DNS/Rendezvous-based resource discovery services only produce network traffic in those situations where they actually make a query. Since clients of the service are not servers, like in a peer-to-peer network, they are simple and do not pay a network or computational cost when not using the service. Also, the DNS infrastructure is federated and allows cooperation among multiple servers.

3   Eureka

Eureka is a network-based resource discovery service to support deployment and run-time integration of components into extensible systems using Rendezvous' DNS-based approach. Eureka's resource discovery service has the following features:

- Resource discovery servers are federated, where additional servers can be set up and connected to an existing resource discovery network or used as the root of another one.

- Publishing and discovery of components can be performed in both wide-area and local-link (i.e., ad-hoc) networks.

- Component providers can submit components to existing resource discovery servers, so it is not necessary for them to maintain their own server.

- Clients do not need to know the specific server that hosts a given component to discover it.

- Domain names under which components are registered provide an implicit scoping effect, as suggested by Rendezvous (e.g., a query for printers under the scope inf.fu-berlin.de produces a list of printers in the computer science department of the Free University Berlin).

Figure 1 is a conceptual view of the Eureka architecture. Each Eureka server has an associated DNS server, whose resource records can be manipulated by the Eureka server. A Eureka server has a client application programming interface (API) that provides access to its functionality. The client API allows clients to publish components, discover available components, and discover other Eureka servers. The Eureka client API provides two options for publishing components. A provider can submit component meta-data and an URL from which the component archive file is accessible or the provider can submit component meta-data and the component archive file itself, which the Eureka server will store in its component repository. In this latter case, Eureka uses its own HTTP server (not pictured in the figure) to make the submitted component archive file URL accessible. Component discovery occurs in the DNS/Rendezvous cloud of the figure, which represents the unified local-link and wide-area networks accessible through mDNS and standard DNS, respectively. The following subsections provide some of the more important technical details of this high-level architecture.

3.1   Technical Details

Given the promise offered by the DNS/Rendezvous infrastructure discussed in section 2.2, Eureka adopted this technical approach. However, not all of Eureka's requirements for component discovery were addressed by this approach; in particular, the following issues still needed to be resolved:

- How to map component meta-data to DNS resource records.

- How to allow either existing DNS servers (i.e., those involved with Internet name-address resolution) or arbitrary DNS servers (i.e., those not involved with name-address resolution) to participate in the same Eureka network.

- How to allow component providers to publish components into a Eureka network without having to maintain their own DNS server.

- How to create a federated network out of the individual servers offering components, so that once a client has an entry point they can then discover other servers participating in the Eureka network.

The specific approach for resolving each of these issues is presented in the following subsections.

3.1.1 Mapping Component Meta-data to DNS Resource Records
As mentioned in section 2.2, DNS-SD describes a convention for naming and structuring DNS resource records for discovering a list of named instances of services using standard DNS queries. A similar mechanism is needed for DNS-based component discovery, referred to in this paper as DNS-CD, for purposes of analogy.

DNS Resource Record	Type	Description
_x-<md5-hash>._x-export._x-package. _x-eureka._tcp.<scope>	PTR	A pointer to the TXT record of a bundle that exports a certain package.
_x-<md5-hash>._x-import._x-package. _x-eureka._tcp.<scope>	PTR	A pointer to the TXT record of a bundle that imports a certain package.
_x-<md5-hash>._x-export._x-service. _x-eureka._tcp.<scope>	PTR	A pointer to the TXT record of a bundle that exports a certain service.
_x-<md5-hash>._x-import._x-service. _x-eureka._tcp.<scope>	PTR	A pointer to the TXT record of a bundle that imports a certain service.
_x-bundle._x-eureka._tcp.<scope>	PTR	A pointer to the TXT record of a bundle.
_x-scope._x-eureka._tcp.<scope>	PTR	A pointer to another scope.
<Bundle-Name>.<scope>	TXT	A TXT record that contains meta-data about a bundle (i.e., the manifest entries); a bundle may have more then one TXT record
<Scope-Name>.<scope>	SRV	A SRV record containing information needed to query the DNS server that hosts a scope (i.e., its port and the name of the host).
<Scope-Name>.<scope>	TXT	A TXT record that contains the unescaped scope name.

Fig. 2. The DNS Resource Records used by Eureka.

DNS-CD defines how to map component meta-data onto the three different types of DNS resource records: PTR, SRV, and TXT. As a model, the DNS-SD approach for service discovery uses SRV records to describe the location of a service, PTR records to list all available instances of a particular service type, and TXT records to convey additional service meta-data; for example, available queues on a printer. Similarly for component discovery, DNS-CD uses PTR records for describing export/import of libraries/services, SRV records for publishing available discovery scopes (defined in the next subsection), and TXT records to contain additional component meta-data.

For example, the following PTR record format is used to point to the TXT record of a component that exports a particular package:

    _x-<md5-hash>._x-export._x-package._x-eureka._tcp.<scope>

The pieces of this string signify that the component exports (_x-export) a certain Java package library (_x-package); the leading part is the content hash of the name of the package (a content hash is used to avoid illegal characters and to limit the length). The <scope> element is a unique name under which resources are registered and is discussed in more depth in the next subsection. Figure 2 shows the various DNS resource record type mappings and query forms that Eureka uses. For each exported/imported package/service of a component, a set of resource records is published and these records can be queried to reconstruct the component meta-data. All queries can be performed via normal DNS queries using normal DNS tools.

3.1.2 Using Existing or Arbitrary DNS Servers

As discussed previously, a Eureka server has an external DNS server associated with it; standard DNS server implementations are freely available and by leveraging them Eureka avoids a duplication of effort. This use of standard DNS server implementations is a first step toward using existing (i.e., involved in Internet name-address resolution) or arbitrary (i.e., not involved in Internet name-address resolution) DNS servers. As part of this first step, Eureka needs a way to externally configure standard DNS server implementations. Fortunately, most DNS server implementations use the DNS Dynamic Update Protocol [22], which allows clients to dynamically manipulate information stored on the server. This protocol is used by Eureka to add, edit, and remove DNS resource records that represent component meta-data. However, this protocol's security mechanisms are too coarse grained for Eureka's requirements.

For example, it is possible to restrict access to a specific domain by means of a shared secret (i.e., user name and password) or topological detail (e.g., source IP address), but once access is granted the client has full access to all resource records. To resolve this issue, Eureka servers have a DNS controller that provides access control for editing the DNS resource records of the DNS server associated with the Eureka server. The controller provides an XML-RPC remote interface that can be used to change the DNS server entries via the DNS Dynamic Update Protocol. The controller mechanism is the only entity that has access to the domains controlled by the associated DNS server, ensured via a shared secret. Since the controller's remote interface only allows adding components, it effectively prevents third parties from having access to arbitrary content. This approach allows any DNS server implementation supporting the DNS Dynamic Update Protocol to be used as the back end of a Eureka server.

To explicitly support using a mixture of existing and arbitrary DNS servers as back ends for Eureka servers, Eureka introduces the concept of a *scope*. A scope is an arbitrary name formulated using domain naming conventions; it does not need to be a valid domain name (i.e., registered with an Internet naming authority). Along with components, scopes are treated as a resource that can be discovered by clients. For each scope, a Eureka server places a PTR resource record into its DNS server that points to SRV and TXT resource records that contain the name of the scope and the name or IP address of the DNS server hosting the scope. Using Eureka's client API, a client can discover the scopes that its Eureka server is aware of and, subsequently, can issue additional queries to find the components that they provide. One constraint of this approach is that scopes must be unique within an Eureka network; how this is enforced is discussed in section 3.1.4.

3.1.3 Publishing Components without a DNS Server

It is important for Eureka to allow providers to publish components without maintaining there own server, since maintaining network servers is a potential security risk for less knowledgeable users. For this reason, publishing components to existing Eureka servers will probably be the preferred way to provide components for most providers. To achieve this, a scope hosted by a server can be either open or closed. An open scope allows arbitrary providers to publish their components into that scope, i.e., onto the hosting server. A closed scope requires a user name and password to publish components into that scope. For an open scope, a provider can use the client API to submit the component meta-data and an URL from which the component archive file is accessible or the provider can submit the component meta-data and the component archive file itself, which the Eureka server will store in its component repository. In this latter case, Eureka uses its own HTTP server to make the submitted component archive file URL accessible.

Since components are published by arbitrary providers, like web pages, it is likely that component references will eventually get stale and will no longer be accessible. To deal with this situation, Eureka provides a garbage collection mechanism for component meta-data. A Eureka server periodically checks whether all components referenced by the meta-data in its associated DNS server are accessible via their given URL. If a component can not be accessed, its meta-data is removed from the server.

3.1.4 Creating a Federated Network of Servers

To ensure that a query for a given resource is found, no matter which entry point into the Eureka network a client is using, Eureka must define a way to interconnect Eureka servers by propagating new scopes to existing servers. As it turns out, DNS provides a mechanism for distributing resource records to other DNS servers. A DNS server that is responsible for a specific domain can be configured as the master of that domain, while other servers may act as slaves that maintain copies of the master's resource records. A slave server periodically checks for changes on the master server and, when changes are found, applies those changes to its copy of the resource records. These mechanisms are well understood and have been in use for a long time in DNS servers.

Using this mechanism it is possible to make every DNS server that takes part in an Eureka network aware of all other scopes by creating a special scope at the root server of a given Eureka network; the root server acts as the master of that scope. When other servers join the Eureka network, they are configured as a slave for that special scope. This then propagates all available scopes to the other servers. Clients of the DNS servers are then free to query this special scope at their DNS server to discover what scopes are available. New scopes are added to the master server by using the DNS controller of the associated Eureka server. The DNS controller for the master server is also responsible for enforcing the uniqueness of scope names.

3.2   Implementation Target Platform

Eureka's implementation targets the OSGi framework, which was defined by the OSGi Alliance [16] to dynamically deploy, activate, and manage service-oriented applications. The OSGi framework defines a unit of modularization, called a *bundle*, that is both a deployment unit and an activation unit. Physically, a bundle is a Java JAR file that contains a single component. The framework provides dynamic deployment mechanisms for bundles, including installation, removal, update, and activation. After a bundle is installed, it can be activated if all of its Java package dependencies are satisfied; package dependency meta-data is contained in the manifest of the bundle JAR file. Bundles can export/import Java package to/from each other; these are deployment-level dependencies. The OSGi framework automatically manages package dependencies of locally installed bundles, but it is not able to remotely discover bundles.

After a bundle is activated it is able to provide service implementations or use the service implementations of other bundles within the framework. A service is a Java interface with externally specified semantics; this separation between interface and implementation allows for the creation of any number of implementations for a given service interface. When a bundle component implements a service interface, the service object is placed in the service registry provided by the OSGi framework so that other bundle components can discover it. All bundle interaction occurs via service interfaces. When a bundle uses a services, this creates an instance-level dependency on a provider of that service. The OSGi framework defines no mechanisms for managing service dependencies.

Eureka is implemented as five OSGi bundles, an external DNS server, and the OSGi standard HTTP service. The five Eureka bundles register various services with the OSGi framework in order to make their functionality available among each other and to third-party bundles.

4 Usage Scenarios

Apart from providing OSGi services to other bundles, Eureka provides interactive user interfaces for the command shell shipped with Oscar [9], an open source implementation of the OSGi framework, and the graphical environment of Gravity [8], a research project studying dynamic assembly of applications. This section presents these two usage scenarios, but first it describes the general component deployment process when using Eureka.

4.1 General Component Deployment Process

There are two options for providing components; the provider can set up a DNS server or can publish his component meta-data to an existing Eureka-controlled DNS server. If the provider is setting up his own server, he may configure the DNS server to be the root of a new independent discovery network or connect it to an existing one. In either case the DNS server must be configured as being responsible for some scopes. If the server is creating a new discovery network, then it must also be configured as a master server for that discovery network; otherwise the server should be configured as a slave of an existing master server. Once the server is properly configured, it is possible to add meta-data about components to the scopes hosted on the DNS server via a Eureka-provided user interface. This component meta-data contains dependencies on libraries and/or services, as well as the libraries and/or services that the component provides. The meta-data should also contain a sufficiently unique name, an URL-accessible archive file, and a description of the component. All this information is mapped onto DNS Resource Records as described in section 3.1.1.

Once the scopes have been populated with component meta-data, it becomes possible to discover components. To discover components, clients query for components that are available in a given scope. Clients discover available scopes by querying the DNS server for known scopes. When a component is discovered in a scope, all of its meta-data is fetched from the scope using standard DNS queries and is processed in some fashion; this processing is dependent on the client that is accessing it. For example, an installer service might provide a user interface that allows the end user to specify a component name to install. In this case, the installer service will query available scopes to find the specified component to install and will then traverse the available scopes again to install the transitive closure of the component's deployment dependencies.

4.2   Oscar Command Shell

Oscar provides a command shell service, implemented as a standard OSGi bundle, to interact with its OSGi framework implementation. A shell command is represented as a service that other bundles can implement to provide their own custom commands. When a bundle registers a shell command service with the OSGi framework, the shell service automatically integrates it into the shell. Eureka registers two commands with the shell: rdc and rds. The rdc command is used to query for bundles and to install a bundle and its transitive closure of deployment-level dependencies. The rds command is intended to simplify the process of providing components by creating configuration files that conform to the necessary formats to enable a DNS server to participate in an Eureka network. Additionally, the rds command allows component providers to link their own DNS server and associated scopes into an existing Eureka network.

Assuming that an Eureka network is properly configured, the following Oscar shell session shows how the end user is able to discover OSGi bundles within the Oscar framework using the rdc command; first the end user lists the available scopes:

```
-> rdc -sd
oscar-bundles.inf.fu-berlin.de.
gravity-bundles.inf.fu-berlin.de.
open-osgi.inf.fu-berlin.de.
local.
```

The end user selects a certain scope and lists the bundles available in that scope:

```
-> rdc -s oscar-bundles.inf.fu-berlin.de.
-> rdc -q
Eureka RDC
Java Rendezvous
Eureka RDS
Eureka Base
DNS Java
```

Finally, the end user selects all available scopes and installs a bundle, which automatically installs the transitive closure of its deployment dependencies:

```
-> rdc -s
-> rdc gravity
Installing dependency: Table Layout...
Installing dependency: Service Binder...
Installing bundle: Gravity...
```

4.3   Gravity

The previous example showed how the Oscar command shell accesses the Eureka network to discovery and install components and the transitive closure of their deployment-level dependencies. This subsection illustrates how Eureka can be used to dynamically resolve instance-level dependencies in an extensible system, called Gravity. Gravity is a research project investigating the dynamic assembly of applications and the impact of building applications from components that exhibit dynamic availability, i.e., they may appear or disappear at any time. Gravity is built as a standard OSGi bundle and provides a graphical design environment for building

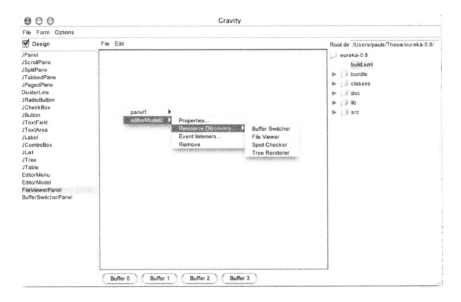

Fig. 3. Gravity showing a list of discovered bundles.

applications using drag-and-drop techniques. Using Gravity, an application is assembled dynamically and the end user is able to switch at any time between design and execution modes. Eureka was integrated into the Gravity user interface to enable end user discovery of components for integration into a running application.

Eureka's enhancements to Gravity occur in the design mode. Eureka adds a menu entry to Gravity's context menu, which appears when the end user right-clicks over a component in the design canvas. This menu entry, called "Resource Discovery," displays a sub-menu that lists all discovered components that have a dependency on any of the service interfaces provided by the component under the mouse pointer; this is achieved by querying the Eureka network for all components that depend on the targeted component's service interfaces. Figure 3 shows Gravity in design mode with the context menu showing a list of components that Eureka has discovered that can integrate with the underlying text editor component. If the end user selects a component from the resource discovery sub-menu, it is automatically installed, including the transitive closure of dependencies, if possible, and made available in Gravity's component palette along the left side of the window in figure 3. From the component palette, the end user is free to drag-and-drop the component into place on the design canvas.

To provide access to the keyword searching capabilities of Eureka, an additional entry was added under the "Options" menu in Gravity's design mode. When selected, a dialog box provides the ability to search for bundles under the available scopes; by default, all available scopes are searched. The end user is free to select specific scopes of interest. Filters can also be applied for the name, vendor, version, and description of bundles. The filters may contain LDAP query syntax, which is the standard filter language used by OSGi. When issuing a query, any discovered bundles are presented in a list, from which the user can choose to install any of them, including the transitive closure of their deployment dependencies.

5   Related Work

Napster is one of the first systems oriented around the peer-to-peer approach to receive wide-scale popularity and its primary goal was to enable file sharing among clients with a special focus on music files. For more details on the advantages and disadvantages of this approach, refer to the discussion in section 2.1.

Over the last few years another peer-to-peer solution has gained attention, the Gnutella protocol [6]. The main advantages of this protocol are based on its simplicity. Due to the fact that only a few message types exist through which peers communicate with each other and that the payload of queries is undefined, the protocol is easy to implement and makes no assumptions about the types of resources that are shared. Due to its simplicity, there are numerous clients available for the Gnutella protocol, such as LimeWire [18]. The Gnutella protocol does have its drawbacks, as discussed in [17]. Gnutella has high network traffic overhead and the only real traffic avoidance mechanism is loop-back discovery, where a node detects messages it has already received and does not forward them again. Also, clients can limit the number of open connections they allow and messages have a time-to-live property so that they do not traverse the entire network.

Sun Microsystems has founded an open community project called JXTA (short for Juxtapose) [19]. The goal of the project is to allow a wide range of applications to make use of distributed computing and targets some of the limitations found in many peer-to-peer systems. JXTA defines a set of simple, small, and flexible mechanisms that can support peer-to-peer computing on many platforms. In order to achieve this goal, a complete protocol is defined and all communication-related messages are based on XML. At the core, operations are provided to create, delete, advertise, join, and leave peer groups. On top of this functionality, peer group services can be built and some tools are given that allow an inside view of JXTA-technologies-based networks, like the JXTA shell for example. On the whole, JXTA introduces some new concepts to the peer-to-peer approach, most noticeably the "peer group" concept and the possibility of context-based querying for services. A peer group is a set of peers with policies regarding joining and leaving the group and the possibility of advertising group-services.

One of the available peer-to-peer applications built on top of JXTA is JXTA Search. The idea of this project is to use server peers with which other peers can register as capable of answering queries for a certain query-space. A query-space is a topic under which a query belongs and all queries made to a server node must commit themselves to a query-space. The server nodes themselves, called JXTA Search Resolvers, can be inter-connected creating a peer-to-peer server network. Since communication is based on XML structured messages, JXTA Search is not limited to queries from inside the JXTA framework and server nodes can be queried via SOAP [23] as well. This makes it possible for all sorts of resources capable of answering SOAP calls to take part in a search, e.g., web sites can register their topics with a server, which could then be searched by peers. The real downside of this approach is that server nodes must be interconnected by hand. Another weak aspect is that the search protocol is heavy, consuming more traffic and processing cycles.

The Service Location Protocol (SLP) [7][10] is an IETF standard for resource discovery of devices that offer network-based services to other devices. SLP Versions 1 and 2 have been published by the Service Location Group. SLP defines a protocol that enables clients to find each other in a network and provide services to each other. A service is a resource that can be used by a device, a user, a program, or another service like a printer. One of the concepts applied in order to structure the services offered in SLP is the notion of scopes. All three types or roles of an SLP network are members of a scope. The purpose of the scope is to provide scalability, limiting the network coverage of a request and the number of replies. SLP focuses on the local-link, not wide-area networks and, currently, no implementations are freely available.

Developed by the Object Management Group (OMG) the Common Object Request Broker Architecture (CORBA) [14] is a reference implementation to aid the development of distributed object-oriented applications. The CORBA Trader [13] provides the possibility of discovering instances of services of particular types. The concept used resembles that of a service-oriented framework. A special registry object, called a trader, supports the trading of objects in a distributed environment. Clients can advertise their services and discover provided services through the trader. Traders can be connected to form a directed graph, called a trading graph, with the information describing the graph distributed among the traders. In this sense traders form a federated system that may span many domains. CORBA, unfortunately, never gained a critical mass of acceptance, so CORBA traders are not ubiquitous like the DNS infrastructure.

Universal Description Discovery and Integration (UDDI) [1] is a specification for distributed registries that allow publishing and discovery of web services. A core concept in UDDI is business publication, where a business is published into the UDDI registry based on a description of the business and the web services it provides. UDDI is a closed federation of registries, where new registries can only be added by existing members. In this federation, all registries replicate all published information, which means that information that is published at one registry is propagated to all other federation members. The downside of this closed federation approach is that it is not simple for arbitrary third-party providers to participate in the federation.

Jini [3] is a distributed Java infrastructure that provides mechanisms for service registration, lookup, and usage. Its provided lookup service is reasonably sophisticated, since it was built for service discovery in networked environments. Jini does not provide sophisticated deployment facilities and relies on the class loading capabilities of Java Remote Method Invocation (RMI) [20]. In general, a protocol is defined that enables clients to find lookup services in a network with which they can register the services they provide in a service registry. Clients then query the registry for services and access them using RMI. An interesting aspect is that services are leased to clients as a means of garbage collection. The downsides of Jini are that it focuses only on services in local-link networks, it is dependent on Java, and the Jini infrastructure is not ubiquitous on the Internet.

6   Future Work

The current Eureka implementation satisfies the needs for resource discovery in the OSGi environment. Eureka still needs to prove its usefulness by being applied in real-world situations; currently, it has only been used for testing purposes. A few other desirable design and implementation issues remain, such as using Apple's mDNS implementation, investigating multi-rooted discovery networks, better tools for manipulating Eureka's XML-based configuration files, and integrating a secure HTTP server for serving components from Eureka.

7   Conclusion

This paper presented Eureka, a resource discovery service to support component deployment and dynamic integration into extensible systems. Eureka targets the resolution of dependencies between components and is implemented on top of the OSGi framework. This implementation specifically solves component deployment and dissemination issues for the OSGi framework using ideas that are general enough for use in any component framework that has dependencies among components.

Eureka uses a network of interconnected DNS servers that advertise component meta-data following the approach of Rendezvous from Apple. The Rendezvous concepts are enhanced by adding the notion of scopes and scope discovery. The scope concept is important because it enables discovery of all participating resource providers and it eliminates the need of the domain names under which resources are published to be real DNS domain names. The resulting approach is a mixture between the client/server and peer-to-peer approaches

References

[1]   Ariba Corp., IBM Corp., and Microsoft Corp., "UDDI Technical White Paper," http://www.uddi.org/pubs/Iru_UDDI_Technical_White_Paper.pdf, September 2000.

[2]   Apple Computer, Inc., "Rendezvous Official Web Site," http://developer.apple.com/macosx/rendezvous/, May 2004.

[3]   K. Arnold et al., "The Jini Specification," Addison-Wesley, 1999.

[4]   S. Cheshire and M. Krochmal, "DNS-Based Service Discovery," Internet Draft, http://files.dns-sd.org/draft-cheshire-dnsext-dns-sd.txt, February 2004.

[5]   S. Cheshire and M. Krochmal, "Multicast DNS," Internet Draft, http://files.multicastdns.org/draft-cheshire-dnsext-multicastdns.txt, February 2004.

[6]   Clip2, "The Gnutella Protocol Specification," Version 0.41, Document Revision 1.2, 2003.

[7]   J. Govea and M. Barbeau, "Comparison of Bandwidth Usage: Service Location Protocol and Jini," Technical Report TR-00-06, School of Computer Science Carleton University, October 2000.

[8]   R.S. Hall and H. Cervantes, "Gravity: Supporting Dynamically Available Services in Client-Side Applications," Poster paper in Proceedings of ESEC/FSE 2003, September 2003.

[9]   R.S. Hall and H. Cervantes, "An OSGi Implementation and Experience Report," Proceedings of IEEE Consumer Communications and Networking Conference, January 2004.

[10] Internet Engineering Task Force, "Service Location Protocol," RFC2608, June 1999.

[11] P. Mockapetris, "Domain Names - Concepts and Facilities," RFC 1034, November 1987.

[12] Napster, LLC., "Official Web Site," http://www.napster.com, January 2004.

[13] Object Management Group, Inc., "Trading Object Service Specification, Version 1.0," http://www.omg.org, May 2000.

[14] Object Management Group, Inc., "Common Object Request Broker Architecture: Core Specification," Version 3.0.2, December 2002.

[15] Open Services Gateway Initiative, "OSGi Service Platform Version 3," http://www.osgi.org, March 2003.

[16] OSGi Alliance, "Official web site," http://www.osgi.org, 2004.

[17] J. Ritter, "Why Gnutella Can't Scale. No, Really," http://www.tch.org/gnutella.html, 2003.

[18] C. Rohrs, "LimeWire Design," http://www.limewire.org/project/www/design.html, August 2001.

[19] Sun Microsystems, "JXTA v2.0 Protocols Specification," Revision 2.1.1, October 2003.

[20] Sun Microsystems, "Java Remote Method Invocation," http://java.sun.com/j2se/1.4.2/docs/guide/rmi/spec/rmiTOC.html, 2003.

[21] C. Szyperski, "Component Software: Beyond Object-Oriented Programming," ACM Press/Addison-Wesley Publishing Co., 1998.

[22] P. Vixie, S. Thomson, Y. Rekhter, and J. Bound, "Dynamic Updates in the Domain Name System (DNS UPDATE)," RFC 2136, April 1997.

[23] World Wide Web Consortium, "SOAP Version 1.2 Part 1: Messaging Framework," W3C Recommendation, June 2003.

Secure Deployment of Components

Mark Grechanik[1] and Dewayne E. Perry[2]

[1] Department of Computer Sciences,
University of Texas at Austin
gmark@cs.utexas.edu

[2] Department of Electrical and Computer Engineering,
University of Texas at Austin
perry@ece.utexas.edu

Abstract. The secure deployment of components is widely recognized as a crucial problem in component-based software engineering. While major effort is concentrated on preventing malicious components from penetrating secure systems, other security violations may also cause significant problems. We uncover a technique that creates a major breach of security by allowing rogue components to interfere with component-based applications by impersonating various generic components. This interference leads to stealing business value of competitive products and causes problems without violating legal agreements. We also present our solution to this problem, called *Secure COmponent Deployment Protocol (S-CODEP)*, and prove its soundness using the authentication logic of Burrows, Abadi, and Needham (*BAN authentication logic*).

1 Introduction

The secure deployment of components is widely recognized as a crucial problem in component-based software engineering (CBSE), and it has a major impact on the overall quality of component-based applications [1,2]. Component-based applications are ubiquitous in today's computing world. Many software vendors provide various generic components for free thereby reducing the cost and time required for development of commercial products that use these components. For example, Microsoft Windows comes with hundreds of generic components ranging from different GUI elements and FTP clients to the sophisticated Internet Explorer browser control.

The deployment of generic third-party components opens their users to different security risks. While major efforts are concentrated on preventing malicious components from penetrating secure systems, other security violations may also cause significant problems. Apart from general widely known security breaches like *buffer overflow* and *denial of service attack*, component deployment introduces CBSE-specific ways to exploit mechanisms incorporated in components and underlying component infrastructures. One of such security problem is the *impersonation* of some component by a surrogate component (e.g. inserting component server objects that act on behalf of their clients) [3] that serves as an *interceptor* [4,5,6] of all pa-

W. Emmerich and A.L. Wolf (Eds.): CD 2004, LNCS 3083, pp. 175–189, 2004.
© Springer-Verlag Berlin Heidelberg 2004

rameter values that clients of the impersonated component provide when invoking its interfaces and all values that these interfaces return to the clients after the execution.

We uncover a technique by which a rogue application legally installed by a user may impersonate a generic component by subverting existing security mechanisms in order to interfere with commercial component-based applications. The goal of this interference is to enable this rogue application to participate in the workflow of commercial applications thereby stealing the business value of competitive products and causing serious problems without violating legal agreements.

Suppose that application A sold by some company is a popular commercial product with a closed architecture that uses proprietary algorithms and techniques to deliver the business value to its users. Application A uses a generic component C that processes some proprietary data. On the other hand, application B is some inferior commercial product of a different company that would like to team up with the company that created product A. However, this partnership either costs company B some amount of money up-front that is B is unwilling to pay, or company A does not want such an alliance perceiving company B as A's potential competitor in the marketplace.

At this point, company B can use a security breach to integrate its application with A's product without violating legal agreements and without making any business alliance with company A. Company B creates a surrogate C' of component C with identical interfaces since all interfaces of C are well-documented. The public interfaces of C' only invoke real interfaces of C. That is, C' impersonates the component C and serves as an interceptor of all parameter values that A provides when invoking interfaces of C and all values that C returns to A after executing its interface methods. In fact, B can control the behavior of application A redirecting some functionality to itself thereby increasing its business value at the expense of A. We give a real-world example of this impersonation technique in Section 2.

When the user installs application B it deploys its surrogate component C' that replaces component C used by A. Since the user does not care about competitive differences between companies A and B s/he does not consider the above-mentioned action of B as a security breach providing that C' does not cause any harm to the computer (and no harm is caused except for a very small and mostly unnoticeable performance penalty due to the interception). Thus, company A may lose its competitive edge due to the security breach, and it cannot even sue company B since its actions do not violate standard license agreements that stipulate that only static modifications of executable programs produced by a company that sells a product, are prohibited.

Existing component and underlying distributed object infrastructures attempt to solve the problem of impersonation by providing special security settings that prohibit the further delegation of client requests by surrogate servers. This security approach can be easily subverted using various techniques that we review in Related Work.

Our solution is a protocol called *Secure COmponent Deployment Protocol (S-CODEP)*. S-CODEP is based on the Kerberos [7] and a generic model of a component infrastructure that we present shortly. By identifying weak links of a component infrastructure in the deployment chain, we apply S-CODEP to eliminate these links. Finally, we prove the soundness of S-CODEP using the BAN authentication logic [8]. *The contribution of this paper is thus in discovering a security breach when deploy-*

ing components under certain settings, analyzing the sources of potential attacks that lead to this breach, proposing a protocol that eliminates this problem and formalizing it, and proving that our solution is sound.

2   A Real-World Motivating Example of the Impersonation

One of the authors (Grechanik) was a consultant to Globeset, Inc., an Austin, Texas based company that developed an infrastructure for secure electronic transactions. As part of this infrastructure the company developed software package called SSL Wallet that was supposed to assist customers with the automatic completion of electronic financial transactions. Globeset established business alliances with some large banks and merchants. These banks wanted customers that carried their credit cards to receive assistance from Globeset. On the other hand, merchants also believed that Globeset would help them to increase their sales since customers liked the automatic payment system, and the company would direct them to participating merchants for products they need.

Globeset ran into a problem when attempting to integrate its SSL Wallet with the AOL browser. AOL has its own proprietary Internet browser that in 1999 used Microsoft Internet Explorer control supplied with Windows as a generic component, around which most of the AOL browser functionality was built. With a customer base of over 20 million users, AOL had its own plans of developing an electronic payment wallet and signing agreements with major banks and merchants. Therefore Globeset received a definite "No" when it asked AOL to form a business alliance that would enable SSL Wallet to work seamlessly with the AOL browser.

Since modifications of the binary code of the AOL browser were prohibited under its license agreement, Grechanik exploited the fact that Globeset's installation program and installed products were granted full administrative privileges by users who purchased SSL Wallet. He (with assistance of other developers) designed a surrogate control that impersonated Microsoft Internet Explorer component and provided information about the usage of the AOL browser at the runtime to the Globeset's SSL Wallet. Once it became clear that a user wanted to buy a product, the SSL Wallet directed the user to a specific merchant's web site and used credit card information to complete a transaction thereby effectively diverting business from AOL. The SSL Wallet was commercialized and successfully used by Globeset's customers.

As of today this security breach is still intact, and to our knowledge no one identified it and took steps to eliminate this problem. We undertake this task with our solution.

3   Our Solution

Our solution consists of three parts. First, we present a model of a generic component infrastructure and analyze it to determine the weakest links that enable security breaches such as our case of impersonation. Then, we describe the protocol S-

CODEP that enables the secure deployment of components. Finally, we prove the soundness of S-CODEP using the BAN authentication logic.

3.1   Assumptions

We make four assumptions. First, we assume that the overall integrity of the operating system cannot be violated (i.e., no external threats can exploit general security breaches that may compromise the overall integrity of the system). It means that no program can modify the kernel of the operating system or change it by installing different system drivers that would otherwise compromise standard security settings. Second, we assume that when installing any program the operating system creates a sandbox effectively protecting the installation from being penetrated by an adversary. The third assumption is that digital certificates and private keys provided by certification authorities (for example, makers of components or third-party companies such as Verisign, Inc.) and carried by programs and components should be trusted and cannot be forged. Finally, no program installed by the user can analyze other programs to determine their control and data flows or can extract their computational logic (i.e. to reverse engineer installed software). Doing such analysis would require significant computational resources and is therefore impractical. It is noteworthy that these assumptions do not go beyond what is normally assumed about various security infrastructures.

3.2   Designators and Definitions

We use the following names and definitions throughout this paper. All principals are designated with uppercase English letters. We designate a commercial application as A and a rogue application that exploits A, as B. A generic component used by A is designated C, and its surrogate installed by B is designated as C'. A component infrastructure is designated by I, and an authentication server that is a part of the operating system is denoted by S. By a component we mean a logical unit of related data (e.g. a file) which comprises logically coupled compiled programs and the format of the file is recognized by the existing component infrastructure. The infrastructure uses a systemwide database with which the file is registered under a unique name, and independently deployed. A component model defines component interaction and composition standards.

4   Weak Security Links in Component Infrastructures

A component infrastructure is a set of system services based on a component standard that ensure the properties of components are immutable and enables rules of component composition and interaction. Known component infrastructures include DCOM/.Net, CCM, and Enterprise JavaBeans. In this paragraph we introduce a generic component infrastructure and analyze it on the subject of weak security links that enable a variety of sophisticated impersonation techniques for which existing security solutions are not adequate.

4.1   Generic Component Infrastructure

A generic component infrastructure model is shown in Fig. 1. It consists of the Component Loader, Classloader, a Finder Service, and a Systemwide Database. Since a component is often a file that comprises logically coupled compiled programs, the Component Loader reads the component file into memory, uncompresses it, and extracts individual programs. However, components are often located in a Systemwide Database that in a simplest case can be a file system. A client refers to a component by its unique name with which the component registers with the Systemwide Database. When the Component Loader receives a request from a Client to instantiate a component, it asks the Finder Service to locate the component.

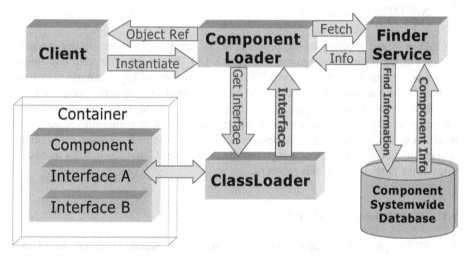

Fig. 1. A model of a generic component infrastructure and interactions among its elements.

When the Finder Service locates the component and provides information about its location, the Component Loader loads this component and asks the Classloader to instantiate classes that provide interfaces needed by the Client. The Classloader accomplishes this job and sometimes instantiates a special library called a Container that provides generic interfaces for certain classes of components. When all classes are instantiated the Component Loader returns a reference to the component that the Client can use to call exposed interfaces for the duration of the session.

4.2   Architectural Security Analysis

Here we perform an architectural security analysis of the generic component infrastructure presented in the previous section. We use the strategy described in [3] for identifying security risks. As the first step we gather information sufficient to understand the structure of the system at a high level (which we did in the previous section), and then we consider how this system operates in a concrete environment.

Concrete implementations (e.g., DCOM, CCM, Enterprise JavaBeans) consist of different modules implementing basic elements of a component infrastructure. These modules are not a part of the underlying operating system and often are user-level programs similar to A and B. It means that B can use binary rewriting [9,10,11] to dynamically modify infrastructure modules or impersonate some of their services similar to the technique for impersonating components. Essentially, if we build an attack tree (i.e., a graph representing the decision-making process of well-informed attackers), then we obtain a large number of possible paths that lead to achieving the security breach by impersonating each element of the generic component infrastructure and then intercepting calls to its interfaces.

5   S-CODEP

S-CODEP is our solution to the problem of the component impersonation security breach created by rogue programs. We base S-CODEP on the same idea that lies in the foundation of Kerberos protocol [7] – to establish shared keys between principals with help from an authentication server. Since the operating system cannot be compromised (by our first assumption), we can use its security layer to act as an authentication server. By our second assumption a program cannot be compromised during its installation. These and other assumptions allow us to establish a secure communication channel between the principal A and the component C that ensures the true identities of the participants of this protocol.

5.1   Description of S-CODEP

S-CODEP exploits the second assumption of secure installation to obtain shared keys from component infrastructure I. During the installation, each principal P sends a message to server S (we mean a security service within an operating system) that contains its identity and a private key that P uses to communicate with S: $\{P, K_p\}$. This operation includes the installation of components. Recall that by our third assumption no program can attempt to reverse engineer other programs to obtain private keys that are used to communicate with S. When S receives this initial message it stores it in a secure storage to which only S can gain access since by our first assumption S cannot be compromised.

A first step is to establish a secure communication channel between A and I so that I can request various services from components securely. To do that, A sends a message encrypted with K_A to S in which it asks S to provide shared key K_{AI} to communicate with component infrastructure I. S receives this message from A and decrypts it with K_A^{-1}. It responds to A with a message encrypted with K_A that contains the session key Ts, shared key K_{AI}, and a message M_{IS} encrypted with K_I that contains the session key Ts, shared key K_{AI}, and the identity of A.

A receives this message from S and decrypts it with K_A^{-1}. It initiates a communication process with I by sending a message encrypted with the shared key K_{AI} to I. This message contains the message M_{IS} encrypted with K_I that A received from S, and a message encrypted with the shared key K_{AI} that contains the identity of A and a timestamp nonce T_A. I receives this message from A, decrypts it, and responds with a message that consists of the incremented timestamp nonce T_A encrypted with the shared key K_{AI}. With reception of the last message from I a secure communication channel is established between A and I.

Suppose that program A needs to instantiate C at some point of time. Using the established secure communication channel with I, A sends a message to I encrypted with the shared key K_{AI} that contains the incremented timestamp nonce T_A, unique identifier of the requested component C, and the description of the requested operation (e.g., to instantiate this component). After receiving and decrypting this message I asks permission from S to establish a secure communication channel with C. That is, I sends a message to S encrypted with K_I that contains I's and C's identities as well as the session key Ts. In this message I asks S to provide a shared key K_{IC} to communicate with component C. S receives this message from I and decrypts it with the key K_I^{-1}. It responds to I with a message encrypted with K_I that contains shared key K_{IC}, and a message M_{CS} encrypted with K_C that contains the session key Ts, the shared key K_{IC}, and the identity of I.

I receives this message from S and decrypts it with K_I^{-1}. It initiates a process of instantiating C by establishing a secure communication channel with C. It does so by sending a message encrypted with the shared key K_{IC} to C. This message contains the message M_{CS} encrypted with K_C that I received from S, and a message encrypted with the shared key K_{IC} that contains the identity of I and a timestamp nonce T_I. C receives this message from I, decrypts it, and responds with a message that consists of the incremented timestamp nonce T_I and reference R_C to the component C, encrypted with the shared key K_{IC}. With reception of the last message from C a secure communication channel is established between I and C. I extracts the reference R_C to the component C and forms a new message comprising the incremented timestamp nonce T_A, unique identifier of the requested component C, and the reference R_C and encrypts this message with the shared key K_{AI}. Then it sends this message to A. After decrypting it A holds the reference R_C to the component C.

When A needs to invoke some interface of C, it sends a message to I that is encrypted with the shared key K_{AI} that contains the incremented timestamp nonce T_A, the reference R_C to the component C, the list of parameter values in the order in which they are specified in the declaration of this interface, and the description of the requested operation (e.g., to invoke an interface of the component). I decrypts this message and invokes the requested interface on behalf of A, and receives the return values. Then it forms a message encrypted with the shared key K_{AI} that contains the incremented timestamp nonce T_A, the reference R_C to the component C, the list of return values, and the description of the requested operation. This concludes the description of S-CODEP.

5.2   BAN Logic Notation

In order to prove that S-CODEP is sound we need to formalize it. We selected BAN formalism [8] for this purpose that is built on a many-sorted model logic. This logic comprises following sorts of objects: principals, encryption keys, and formulas. Principals are designated with uppercase English letters, and K_{AB} denotes a shared key between principals A and B. The symbols P and Q range over principals; X and Y range over statements; and K ranges over encryption keys.

BAN defines following constructs:
- **P believes X** : the principal **P** may act as if **X** is true;
- **P sees X** : **P** receives and reads message **X** after decrypting it;
- **P said X** : **P** sent a message containing statement **X** at some time;
- **P controls X** : **P** has jurisdiction over **X** meaning that the principal **P** is an authority on **X** and should be trusted in this matter;
- **fresh(X)**: **X** has not been sent in a message at any time before the current run of the protocol;
- $\mathbf{P} \xleftrightarrow{K} \mathbf{Q}$: **P** and **Q** use shared key **K** to communicate and this key can never be discovered by any principal except for **P** and **Q**;
- $\mathbf{P} \underset{\rightleftharpoons}{\overset{X}{=\!=}} \mathbf{Q}$: Only **P** and **Q** and principals they trust know secret **X** ;
- $\{X\}_K$: an abbreviation for an expression that **X** is encrypted using key K, and
- $\langle X \rangle_Y$: **Y** is a digital certificate or password that is combined with **X** to prove the identity of the sender of this message.

Authentication protocols are described as sequences of messages, each message is written in the form $\mathbf{P} \longrightarrow Q$: message meaning that principal **P** sends message to the principal **Q**.

5.3   BAN Logical Postulates

The authentication logic of BAN is based on a set of postulates that we use to prove certain properties of S-CODEP. Here we describe these postulates and explain their meanings.

A shared key postulate expressed in (Eq 1) states that if P believes that the key K is shared with Q and sees X encrypted under K, then P believes that Q once said X. This rule is also called a *message meaning rule*.

$$\frac{P \text{ believes } Q \xleftrightarrow{K} P \quad P \text{ sees } \{X\}_K}{\vdash P \text{ believes } Q \text{ said } X} \qquad \textbf{(Eq 1)}$$

A variant of this rule for shared secrets is expressed in (Eq 2) and states that if P believes that the secret Y is shared with Q and sees $\langle X \rangle_Y$, then P believes that Q once said X.

$$\frac{P \text{ believes } Q \underset{Y}{\rightleftharpoons} P \quad P \text{ sees } \langle X \rangle_Y}{\vdash P \text{ believes } Q \text{ said } X} \qquad \textbf{(Eq 2)}$$

Nonce is a term used to describe a message whose purpose is to be fresh, i.e., this message was not sent at any time before the current run of the protocol. A postulate expressed in (Eq 3) is called *the nonce-verification rule* and states that if P believes that X has been sent in the present run of the protocol and that Q once said X, then P believes that Q believes X.

$$\frac{P \text{ believes fresh}(X) \quad P \text{ believes } Q \text{ said } X}{\vdash P \text{ believes } Q \text{ believes } X} \qquad \textbf{(Eq 3)}$$

(Eq 4) is the jurisdiction rule stating that if P believes that Q has jurisdiction over X then P trusts Q on whether X is true.

$$\frac{P \text{ believes } Q \text{ controls } X \quad P \text{ believes } Q \text{ believes } X}{\vdash P \text{ believes } X} \qquad \textbf{(Eq 4)}$$

(Eq 5) expresses the fact that if P sees an encrypted message, then it can also see its content. Finally, (Eq 6) states that if any part of a message is fresh, then the entire message is also fresh.

$$\frac{P \text{ believes } Q \xleftrightarrow{K} P \quad P \text{ sees } \{X\}_K}{\vdash P \text{ sees } X} \qquad \textbf{(Eq 5)}$$

$$\frac{P \text{ believes fresh}(X)}{\vdash P \text{ believes fresh}(X,Y)} \qquad \textbf{(Eq 6)}$$

5.4   Formalization of S-CODEP

At this point we are ready to provide a formal description of S-CODEP. The protocol consists of ten mandatory initial messages whose purpose is to establish secure communication channel between A and I. Once this task is accomplished, A proceeds to request invocations of C's interfaces and I returns the results of these invocations. Idealized messages that accomplish this task of interface invocations are shown below as Messages N and N+1.

Message 1: $A \longrightarrow S: \{A, I\}_{K_A}$

Message 2: $S \longrightarrow A: \left\{T_s, K_{AI}, \{T_s, K_{AI}, A\}_{K_I}\right\}_{K_A}$

Message 3: $A \longrightarrow I: \{T_S, K_{AI}, A\}_{K_I}, \{A, T_A\}_{K_{AI}}$

Message 4: $I \longrightarrow A: \{T_A + 1\}_{K_{AI}}$

Message 5: $A \longrightarrow I: \{T_A + 2, C, \text{instantiate}\}_{K_{AI}}$

Message 6: $I \longrightarrow S: \{I, C, T_S\}_{K_I}$

Message 7: $S \longrightarrow I: \left\{K_{IC}, \{T_S, K_{IC}, I\}_{K_C}\right\}_{K_I}$

Message 8: $I \longrightarrow C: \{T_S, K_{IC}, I\}_{K_I}, \{I, T_I\}_{K_{IC}}$

Message 9: $C \longrightarrow I: \{T_I + 1, R_C\}_{K_{IC}}$

Message 10: $I \longrightarrow A: \{T_A + 3, C, R_C\}_{K_{AI}}$

. . . .

Message N: $A \longrightarrow I: \{T_A + N + 3, R_C, \{p_1, p_2, ..., p_q\}, \text{invoke(interface)}\}_{K_{AI}}$

Message N+1: $I \longrightarrow A: \{T_A + N + 4, R_C, \{r_1, r_2, ..., r_t\}, \text{invoke(interface)}\}_{K_{AI}}$

Message N+2: $A \longrightarrow I: \{T_A + N + 5, R_C, \text{terminate}\}_{K_{AI}}$

Formalization of S-CODEP allows us to make assumptions that we use to prove the soundness of this protocol. Messages 1 to 4 establish the fact (A 1) that principal P communicating with component infrastructure I believes that I and P communicate using shared key K_{PI}. Protocol messages 5 to 10 ensure that the principal P receives messages from the real component C via I and reads them after decrypting using key K_{PI}. We specify this fact in our assumption (A 2). Since we include encrypted none T_C in each message, we state that the freshness of messages that P sees is always guaranteed (A 2). Finally, since I is responsible for handling the lifecycle of C we state that P believes that I has the authority over C in our assumption (A 2).

$$P \text{ believes } I \xleftrightarrow{\ K_{PI}\ } P \qquad\qquad\qquad \textbf{(A 1)}$$

$$P \text{ sees } \{T_C, C\}_{K_{PI}} \qquad\qquad\qquad \textbf{(A 2)}$$

$$P \text{ believes fresh}(T_C) \qquad\qquad\qquad \textbf{(A 3)}$$

$$P \text{ believes } I \text{ controls } C \qquad\qquad\qquad \textbf{(A 4)}$$

5.5   Proof of Soundness of S-CODEP

Given S-CODEP we need to be sure that every time a principal invokes interfaces of component C it actually communicates with the real component C and not some intercepting surrogate C'. Proving this property is in fact equal to establishing that the model of the protocol is sound, that is, it does not lead to wrong behavior when some intercepting surrogate C' can impersonate the real component C.

Theorem. When principal P communicates with C it believes that C is true (i.e., P believes C).

Proof.
We start with the assumptions (A 1), (A 2), (A 3), and (A 4). Here T_C stands for nonces used in S-CODEP as part of secure communications between A, I, and C. By applying the BAN message meaning rule (Eq 1) and the assumptions (A 1) and (A 2), we derive

$$\frac{P \text{ believes } I \xleftrightarrow{\ K_{PI}\ } P \quad P \text{ sees } \{T_C, C\}_{K_{PI}}}{\vdash P \text{ believes } I \text{ said } \{T_C, C\}} \qquad \textbf{(Eq 7)}$$

In the next step of our proof we take assumption (A 3) and apply (Eq 6) to obtain the following result shown in (Eq 8).

$$\frac{P \text{ believes fresh}(T_C)}{\vdash P \text{ believes fresh}(T_C, C)} \qquad \textbf{(Eq 8)}$$

In the penultimate step of our proof we take rules (Eq 3), (Eq 7), and (Eq 8) and obtain

$$\frac{P \text{ believes fresh}(T_C, C) \quad P \text{ believes } I \text{ said } \{T_C, C\}}{\vdash P \text{ believes } I \text{ believes } \{T_C, C\}} \qquad \textbf{(Eq 9)}$$

Finally, we take assumption (A 4) and inference rule (Eq 4) and obtain

$$\frac{P \text{ believes I controls } \{T_C,C\} \quad P \text{ believes I believes } \{T_C,C\}}{\vdash P \text{ believes } \{T_C,C\}} \quad \textbf{(Eq 10)}$$

which is the statement of the theorem we need to prove. □

6   Related Work

While the areas of component deployment and software security are, each on its own, rife with excellent publications, the intersection of these areas of research yields few but memorable results. It is widely recognized that no single technique can produce completely trusted components [12]. The uniqueness of this paper is in identifying a problem that leads to creation of untrustworthy components and in using sophisticated algorithms developed in the area of secure communication protocol to solve it.

The Trusted Components Initiative (TCI) is a cooperative effort to provide the software industry with methods, techniques and tools for building high-quality reusable components, thereby elevating the general level of trust that software users, and society at large, can have in these components [**Fehler! Verweisquelle konnte nicht gefunden werden.**]. TCI's web site contains a page with references to the growing number of publications in this area.

One of main research directions in secure component deployment is in providing strong authentication control of access to and from components [14,15]. A number of techniques and algorithms are designed to prevent malicious components to gain access to computers inside secured networks, or to prevent components to access domains for which they do not have a proper authorization. However, these solutions fall short to solve the problem that we pose in this paper since this trick exploits the inability of component infrastructures to prevent two programs with equally high security privileges from interfering with each other via a commonly used generic component.

Software fortresses is an approach for modeling large enterprise systems as a series of self-contained entities [16]. Each such entity is called a fortress and it makes its own decisions about the underlying platform, data storage, and security mechanisms and policies. Fortresses communicate with one another through carefully designed mechanisms. Once a component is allowed inside a fortress it gains access to all other components within the same fortress. No mechanisms are offered to solve the impersonation problem that we presented in this paper.

Existing component and underlying distributed object infrastructures attempt to solve the problem of impersonation by providing special security settings that prohibit the further delegation of client requests by surrogate servers. For example, DCOM [17] defines four impersonation levels:

- Anonymous level completely hides the credentials of the caller;
- Identify level enables objects to query the credentials of the caller. Under this level access control lists are checked and no scripts can be run against remote computers;

- Impersonate level enables objects to use the credentials of the caller, and
- Delegate level enables objects to permit other objects to use the credentials of the caller.

This security approach can be easily subverted using various techniques. It is noteworthy that impersonation is a useful technique and is often required to implement different software architectures [6] so turning it off may not be allowed at all. However, even when security settings are explicitly set to prohibit impersonation it may still be possible to implement it with clever tricks. For example, since programs that are installed on the same computer under high administrative privileges may modify security settings during the installation, the security attribute prohibiting impersonation can be simply turned off. A more complicated example of bypassing security setting that prohibits impersonation is installing a daemon that instantiates a real component and communicates with a surrogate component by using some inter-process communication channel.

CORBA and CCM implementations may use security services defined by the Object Management Group's standards [18]. Authorization Token Layer Acquisition Service (ATLAS) describes the service needed to acquire authorization tokens to access a target system using the CSIv2 protocol. This design defines a single interface with which a client acquires an authorization token. This token may be pushed, using the CSIv2 protocol in order to gain access to a CORBA invocation on the target. This specification solves the problem of acquiring the privileges needed for a client to acquire a set of privileges the target will understand.

The Common Secure Interoperability Specification, Version 2 (CSIv2) defines the Security Attribute Service that enables interoperable authentication, delegation, and privileges. CORBA Security Service provides a security architecture that can support a variety of security policies to meet different needs. The security functionality defined by this specification comprises a variety of mechanisms such as identification and authentication of principals and authorization and infrastructure based access control. While CORBA and CCM security specifications provide a protection against the impersonation threat in general by introducing different authentication levels similar to DCOM, this protection can be easily subverted using the techniques described above.

Some component infrastructures make the task of impersonation of components simpler. A common technique in Windows platforms is emulation [19]. Each COM component (or dynamically linked library (DLL)) has a GUID (Globally Unique IDentifier). The Windows registry is a database of DLLs organized by GUIDs. A client loads a DLL by invoking a system call with the DLL's GUID; the registry is searched for the location of that DLL. Emulation is a registry technique that replaces an existing DLL with an intermediary DLL that implements the same COM interfaces and has the same GUID. When a client requests a particular DLL, the intermediary is loaded instead. In turn, the intermediary loads the shadowed DLL and acts as a "pass-through" for all client requests. Thus the intermediary can monitor call traffic for a COM interface unobtrusively.

7   Conclusion

Secure deployment of components is widely recognized as one of the crucial problems in component-based software engineering. The contribution of this paper is first in discovering a technique that creates a major breach of security by allowing rogue components to interfere with component-based applications by impersonating various generic components. This interference leads to stealing business value of competitive products and causes serious problems without violating legal agreements. Our second contribution is a solution to this problem that we call Secure COmponent Deployment Protocol (S-CODEP). We prove its soundness using the authentication logic of Burrows, Abadi, and Needham (BAN authentication logic). We know of no other work that addresses the problem that we present in our paper and solves it.

Acknowledgments. We warmly thank Don Batory for reading this paper and providing useful comments, suggestions, and corrections.

References

1.   Meyer, B.: The Grand Challenge of Trusted Components. The 25th International Conference on Software Engineering, Portland, OR, (2003)
2.   Szyperski, C.: Component Software: Beyond Object-Oriented Programming. ACM Press, Addison-Wesley (1998)
3.   Viega, J. and McGraw, G.: Building Secure Software. Addison-Wesley (2002)
4.   Brown, K.: Building a Lightweight COM Interception Framework, Part I: The Universal Delegator. Microsoft Systems Journal, 14 (1999) 17-29
5.   Brown, K.: Building a Lightweight COM Interception Framework, Part II: The Universal Delegator. Microsoft Systems Journal, 14 (1999) 49-59
6.   Schmidt, D., Stal, M., Rohnert, H., and Buschman, F.: Pattern-Oriented Software Architecture. John Wiley & Sons, 2 (2001) 109-140
7.   Tung, B.: Kerberos: A Network Authentication System. Addison-Wesley (1999)
8.   Burrows, M., Abadi, M., and Needham, R.: A Logic of Authentication. ACM SIGOPS Operating Systems Review 23(5) 1989
9.   Romer, T., Voelker, G., Lee, D., Wolman, A., Wong, W., Levy, H., and Bershad, B.: Instrumentation and Optimization of Win32/Intel Executables Using Etch. USENIX Windows NT Workshop, Seattle, WA (1997)
10. Hunt, G.: Detours: Binary Interception of Win32 Functions. Proc. 3rd USENIX Windows NT Symposium, Seattle, WA (1999)
11. Larus, J. and Schnarr, E.: EEL: Machine-Independent Executable Editing. SIGPLAN Conference on Programming Language Design and Implementation (PLDI) (1995)
12. Meyer, B., Mingins, C., and Schmidt, H.: Providing Trusted Components to the Industry. IEEE Computer (1998) 104-115
13. The Trusted Components Initiative: http://www.trusted-components.org/
14. Bagarathan, N. and Byrne, S.: Resource Access Control for an Internet User Agent. The 3rd USENIX Conference on Object-Oriented Technologies and Systems (1997)

15. Lindqvist, U., Olovsson, T., and Jonsson, E.: An Analysis of a Secure System Based on Trusted Components. Proceedings of 11th Ann. Conf. Computer Assurance, (1996) 213-223

16. Sessions, R.: Software fortresses : modeling enterprise architectures. Addison-Wesley, (2003)

17. Brown, N. and Kindel, C.: Distributed Component Object Model Protocol - DCOM/1.0. Internet Draft, January 1996. http://www.microsoft.com/oledev/olecom/draft-brown-dcom-v1-spec-02.txt

18. Object Management Groups security standards:
http://www.omg.org/technology/documents/formal/omg_security.htm

19. MSDN Library: http://msdn.microsoft.com/library/default.asp?url=/library/en-us/dnesscom/html/classemulation.asp

JPloy: User-Centric Deployment Support in a Component Platform

Chris Lüer and André van der Hoek

School of Information and Computer Science
University of California, Irvine
Irvine, CA 92697-3425
USA
{chl,andre}@ics.uci.edu

Abstract. Based on a vision that, in the future, applications will be flexibly built out of small-grained components, we argue that current technologies do not adequately support component deployment in such a setting. Specifically, current technologies realize deployment processes where most decisions are made by the application manufacturer. When using small-grained components, however, the component user needs to have more control over the deployment process; *user-centric deployment* is needed. In this paper, we describe our initial efforts at providing user-centric deployment. We present JPloy, a prototypical tool that gives a user more control about the configuration of installed Java components. JPloy extends the Java class loader so that custom configurations can be applied to existing components, without having to modify the components themselves. For example, name space or versioning conflicts among components can be elegantly resolved in this way. We demonstrate JPloy by applying it to an example application.

1 Introduction

It is assumed that in the future, applications will consist out of large numbers of independently developed, reusable components. The role of the *application builder* will emerge (see Figure 1): application builders compose applications out of reusable components licensed from a number of different component manufacturers. In such settings, application builders need to have control over the deployment of individual components, so that they can determine the structure of the application that is built. Furthermore, they should not have to program extensive amounts of code, rather, they should be able to *compose* applications. To enable this kind of user-centric composition, new deployment technologies are needed.

Current support for the deployment and composition of component-based applications can be divided into two kinds of approaches: component platforms and deployment tools. Current component platforms [15], such as Java [3], Dotnet [6], Koala [22], or ArchStudio [19], make it possible to configure applications at the user's site (i.e., they support deployable components). The process of installing and configuring components, however, is manual and error-prone. Current deployment tools, on the

W. Emmerich and A.L. Wolf (Eds.): CD 2004, LNCS 3083, pp. 190-204, 2004.
© Springer-Verlag Berlin Heidelberg 2004

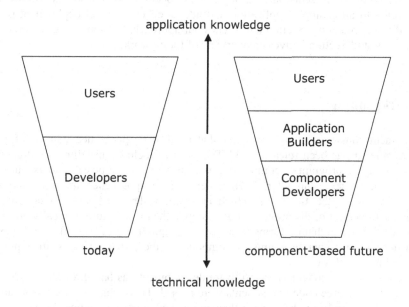

Fig. 1. Traditional and component-based development scenarios.

other hand, do not support deployable components; they assume that applications are configured mainly at the manufacturer's site.

We believe that there is a need for a blending of the two approaches, in effect creating a deployment technology for component platforms that is *user-centric*. This would put full control of the application structure into the hands of an application builder located at the user's site, and thus would leverage the full potential of deployable components. As a consequence of the shift from manufacturer-centric to user-centric deployment, deployment support has to move from a dedicated deployment tool (such as an installer) into the component platform. This is because, in a manufacturer-centric setting, deployment is an occasional activity; it is performed only when a new product version is available or when the user's computer system changes. In a setting with small-grained deployable components, activities such as installing and configuring components must be performed continuously. For example, if an application consists of large numbers of components, updates for individual components will frequently be available. Even if a user chooses to perform these updates manually at a later point of time, the number of components and the complexity of their relationships will make tool support indispensable.

In this paper, we present JPloy, a tool that provides deployment support for Java components. JPloy extends the Java runtime environment so that it can read in *configuration files*, which are used to connect and adapt deployed components. In particular, configuration files specify the usage relations between components, and how components are modified at runtime. The remainder of this paper is structured as follows. In Section 2, we discuss the background of deployment technologies. Section 3 identifies what we consider core requirements for a user-centric deployment technology, and Section 4 presents our approach, JPloy. Section 5 demonstrates how we applied JPloy to an example application and addressed two critical deployment problems of this application. Section 6 evaluates our approach, Section 7 discusses related approaches, and Section 8 gives an overview of future work.

2 Background

Deployment consists of those activities that need to be performed with a software product after it has been released [11]. Deployment includes installing, configuring, and updating the program or component; its goal is to make it possible to execute the program on a user's computer. Current deployment approaches are *manufacturer-centric*; this means that the way in which a program is deployed is largely determined by the manufacturer of the program. For example, the manufacturer typically provides an installation script that performs the automatic deployment of the software. If a program depends on other programs or components, these dependencies are typically specified in a rigid way.

Historically, component-based software development has had three stages [26]. In the first stage, source code components were reused. These components disappear after compilation and thus have no influence on deployment activities. In the second historical stage, the manufacturer can link binary components into different products from a product line. Current deployment tools (for example, the Software Dock [11] [13], Bark [24], or RPM [5]) are designed to support this stage of component technology. They assume that all available forms of an application are determined before it is shipped to the user's site, and hence the user's control over the application structure is limited. All deployment activities are controlled by the manufacturer. Typical deployment activities in such a setting are:

- *Release:* the activity of ending development and making the software product ready to be shipped.
- *Retire:* its opposite, performed when support for a product is terminated.
- *Install:* the activity of copying a product to a user's machine and preparing it so that it can be used.
- *Remove:* its opposite, removing all traces of a product from the user's machine.
- *Update:* a partial remove and install; typically used when a new version of the software product is released and downloaded.

Current and future component systems, however, must be designed to support *deployable components* (stage 3) [15]: components that can be deployed individually, and that are composed into different applications at the user's site. This means, that in this stage, the two steps of configuring and shipping code have been swapped: first, components are shipped to the user; only afterwards, they are configured into applications.

3   Requirements

To make user-centric deployment a reality, certain requirements must be met. In this section, we identify three requirements that we consider to be at the core of any solution to user-centric deployment. *Interference-free deployment* requires that deploying one component should not change the behavior of other deployed components. *Independent deployment* requires that components can be deployed, as far as possible, independently from each other; especially, this criterion implies absence of strict dependencies. Further, user-centric deployment requires *compatibility with legacy components*.

3.1 Interference-Free Deployment

Installation and configuration of components should not change the behavior of already installed components. This is a general requirement of deployment technologies and this holds as well in user-centric deployment. As a consequence, installing and configuring of components needs to be performed without side-effects or irreversible changes [9].

To realize interference-free deployment, a component platform must not:

- overwrite information in configuration files during install or configuration;
- occupy a location in a namespace that is also used by a previously installed component; for example: a component uses the same name as another one, so that one of the two components cannot be accessed any longer; and
- change global properties of a system such as environment variables or class paths.

A special case of interference-free deployment is concurrent deployment of versions. Since two components in one applications may require different versions of the same component (or, in the general case, two different applications use two different versions of the same component), it has to be possible to install and configure several versions of one component at the same time [20].

3.2 Independent Deployability and Absence of Strict Dependencies

Since components are units of deployment, there should be no strict dependencies among them. A strict dependency is a dependency that can be resolved only by one component. Instead, if a component requires another component, this requirement has to be formulated in terms that allow several options of how to fulfill requirements, thereby changing the model from manufacturer-centric to user-centric deployment. In particular, the prohibition of strict dependencies is needed to enable competition among component developers, and to give full control over which components are employed in an application to the application builder.

In the absence of strict dependencies, a component platform needs to provide mechanisms to specify dependencies that are not based on component identities. I.e., a dependency has to be specified on a higher level than the level of component names. It must be possible to deploy each component individually; and the application builder at the user's site must be able to decide on the concrete configuration of an application.

An implication of independent deployability is the need to deploy configurations (or, architectures) independently from components. Since components cannot contain strict dependencies, the actual instantiations of component interactions have to be stored elsewhere.

3.3 Compatibility with Legacy Code

A platform that is not backwards-compatible to legacy code will be impracticable due to the large number of components that already exist. A component deployment platform needs to be able to support legacy code without much effort on the application builder's part. For example, legacy code may be wrapped in some way to make it compatible to the platform. It may be possible to create such wrappers in part automatically. A consequence of backwards compatibility is that user-centric deployment support may not reduce the expressiveness of the platform, i.e., it cannot restrict the space of valid executable files.

3.4 Other Requirements

We can certainly identify many additional requirements that build upon the core requirements. Two interesting such requirements are transparent updating and incremental builds. Transparent updating requires a mechanism that can automatically install and configure updates of deployed components; since a user's system may consist of a very large number of components, manual updating would not be feasible. Incremental builds requires the ability to configure and test partial applications. For the purpose of this paper, we focus on the core requirements in order to establish a base on which we and others can build.

4   The JPloy Approach

4.1 Motivation of the Approach

Support for component deployment could be provided either by a programming language, by external tools, or by a component platform. Language level support has the disadvantage that deployment information will be lost after compiling. Since components are generally shipped in compiled form, programming language support would not be helpful in assisting an application builder. External tools can modify existing components by editing their binary representation; but this is generally undesirable since it has the potential to create a large number of different binary component versions. This leaves us with the component platform as the optimal location for deployment support: the component platform can modify compiled components at runtime and on-the-fly, without requiring source access and without multiplying the number of component files.

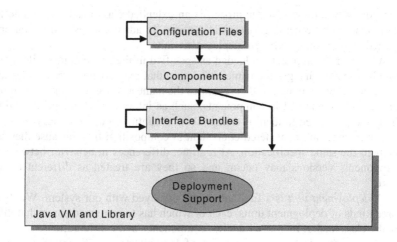

Fig. 2. Architecture of a JPloy application. Arrows represent *uses* relations.

There are two possible ways to add deployment support to a component platform: extending the application programming interface (API) of the platform, or modifying the loading and linking mechanisms of the platform. Additional tools that are external to the platform can be used with both approaches.

When extending the API of the platform, byte code instructions or operations in the base library are added. This makes it possible for components to call platform functionality that ensures proper installation and configuration. But for this approach to work, components need to be required to call this functionality at the appropriate times. This may be hard to enforce, and makes the use of legacy components that were not specifically written for the platform impossible.

We choose the second approach: extending the loading and linking mechanisms. This approach has the advantage that all modifications to the platform are transparent to components. This simplifies the development of new components and at the same time enables the use of legacy components.

To implement the approach, we had to select a component platform. Currently there are two industrial-quality component platforms, Dotnet [6] and Java [27]. We selected the Java platform, since it provides a well-documented solution for extending its loading and linking mechanism: the Java class loader [14]. Our solution extends the Java class loader, so that it can read in configuration files and modify binary code (i.e., Java class files) in an appropriate manner while the code is being loaded into memory.

Figure 2 shows the architecture of a running system under this approach. At the bottom, one can see the Java platform, which consists of a virtual machine and a class library. Inserted into the platform is the deployment support module, which extends the functionality provided by the platform. In particular, the deployment support module interprets configuration files and interface bundles to instantiate a desired application.

4.2 Extended Class Loader

The core technology of our approach is an extended class loader. It is able to avoid name clashes by renaming classes at runtime, to adapt classes and operations when needed, and to handle different deployment units.

Whenever a component is loaded as specified in the configuration file, the renaming class loader changes the names of classes that may create name clashes to appropriate new values. In effect, this separates the namespace used to identify components (and entities contained in components, such as interfaces) at composition time from the namespace used to identify components at runtime. For example, two versions of one component are considered equivalent at composition time because they both implement the same specification. At runtime, differences in behavior between the two components versions may occur, and so they are treated as different components there.

A *deployment unit* is a file that can be deployed with our system. We distinguish three kinds of deployment units, each of which has to be treated somewhat differently by the class loader: interface bundles, components, and configurations.

An *interface bundle* is a collection of Java interfaces. The interfaces are used to specify components in a given domain. Public interfaces need to be deployed separately from components since each interface can be implemented by several classes contained in several components. Thus, an interface bundle specifies data types in a domain, but does not contain any implementation code.

A *component* is a collection of class files, typically in the form of a jar file. Any Java class files can be used, including legacy code. All public classes in the component are by default its provided services. All classes that are used by classes in the component and are not contained in the component are its required services.

Any name in a component that refers to an external entity (such as a class or method that is not defined inside the component) is subject to renaming by the extended class loader. For example, if class C refers to class D, and D is not defined in the same component, the class loader uses a configuration file to determine which class in which component is supposed to stand in for D. The class loader will then, during loading time, replace all references to D with references to the stand-in.

A *configuration* is a file that specifies how a set of components interoperate. It lists 1) the components that are needed, 2) how they are connected, and 3) optionally, adaptations. Configurations are created and edited by application builders in order to define applications, exchange components in an existing application, etc. Thus, they are stored in a human-readable form. Each component may be used in any number of configurations. When the extended class loader encounters a configuration, it treats it as a set of instructions on how to treat entities that occur inside of components.

The conceptual difference between a component and a configuration is that components cannot refer to other components or to configurations. They refer only to programming-language entities such as classes, and all matching between the names of classes outside of a component and the components that provide an implementation to them will be done by the extended class loader. Configurations, on the other hand, can refer to components and to other configurations. Components can refer to interface bundles, though; and interface bundles can refer to other interface bundles. Referring to interface bundles is needed to enable type checking as normally done by a typed component platform.

4.3 Configuration Language

The syntax of configuration files currently consists out of the following commands; see Figure 3 for an example configuration.

1. A command for importing a new component and assigning it an alias (lines 1-5 in the example). All components that are imported in this way can be referred to in other parts of the configuration, and may be executed as part of the application. Currently, components are identified by a local file name. In a later version of the system, a uniform resource identifier will be used instead, so that configurations will be independent of location.

2. The main command (line 7). It is needed to declare the entry point for execution; i.e., with which component execution starts when the configuration is executed. The main component is required to include a main class, i.e., a class that has an operation with the signature of a Java main method. The information which class in the main component is the main class is taken from the component's manifest; alternatively the name of the main class can be given as a parameter to the "main" command.

3. The use command (lines 9-12) defines a usage relationship between two components; a set of use commands thus defines the architecture of the application. A use B means that A is allowed to access features provided by B. Without such a command, all attempts by A to use features in B will fail. However, it is not enforced that A actually uses any of the features in B. In a sense, this command is a replacement for the Java class path, which is a simple way to declare which components provide the features needed by an application. The disadvantage of the class path is that it does not allow to define individual relations between components; all relations are all-to-all (every component that is part of the application can access any other).

4. The replace command (line 14) removes a class from a component, and replaces all references to it by something else. This allows an application builder to replace parts of a component that are not compatible with the current application, and to replace them by alternatives (see Section 5.2). The command syntax is: *requiring_component* replace *old_class new_class*. This will cause two actions to happen: one, *old_class* is never loaded from component *requiring_component*. Two, all references to *old_class* in *requiring_component* will be replaced by references to *new_class*, which will typically not be located in *requiring_component*, but in one of the components that provide features to it (example: *new_class* is located in component B, and there is a command: *requiring_component* use B).

5. The wrap command (not shown) wraps a feature (a class or operation) with another name whenever it is used by the given component. In a case where component A expects a feature called X, and component B provides this feature under the name Y, the wrap command provides a simple way to resolve this problem. The command is equivalent to writing a wrapper class; it serves as a simple means to adapt a component in the case of an incompatibility.

Naming conflicts between components are avoided automatically; this does not require the use of a special command. This means that, whenever a component is loaded, the extended class loader checks whether its names conflict with those of any previously loaded components, and if so, all concerned classes are automatically re-named.

5 Example

In the following, we will detail two exemplary situations that illustrate how JPloy can be used to solve practical software development problems. Problem 1 deals with concurrent versioning; JPloy is used to deploy an older and a newer version of the same component simultaneously. Problem 2 addresses the architectural modification of an existing application; here JPloy allows a reconfiguration of the application without source code manipulation.

5.1 Problem 1: Concurrent Versioning

We recently developed a component-based developed environment called Wren [17], which uses the Argo/UML [1] graphical design tool, and the xArch [8] architecture description language. When integrating these technologies, a version conflict occurred. Both Argo and xArch use XML files to store their configuration; but Argo (in the version employed) uses an older version of the same library. As a consequence, it was not possible to integrate the application as planned. It is not possible on the Java platform to load two different packages with the same name simultaneously; and it was not possible to replace one of the two versions by the other, because the two versions were not compatible with each other.

To solve this problem, a separation between the development-time component namespace and the deployment-time component namespace is needed. It is useful that the two implementations of the XML component have the same name at development time, since they are intended to solve the same problem, and to implement the same specification. A developer would not choose to use both at the same time, instead he/she would settle on the newer version. But at deployment time, this choice may not exist; a separate namespace is needed to avoid problems like this. Thus, each component implementation should have its own identifier at deployment time, no matter which specification it implements.

Using JPloy, we can specify the architecture of the application as a uses-graph (see Fig. 3 for the JPloy notation). This allows us to map different versions of the same package to different requirers: the Argo component is paired with the (older) Xerces version of the XML component, while the xArch component is implicitly paired with the newer version of the XML component that is contained in the Java platform library (since component `xarch` has no `use`-command that connects it to an XML component, the only place where it can access XML features is in the platform).

```
1    wren        = c:\wren\wrenclient.jar
2    argo        = c:\wren\argouml.jar
3    xarch       = c:\wren\xarchlibs.jar
4    xerces      = c:\wren\xerces.jar
5    argoinit    = c:\wren\argoinit.jar
6
7    wren main
8
9    wren use argo
10   wren use xarch
11   argo use xerces
12   argo use argoinit
13
14   argo replace
          org.argouml.application.PreloadClasses
          edu.uci.wren.PreloadClasses
```

Fig. 3. JPloy configuration for the example application.

At runtime of the application, the JPloy class loader checks, whenever a class from the XML package is requested, which component is requesting it. If the requester is a part of Argo or of Xerces, the class is loaded from Xerces; if the requester is a part of xArch, then the class is loaded from the platform library.

5.2 Problem 2: Reconfiguration of a Third-Party Application

In the Wren project from example 1, we reused code from the Argo project for drawing customized design diagrams. Since Argo is a full-featured UML tool, only a small part of its diagramming functionality was needed. Unfortunately, Argo performs extensive initializations at program start time in order to avoid performance overheads later; but since we were reusing only a small part of its functionality, most of this lengthy initialization was unneeded in our project. We decided to modify Argo's code in this respect; this did not prove very difficult, because Argo is a well-documented open source project.

However, modifying Argo in this way created a maintenance and deployment problem. The code modification could not be integrated into the standard Argo code base, since it contradicted the purpose of the project (providing full-featured UML modeling support); it applied only to our use of it. Hence, both the original Argo component and the modified one had to be maintained and deployed separately; each time a new Argo version was released, the modification had to be edited in manually. Also, the code distribution was redundant: people using both Wren and Argo had to have available two almost, but not quite, identical copies of the Argo component.

To solve this problem, we used a JPloy configuration that contained the `replace` command: we replaced the initialization class in the Argo component (`org.argouml.application.PreloadClasses`) with an abbreviated version (`edu.uci.wren.PreloadClasses`; see Figure 3). The effect of this is that the Argo component is loaded without the original initialization class, and instead it requests this class from component `argoinit`, which was written by us and only contains the simplified initialization class. In this way, when the program is executed, we save the initialization overhead that is normally needed for the Argo component to work, but which is not needed for our specific use of it.

This example shows how JPloy configurations can be used to override architectural constraints that are embedded in the code of a component. Doing so requires some knowledge of the internal structure of the component, but so does modifying the source code. The advantage of our approach, though, is that no maintenance problem occurs, and that the component can be simultaneously deployed both with and without the modification.

6 Evaluation of the Approach

JPloy is an initial implementation of a deployment tool. In this section, we briefly discuss how it compares to the requirements stated in Section 3, and what its limitations are.

Requirement: interference-free deployment. JPloy's capability to automatically avoid name conflicts solves an important part of the problem of interference-free deployment. There is no case in which a component cannot be installed because another component that conflicts with it is already installed. Also, the strict separation between components and configurations prevents many possible side-effects of deployment operations. For example, in some system an update operation may accidentally remove components that are still needed by some applications.

However, there are other aspects of interference-free deployment. For example, when a component modifies an operating system variable, this will interfere with the behavior of other installed components. More research is needed to determine how these kinds of interferences between components can be avoided.

Requirement: independent deployability. Independent deployability is given by the fact that every component can be replaced by another, compatible one. There is a strict separation between specifications and components; for any specification, there may be any number of components implementing it, so that any component is replaceable. When a component refers to features from another component in its code, this dependency can always be remapped to another component at runtime.

To replace a given component used in an application, all that needs to be done is to replace the identifier of the old component with the identifier of the new component in the application's configuration file.

Requirement: compatibility to legacy components. This is given through the transparency of the JPloy approach. Most legacy components will continue to work without change; the only exception is components that use reflection. A renaming class loader cannot correctly work with reflection, because reflection allows Turing-complete modifications of code.

We note that a main limitation of the current system is its reliance on close compatibility of the components that are used together (as with many CBSE approaches to date). In practice, glue code is often needed to make components that are not completely compatible interoperate with each other. See Section 8 for a discussion on how we believe that JPloy lays a basis for an effective and elegant solution to this problem.

7 Related Work

In the following paragraphs, we briefly summarize the most relevant related systems.

Jiazzi [18] is a linker that can compose applications out of Java components and Jiazzi scripts. The scripts determine the structure of the application, and according to the information in the scripts, the linker will modify the Java class files of the components so that together they form the desired application. JPloy has in common with Jiazzi the ability to impose a configuration on a set of preexisting components. The disadvantage of Jiazzi, however, is that it modifies the actual component files, thus creating a number of variants of each component in the file system. JPloy does not modify files; all modifications happen exclusively at runtime.

MJ [7] is an extension of the Java platform that introduces a module concept. Modules are defined in module files; each module consists out of a number of classes and has well-defined uses relations. Modules are enforced at run-time by an extended class loader. MJ utilizes a similar technique as JPloy, but it does not have the focus on user-centric deployment.

Eclipse [2] is an integrated development environment for Java with an advanced plug-in concept. A plug-in is a component that can be integrated into the environment. Eclipse has in common with JPloy the ability to define use-relations between components. It accomplishes this by giving each component a metadata file that describes which other components it is allowed to use. Unlike JPloy, the Eclipse model is limited to acyclic dependency graphs.

Dotnet [6] is the core programming platform of recent Microsoft operating systems. It includes a component concept called *assembly*. Dotnet has the ability to concurrently deploy multiple versions of the same component. However, it does not support independent deployability; a component is typically tightly linked to components that provide services to it.

Hnětynka and Tůma [12] discuss name clashes on the Java platform in detail. They present a solution based on the Sofa component model that employs a renaming class loader to automatically avoid name clashes in a way similar to our approach. However, their solution does not address other deployment issues.

OSGI [4] is a standard for home appliance software components; it is implemented among others by the Oscar [10] project. OSGI provides capabilities for connecting components by extended class loaders; especially, it allows components to define uses-relations among themselves.

8 Future Directions

We believe that the our approach presents a powerful basis for component connection and adaptation at deployment time. Two areas of extensions to the approach are interaction styles and glue code; the concepts of the extended class loader and of configuration files will make integration of these extensions straightforward.

Interaction styles are restrictions on the way components may interact. They are known from the field of software architecture [25], where they form part of architectural styles. For example, the event-based style (also known as indirect invocation [21]) postulates that all communication must be performed through events; subscribers subscribe to event sources, and are notified when new events are published. Interaction styles are often essential for the architecture of an application. Hence, when using a given premanufactured component in a certain architecture, it may be necessary to adapt the interaction style of the component to the one required by the architecture. When done manually (assuming source code is available), this may be a labor-intensive task; when switching from a procedural to an event-based interaction style, all procedure calls that cross component boundaries need to be modified.

We plan to extend the JPloy configuration language to allow users to specify an interaction style for a configuration. Then, the JPloy runtime environment will generate the appropriate interaction code and enforce the interaction style when the components are deployed. While not all possible interaction styles can be automatically generated and enforced, we expect that our approach will be able to cover a selection of relevant interaction styles.

Glue code is the common name for code that is written to make independently developed components interoperate. It resolves the different syntactic and semantic incompatibilities that typically exist between components without adding much functionality.

Glue code is often considered essential for application composition, because it is unlikely that two components from different sources will be completely compatible with each other. But at the same time, glue code is often highly mechanical in nature, consisting only out of simple mappings between syntactically incompatible interfaces with the same underlying semantics. We will extend JPloy to generate glue code for syntactical component mismatches. The configuration language will also include support for easily specifying small parts of code that can be used in cases where the automatically generated code is insufficient.

The run-time code manipulation capabilities of a JPloy-like tool can potentially be useful for other problem areas besides component deployment, for example program compaction [16]. Subject-oriented programming tools such as HyperJ [23] provide similar capabilities for the purpose of multidimensional separation of concerns.

9   Conclusions

In this paper, we defined user-centric deployment and argued that current deployment approaches are insufficient in this respect. We identified a set of requirements for a possible solution, and presented JPloy, an initial approach towards addressing user-centric deployment in the Java platform. JPloy realizes interference-free deployment and independent deployability of components by extending Java's mechanism for loading compiled code into memory. JPloy does not require source code access and works with legacy components.

We applied JPloy to two deployment problems (concurrent versioning, and reconfiguration of a legacy application), and showed how it can be used in these situations. While we certainly recognize that JPloy is not a complete solution at this moment in time, we believe that its approach establishes a solid core for addressing the full spectrum of issues in a user-centric deployment environment. Our future work will build upon this core and work towards providing capabilities for injecting interaction styles and glue code into applications.

References

1. Argo/UML, http://argouml.tigris.org/.
2. Eclipse.org, http://www.eclipse.org/.
3. Java 2 Platform, Standard Edition, v 1.4.0 API Specification, 2002. http://java.sun.com/j2se/1.4/docs/api/index.html.
4. Open Services Gateway Initiative, http://www.osgi.org/.
5. RPM Package Manager, http://www.rpm.org/.
6. Box, D. *Essential .NET.* Addison-Wesley, Boston, 2002.
7. Corwin, J., Bacon, D.F., Grove, D. and Murthy, C. MJ: A Rational Module System for Java and its Applications. In *OOPSLA 2003: 18th Conference on Object-Oriented Programming, Systems, Languages, and Applications*, ACM, New York, 2003, 241-253.
8. Dashofy, E.M., van der Hoek, A. and Taylor, R.N. An Infrastructure for the Rapid Development of XML-Based Architecture Description Languages. In *Proceedings of the ICSE 2002 International Conference on Software Engineering*, ACM, New York, 2002.
9. Dolstra, E., Visser, E. and Jonge, M.d. Imposing a Memory Management Discipline on Software Deployment. In *International Conference on Software Engineering (ICSE)*, 2004, to appear.
10. Hall, R.S. and Cervantes, H. An OSGi Implementation and Experience Report. In *2004 IEEE Consumer Communication and Networking Conference*, 2004.
11. Hall, R.S., Heimbigner, D. and Wolf, A.L. A Cooperative Approach to Support Software Deployment Using the Software Dock. In *Proc. 1999 International Conference on Software Engineering*, ACM, New York, 1999, 174-183.
12. Hnetynka, P. and Tuma, P. Fighting Class Name Clashes in Java Component Systems. In *Proceedings JMLC 2003*, Springer, 2003.
13. van der Hoek, A., Hall, R.S., Heimbigner, D. and Wolf, A.L. Software Release Management. In *Proceedings of the Sixth European Software Engineering Conference*, Springer, Berlin, 1997, 159-175.
14. Liang, S. and Bracha, G. Dynamic Class Loading in the Java Virtual Machine. *Sigplan Notices*, *33* (10), 1998. 36-44.
15. Lüer, C. and van der Hoek, A. Composition Environments for Deployable Software Components, Technical Report UCI-ICS-02-18, Dept. of Information and Computer Science, University of California, Irvine, 2002.
16. Lüer, C. and Hoek, A.v.d. Architecture-Based Program Compaction. In *First Workshop on Reuse in Constrained Environments (RICE 2003) at OOPSLA 2003*, Anaheim, California, 2003.
17. Lüer, C. and Rosenblum, D.S. Wren—An Environment for Component-Based Development. *Software Engineering Notes*, *26* (5), 2001. 207-217.
18. McDirmid, S., Flatt, M. and Hsieh, W.C. Jiazzi: New-Age Components for Old-Fashioned Java. In *Proceedings of the ACM Conference on Object-Oriented Programming, Systems, Languages, and Applications*, 2001.
19. Medvidovic, N., Oreizy, P., Taylor, R.N., Khare, R. and Guntersdorfer, M. An Architecture-Centered Approach to Software Environment Integration, Technical Report UCI-ICS-00-11, University of California, Irvine, Irvine, 2000.
20. Meijer, E. and Szyperski, C. Overcoming Independent Extensibility Challenges. *Communications of the ACM*, *45* (10), 2002. 41-44.
21. Notkin, D., Garlan, D., Griswold, W.G. and Sullivan, K. Adding Implicit Invocation to Languages: Three Approaches. In Nishio, S. and Yonezawa, A. eds. *Object Technologies for Advanced Software*, Springer, Berlin, 1993, 489-510.

22.   van Ommering, R., van der Linden, F., Kramer, J. and Magee, J. The Koala Component Model for Consumer Electronics Software. *Computer, 33* (3), 2000. 78-85.

23.   Ossher, H. and Tarr, P. Hyper/J: Multi-Dimensional Separation of Concerns for Java. In *Proc. of the International Conference on Software Engineering (ICSE) 2000*, ACM, New York, 2000, 734-737.

24.   Rutherford, M.J., Anderson, K., Carzaniga, A., Heimbigner, D. and Wolf, A.L. Reconfiguration in the Enterprise Java Beans Component Model. In *Component Deployment: IFIP/ACM Working Conference*, Springer, Berlin, 2002, 67-81.

25.   Shaw, M. and Garlan, D. *Software Architecture*. Prentice Hall, Upper Saddle River, 1996.

26.   Szyperski, C., Gruntz, D. and Murer, S. *Component Software*. Pearson Education, London, 2002.

27.   Yellin, F. and Lindholm, T. *The Java Virtual Machine Specification*. Addison Wesley, 1998.

On the Performance of SOAP in a Non-trivial Peer-to-Peer Experiment

Tom Van Cutsem, Stijn Mostinckx,
Wolfgang De Meuter, Jessie Dedecker*, and Theo D'Hondt

Programming Technology Lab
Department of Computer Science
Vrije Universiteit Brussels
Pleinlaan 2, 1050 Brussels, Belgium
{tvcutsem,smostinc,wdmeuter,jededeck,tjdhondt}@vub.ac.be

Abstract. This paper reports on the experiences we gained while trying to build an interpreter for a new programming language aimed at developing strong mobile software. The interpreter is actually a distributed virtual machine that can be used in a peer-to-peer setting on a heterogeneous platform. In our quest for an experimental implementation, simplicity and portability led us to using a combination of Java and SOAP technologies. The paper reports on the problems we encountered in this experiment and shows that SOAP is inadequate in peer-to-peer communication that cannot afford fat servers to run on all nodes.

1 Introduction

The topic of our research is the design of programming languages that simplify the construction of strongly mobile applications. This fits in what has been called "Ambient Intelligence" (AmI) by the European Council's IST Advisory Group (ISTAG, [6]). The vision of AmI is that soon individuals will be surrounded by a dynamically configured processor cloud running smoothly integrated applications. In this context, we conduct experiments in language design in order to distil language concepts that will facilitate writing mobile applications. The languages we design are typically dynamically typed, reflective and have built-in provisions for distribution and mobility.

The current scion of our language family is called Pic% (pronounced Pic-oh-oh). It is an object-oriented mobile extension of a language family called Pico (D'Hondt, [5]). Pico has been extended in various experimental ways, ranging from distributed agents (Van Belle and D'Hondt, [11]) to objects and delegation (De Meuter et al.,[4]). The experiment described here is a unification of these two. Hence, the scion discussed here features:

- **Minimality**: Ordinary calculus syntax is used and the concept space is restricted to basic values, functions and tables (D'Hondt, [5]): Pico can be seen as an attempt to recover as many concepts of Scheme (Abelson and Sussman, [1]) as possible given a conventional infix syntax restriction.

---

* Research Assistant of the Fund for Scientific Research Flanders, Belgium (F.W.O.)

W. Emmerich and A.L. Wolf (Eds.): CD 2004, LNCS 3083, pp. 205–218, 2004.
© Springer-Verlag Berlin Heidelberg 2004

- **Strong reflection**: All entities, including parse trees are first-class. More-over, they can be easily inspected *and* changed by the programmer.

- **First-class computational state**: Computations are first-class entities, similar to Scheme **continuations**. This enables *Strong Code Mobility*, such that *running* programs can transparently migrate to another machine[1]. In Pic%, programs can grab their own computational state, transmit it over a wire, and, upon arrival, resume the computation.

- **Prototypes**: Pic% features prototypical objects (De Meuter et al., [4]) which are created 'ex nihilo' (without classes!) or by cloning existing objects. The absence of classes is very adequate in a language aimed at strong mobility since no (transitive closures) of classes have to be transmitted.

We adhere the vision that language design is an iterative experimental activity. In an experimental implementation, test applications can be written in the language. This allows one to detect unforeseen interactions in its concept space. Very often, these are reflected by similar interactions between its implementation components, such as the VM core and the distribution layer in our case. Based on these experiments, the language and its implementation are further polished and another iteration cycle can be entered. In our case, we wanted to experiment in a *realistic* processor cloud constellation with PDA's, PC's, mobile phones, etc. The limited computational power of some of these forced us reconcile *efficiency* with *portability* as good as possible. Thus, our evaluator had to be constructed using portable lightweight technology, which led us to Java[2] and to SOAP (World Wide Web Consortium, [13]) for the networking and mobility of our *experimental* distributed evaluator. The latter choice was made because SOAP (Simple Object Access Protocol) is claimed to be a lightweight object exchange protocol. Furthermore, SOAP is claimed to be deployable in all kinds of network topologies (client-server, n-tier or peer-to-peer) (Snell et al., [7]). Unfortunately this turned out to be untrue. The point of this paper lies in sharing our experience with the SOAP technology and in arguing why we found SOAP to be unsuitable in order to successfully finish our project. We explain why SOAP is not suitable in a peer-to-peer setup with small devices without huge amounts of memory and without fast processors.

In the following section, we explain a bit more about the mobile Pico version in order to give the reader a good feeling of the flexibility we were after. In section 3 we give an overview of the (sometimes hyped) arguments that led us to the technological platform with which we tried to implement our interpreter. In section 4 we give a thorough overview and analysis of the problems we encountered using this technology. Finally, section 5 concludes.

---

[1] Note that this is much more expressive than *weak mobility*, which is about moving "dead" code (cfr. Java Applets).

[2] We often violated the "rules of good object-oriented practice" for efficiency reasons.

2 Context

As explained our research is about new language concepts for programming distributed and mobile systems in the context of AmI. We believe that current distributed programming languages and middleware solutions (such as Java RMI and CORBA) are too static to match the dynamicity encountered in open distributed environments. Therefore we designed a highly dynamic mobile object-oriented extension of Pico as an alternative (De Meuter et al., [4]). It is not our intent to present its features in detail, but because they influenced our design decisions we briefly explain them in following subsections to give the reader a basic feeling.

2.1 Remote Object Lookup

The first important aspect of our model is how objects find other objects in the network. Given our setting (a heterogeneous, pervasive peer-to-peer environment) we want a system to lookup objects as declaratively as possible. To this extent, our remote object lookup is a distributed generalisation of the lobby concept introduced in Self (Ungar and Smith, [10]). A lobby is an object that denotes a set of processes. Each process can register itself in a lobby and can request other members of a lobby. This is the way a process can lookup other processes in our model. An object is made accessible to remote processes by publishing it under a given name:

```
anObject.publish("alias");
```

To retrieve the remote reference to the service object from `processA` we can write:

```
remoteObject : remoteProcess.alias;
```

2.2 Message Passing

Once we have referenced a remote object we may want to send messages to it. Message sending between local and remote objects happens transparently and is handled by a variation of *wait-by-necessity* (Caromel, [3]). When a message is sent to a remote object, then it is invoked asynchronously (the sender does not block until the message has been performed). The return value of such a remote method invocation is an *awaited object*. When the remote object has received the method call and has computed the result the awaited object *becomes* the real object. The sending process will only wait when the awaited object is sent a message and has not yet *become* the real result. Below is an example of the remote message passing semantics:

```
result = remoteService.perform(aRequest); // does not wait
remoteObj.processResult(result); // does not wait
result.operation() // waits till 'result' is a true object
```

The first expression asynchronously sends the **perform** message to the **remoteService** object and the variable **result** now contains an awaited object. The second expression uses the reference to the **result** object as a parameter. The third expression is a message that is sent to the **result** object. It is only in the last expression that the process will block until the awaited object has become the result that has been computed by the **remoteService** object.

2.3 Mobility

Issues such as partial failures and efficiency can be anticipated using object mobility. In our language all objects understand the **move** message by default. A move method can move any object graph up to a certain cut-off point to any location. This way it is possible to both pull an object to your process as well as to push it to another process. Strong mobility comes for free in our language, because in Pic% the computational state of a process is first-class and also represented as an object (which understands the **move** method). Below is an example of object migration:

```
anObject.move(destination, pruningExpression);
```

The second parameter is a pruning expression that determines what part of the object graph should migrate. Objects that are pruned away are replaced by remote references to the objects that stayed behind on the source process.

3 Architecture and Implementation

Now that we have given a short overview of the distribution and mobility features of Pic%, we can turn our attention to the experimental implementation we built; the main topic of this paper. As already said, Pic% was implemented in Java and the distribution and mobility layer of the interpreter was conceived using SOAP. SOAP stands for Simple Object Access Protocol. It is presented as a lightweight protocol intended for exchanging structured information in a decentralized, distributed environment (World Wide Web Consortium, [13]). The protocol is independent from its protocol binding. HTTP is frequently used as protocol binding, but others such as SMTP can be used as well. The content of a SOAP message is written in XML (World Wide Web Consortium, [12]). A SOAP message contains one main information element, the *envelope* which is divided into several information subelements. The most important subelements are header, body and fault information elements. The *header* specifies the execution directives (such as transaction information) of the message. The SOAP *body* element is optional and contains application specific element information items. A SOAP *fault* element provides a structured way to report various errors that ocurred while processing a message.

One of the design goals of SOAP was the ability to encapsulate and exchange remote procedure calls (RPC). This resulted in SOAP-RPC, a set of rules that specify how a remote procedure call must be embedded in a SOAP envelope.

Our implementation uses SOAP-RPC with HTTP as protocol binding to communicate between the different interpreters of our language. More information on the structure of SOAP messages in the context of our application is given later in this section.

The Apache Software Group developed a library called Apache-SOAP (The Apache Software Foundation, [9]), which is considered to be a modern implementation of the SOAP specification. As said above, we used HTTP as protocol binding, which requires a special kind of HTTP server that supports Web Services (often called an application server). In our experiments, we used the Tomcat (The Apache Software Foundation, [8]) application server . This server is then used by the Apache-SOAP library as the communication layer for the implementation of the Web Service. In our case, the Web Service is a wrapped Pic% interpreter whose methods are remotely invocable. Hence, one Pic% interpreter can "talk SOAP-RPC" (over an HTTP binding) to a Web Service that encapsulates another Pic% interpreter. Figure 1 identifies these different large components that are involved in the communication of two Pic% interpreters.

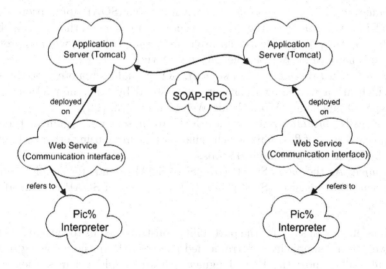

Fig. 1. Distribution Components involving SOAP

The following subsections give a more in-depth discussion of the implementation and the concrete setup of the experiment.

3.1 Implementation Choices

We wanted our language to be a medium for writing experimental, yet *real world* applications. By this, we mean that experimental programs written in Pic% should immediately work in the context of PDAs and mobile phones as well as on traditional PC's. Hence our choice for Java since a virtual machine currently exists for all these platforms.

Another important issue was which networking mechanism to choose from. Although we were no experts in the field of networked objects, we documented ourselves on several existing techniques that were available given the Java restriction. Using documentation, such as a.o. (Snell et al., [7]), we made our decision in favor of SOAP based on the following other arguments:

- *Text-based protocol:* Unlike most of the other available technologies (such as Java RMI and CORBA) SOAP is text-based. This is as a matter of fact an advantage as many of the binary protocols risk getting blocked by firewalls that shield the several *administrative domains* in which most of the internet is currently divided (Cardelli and Gordon, [2]).
- *Independent of implementation language:* The current implementation is done in Java, as it is at this point the most promising platform available for the platforms we target. Nevertheless we thought it would be an extra benefit if we could later on write interpreters in other languages. SOAP will allow us to communicate with interpreters written in other programming languages. This was an important argument not to choose for Java RMI.
- *Independent of transport layer:* Nearly all current SOAP applications use the HTTP protocol. Nevertheless, this is not compulsory so that we can change this to transport protocols that are more oriented towards wireless protocols like Bluetooth or WiFi in the very near future.
- *Standardized communication support:* SOAP enables remote procedure calls which are a well known concept, understood by different packages for all types of languages (World Wide Web Consortium, [13]).
- *Extensible medium:* Since we use XML to present our argument types, we have a degree of flexibility which is harder to achieve using other technologies which generate precompiled stubs.
- *Simple:* As the name SOAP (the 'S' of SOAP stands for simple) and documentation suggests (Snell et al., [7]), the usage of SOAP is claimed to be simple.

In brief, we can say that the portability constraint led us to Java and that the lightweight and simplicity constraints led us to SOAP. In the following sections, we will explain how the Pic% language features explained in section 2 were implemented using this technology.

3.2   Representing Processes

As explained in section 2 a Pic% process can be registered in a lobby, so that it becomes accessible for other Pic% processes. In Java such a Pic% process is represented as an instance of `ProcessServer`. The public interface of such a `ProcessServer` consists of the set of methods making up the Web Service encapsulating a Pic% process. Hence, a `ProcessServer` class implements all methods necessary for interprocess communication. The `ProcessServer` Web Service is an object which is "deployed" on the application server through a so-called deployment descriptor. Such deployment descriptors are XML files containing several configuration parameters for the service such as a unique identifier, the object's class, the set of invocable methods and so on.

As for Apache-SOAP, it was designed in such a way that its Web Services are indistinguishable from 'normal' Java classes at the source code level. This means that one does not need to write a single line of code to promote a Java object to a Web Service. All necessary information must be given in a deployment descriptor and Apache-SOAP will take it from there. When a web server receives an HTTP POST request carrying a SOAP call, it will automatically deserialize arguments into Java objects, call our ordinary Java method and respond by serializing the return value of the method.

3.3 Remote Object Lookup

When the programmer accesses the public fields of a process object (like in section 2.1 when we execute remoteProcess.alias to lookup the published object), we construct a SOAP call to the underlying remote ProcessServer object. The requesting process spawns a new Java Thread which is going to perform the SOAP-RPC call. The return value is an awaited object (Caromel, [3]) that will eventually become a proxy to the requested object. This reflects the implementation of what was described in section 2.2.

Shown below is the actual message sent by the call Thread when processB is requesting a public object called alias residing on processA. Default SOAP and XML namespaces are replaced by an ellipsis because the messages otherwise become too verbose.

```
<?xml version='1.0' encoding='UTF-8'?>
<SOAP-ENV:Envelope xmlns:SOAP-ENV="..."
                   xmlns:xsi="..."
                   xmlns:xsd="...">
   <SOAP-ENV:Body>

      <ns1:getPublicObject xmlns:ns1="processA"
                          SOAP-ENV:encodingStyle="...">
       <name xsi:type="xsd:string">alias</name>
       <sender xmlns:ns2="..."
               xsi:type="ns2:ProcessId">
        <processId xsi:type="xsd:string">processB</processId>
        <processURL xsi:type="ns2:java.net.URL">
          <value xsi:type="xsd:string">URL to B</value>
        </processURL>
       </sender>
      </ns1:getPublicObject>
   </SOAP-ENV:Body>
</SOAP-ENV:Envelope>
```

The SOAP call contains name and sender attributes, which contain respectively the alias of the remote object we want to get a reference to and the requesting process identification. This process is identified by a pair (`name, url`) that uniquely identifies a process. The SOAP message below is the content of the HTTP response:

```
<?xml version='1.0' encoding='UTF-8'?>
<SOAP-ENV:Envelope xmlns:SOAP-ENV="..."
                   xmlns:xsi="..."
                   xmlns:xsd="...">
  <SOAP-ENV:Body>
    <ns1:getPublicObjectResponse xmlns:ns1="processA"
                                 SOAP-ENV:encodingStyle="...">
      <return xmlns:ns2="urn:picoo.vub.ac.be"
              xsi:type="ns2:RemoteObject">
        <!-- serialized version of a RemoteObject -->
      </return>
    </ns1:getPublicObjectResponse>
  </SOAP-ENV:Body>
</SOAP-ENV:Envelope>
```

The method returns successfully and sends the public object to the requesting process. Even though the serialized representation of the proxy is omitted, we have printed the XML messages here in order to illustrate the amount of data that is actually sent over the network.

3.4   Message Passing

Recall that our programming model specifies messages to remote objects to be sent asynchronously, but always immediately return an awaited value which still might have to *become* its actual value. Nevertheless, in the implementation we resorted to a well-established encoding of synchronous SOAP-RPC calls. As illustrated in the above code, for the remote object lookup this problem was solved using a call thread. We cannot apply this scheme to implement message passing, however, because messages sent to remote objects are not handled by the remote process immediately. Instead, the remote process *schedules* such messages in a queue and handles them whenever computing resources are available. We therefore model asynchronicity of remote messages explicitly by using a *callback* mechanism. As an example, consider the evaluation of `remoteObj.m(x)` from within `processA`, where `remoteObj` represents an object on a remote process, say `processB`. The evaluator on `processA` will first perform a SOAP-RPC call to `processB` to initiate the computation of the message send, supplying a return address as an extra argument.

   `processA` maintains a mapping of return addresses onto `AwaitedObjects` that still have to *become* their real value. Thus, the return address is an identifier for some awaited object which needs to be "replaced" by the function's return value when it is computed. Given this information, `processB` can schedule the request in its queue. When the request is eventually evaluated, the return value of the function needs to be sent back explicitly to the caller.

In short, message passing is made asynchronous by using two synchronous SOAP-RPC calls, one to signal a remote method invocation, the other to return the result.

4   Experiment Results

Throughout the development of the Pic% interpreter, we encountered several weaknesses relating both to the concepts underlying SOAP as well as to the specific libraries we used. This section discusses these problems. In our argument we clearly make the distinction between problems inherent to SOAP and those one might encounter when applying the model using contemporary technology. The latter problems are also important since the software we used is a reflection of the technological state of the art of the field. A developer choosing to use SOAP can be confronted with its technical issues just as likely as its conceptual issues.

4.1   The Client-Server Model

The first problem basically boils down to the fact that SOAP is claimed to be applicable in any distribution topology including client-server applications and peer-to-peer. This turns out not to be the case.

Conceptual problems Usually, SOAP provides "service objects" that perform a potentially complex operation, for relatively simple clients. This can indeed be observed by looking at most programs that currently use SOAP. A prototypical example of the usage of SOAP in internet environments is a web service offering the latest stock exchange information. This means there is one *heavyweight* service object, containing a database of stock quotes of a given stock exchange, updated on a regular basis. *Lightweight* clients can then query for the stock quote of a company, e.g. using a company's ticker tape symbol. Other concrete examples include Amazon's [3] SOAP interface for retrieving product information and Google's [4] SOAP interface for retrieving search results. In all these cases the topology is basically client-server with heavyweight servers and lightweight clients. This is not a coincidence. Its (essentially service-based) design, clearly reveals that SOAP was basically designed to offer 'fat' services that perform tasks for 'thin' clients rather than for a truly interoperating set of collaborative entities. Such a setup, which should clearly be our aim given our context of communicating interpreters, requires an architecture that SOAP apparently cannot offer, despite its promising claims. After all, in our setting, SOAP forces every Pic% interpreter to be a (heavy) web service, since each interpreter must be able to act both as a server and as a client. This is too heavyweight a setup for our purposes. The technology is inherently too complex in order to run on small devices with limited computing power.

---

[3] http://www.amazon.com/webservices

[4] http://www.google.com/apis

Technological problems In the Apache-SOAP library, the most natural way to write a distributed application is by using HTTP as protocol-binding. This automatically implies a client-server architecture and that each embedded device needs to run an application server. Another possibility is to use SMTP as protocol-binding which would worsen the situation because we would need to run both an SMTP and a POP server.

The cost of the innate client-server architecture is further aggravated by the fact that Java objects which act as a SOAP service must be **deployed** on an application server, like Apache Tomcat. The application server runs a Web Service, which unfolds the HTTP requests and passes them on to the SOAP layer. Hence, before communication between two computer nodes can occur we have to pass through three layers:

1. the application that needs to communicate (a Pic% interpreter) has to pass communication through the web service.
2. the web service on its turn has to interact with the application server.
3. the application server has to interact with the low level communication layers, such as TCP/IP.

This need for layers immediately presents performance problems of using SOAP in the context of lightweight mobile machines, which do not always have the computing power to run an application server with deployed web services listening for incoming HTTP requests.

4.2   XML Serialization

The second problem basically boils down to the fact that XML is not very well suited for encoding object graphs to be transported over a network.

Conceptual problems Choosing SOAP as a communication medium between components implies using XML to encode the data being communicated. Using XML has the obvious advantage of ensuring portability across platforms and languages. One could use a proprietary protocol and wrap this data in an XML message, but this would nullify the reasons for using XML or even SOAP in the first place. Converting objects to another representation for the purposes of storing them on disk or sending them over a wire is called **serialization** (also called *pickling* or *marshalling*). Using XML for this in our context implies that we have to be able to *represent* any first-class value of our programming language in XML, as any such value can be transported over a wire to another interpreter We thus faced the problem of having to serialize any Pic% value (such as a number, a function, an array of strings, the runtime stack, ...) to XML. This is more problematic than one would imagine at first sight.

First, Pic% objects, like most objects in other object-oriented languages, basically consist of data fields and methods, more generally known as slots. Since objects can contain other objects in their slots, objects and other values are connected with each other in a graph-like manner (a so-called *object graph*). Of

course, this object graph may contain cycles, meaning there are objects pointing (directly or indirectly) to themselves. A serialization algorithm should be
able to cope with such cases. Unfortunately, XML is designed to describe **tree**
structures. **Graph** structures, however, are more complex and require the use
of "pointers" to avoid the duplication of graph nodes. Serializing such object
graph results in pretty complex, but – more importantly – in very large XML
files. We have experienced more than a factor 10 when going from a pointer
representation to an XML representation.

But the situation is even worse. One must make sure that, when reconstruct-
ing an object graph from the XML representation on the receiver side (called
deserializing an object), object identity is maintained. As an example, consider an object o having two slots, one containing some value $v1$, and the other
containing a value $v2$. If $v1 == v2$ before o is sent over the network, then it
should hold that $v1' == v2'$, given that $v1'$ and $v2'$ are the reconstructed versions of $v1$ and $v2$. In general, any two objects pointing to the same object before
serialization should also point to the same object after deserialization. This requires a complex encoding of 'pointers' in the XML files sent around. But apart
from the complexity it also poses some serious conceptual problems. An object
that reaches a process in two different ways should still be equal to itself. This
requires an encoding of pointers in XML that is 'globally consistent' over different machines. Assuring this global consistency actually means implementing a
distributed memory management system in XML!

Technological problems The Apache SOAP library was very minimal in its support for serializing Java objects to XML. Therefore, we had to write our own
serialization algorithm capable of safely (i. e. avoiding aforementioned pitfalls)
transporting any Pic% object graph across the network.

Apache-SOAP provides standard serializers to map primitive Java types and
Arrays, Maps, Dates etc. into XML using standard SOAP encoding (see World
Wide Web Consortium ([13]), section 5). It also provides the necessary deserial-
izers to transform the XML back into the proper Java objects. However, when
(de)serializing arbitrary Java classes, things get more difficult. Apache-SOAP
provides a generic *BeanSerializer* capable of (de)serializing arbitrary Javabeans.
This serializer was impractical for us to use for a number of reasons:

- Our implementation classes do not adhere to the Bean model in that we
  do not allow (for security reasons) all instance variables of our classes to be
  accessed or changed by accessor or mutator methods, and that we do not
  want to provide no-args constructors for them. Writing accessors for every
  instance variable would break encapsulation of Pic% objects. In a mobile
  context this kind of security breaching is totally unacceptable.
- Since we have knowledge of the structure of the classes that we serialize, a
  dedicated (de)serializer would outperform the generic Bean serializer.
- Some Pic% objects require special serialization to preserve object identity.
  Other objects can be singletons, requiring the deserializer to return just the
  existing singleton instance instead of creating a new one.

Because of all these technical problems, we ended up writing a serializer capable of (de)serializing specific Pic% interpreter objects. Dedicated (de)serializers were written for Pic% objects that required special (de)serialization needs. This serializer maintains object identity and handles circular structures. Although not impossible, all this code put extra burden on the machinery it is supposed to run. This was no longer adequate in the context of the lightweight devices we are targeting.

4.3   XML and Typing

Another issue in the transformation between object graphs and XML documents in a statically typed language like Java are **typing** problems. Unfortunately, Apache SOAP bases its serialization on *static* types as specified in method signatures. Of course, in an object-oriented setup that uses inheritance, serialization should logically be performed on *dynamic* types since one wants the 'real' object to be serialized and not only the part indicated by the static (abstract) type it is assigned at that particular moment. When Apache SOAP wants to serialize an object, it retrieves an associated serializer for such objects based on the static type of the variable in which it resides. We therefore explicitly had to override framework methods to circumvent this strategy and to retrieve serializers based on the dynamic type. This is necessary since e.g. many methods in our language implementation operate on abstract classes. One cannot write serializers for such abstract classes. Moreover, subclasses may require special serialization behaviour which cannot be expressed at the level of the superclass.

4.4   Performance Issues

Last, but not least, as already suggested a few times, SOAP (and XML) suffers from some serious performance problems.

Conceptual problems Using SOAP in our setting gives rise to two performance bottlenecks. The first is the limited amount of bandwidth usually available for communication between small mobile devices. To circumvent this drawback, small-size messages and data representation are essential. But, obviously, XML is not a very compact data description language. As already indicated, we observed a factor 10 difference between a tree and its XML representation.

Another drawback of SOAP is that the use of XML leads to speed performance penalties both due to the construction of XML documents and due to parsing them back to object graphs upon reception. In the first part, a lot of verbose information has to be written to the XML document which would not be included in a binary serialization. Concerning the second part, parsing XML is a costly operation. Indeed, apart from the program logic that actually deserializes the flattened object graph, there is also a lot of parsing code active that is merely about XML parsing. Actually, XML puts an extra 'parsing indirection' between the object graph representation and its flattened representation. The point here is that SOAP's use of XML implies generality and thus a larger overhead in parsing. This imposes a significant performance bottleneck on SOAP message reception. Thus, binary protocols outperform XML not only in size but also in speed. Lightweight devices like cellular phones will probably not be able to cope with such costly operations when large object-graphs are transmitted.

Technological problems Apart from these conceptual problems presented abstractly, we can shed some light on the concrete difficulties we encountered in our implementation. In the following, we show that the size and overhead associated with the XML representation of Pic% objects is *really* substantial.

When transmitting Pic% values, every node in the XML structure requires:

– an **xsi:type** element denoting the **dynamic** Java type of the serialized object, qualified by an XML namespace denoting the encoding style used.
– a **picoId** element uniquely identifies a given XML part. It acts as an address to which one can refer later on in the XML document in the case of multiple references. This was already explained in section 4.2.

The following XML excerpt shows part(!) of a SOAP body, representing a serialized version of the Pic% function f():void. This is about the simplest function we can write in Pic% as it is a function without arguments that always returns the void value, Pic%'s null-value. The generated XML is incredibly verbose:

```
...
<argument xsi:type="ns2:edu.vub.picoo.grammar.AGFunction">
  <_picooId_ id="1"/>
  <name_ xsi:type="ns2:edu.vub.picoo.grammar.AGText">
    <_picooId_ id="2"/>
    <text xsi:type="xsd:string">f</text>
  </name>
  <parameters xsi:type="ns2:edu.vub.picoo.grammar.AGTable">
    <_picooId_ id="3"/>
    <table xmlns:ns3="http://schemas.xmlsoap.org/soap/encoding/"
        xsi:type="ns3:Array"
        ns3:arrayType="ns2:edu.vub.picoo.grammar.PicoValue[0]">
    </table>
  </parameters>
  <body xsi:type="ns2:edu.vub.picoo.grammar.AGVoid">
    <_picooId_ id="4"/>
  </body>
</argument>
...
```

Although we have not performed any scientifically founded measurements, one has to admit that the amount of data actually transmitted is tremendous compared to the simplicity of the Pic% function. As good as all experiments we conducted seem to indicate that, in general, an XML representation is at least 10 times bigger than the corresponding binary representation.

5   Conclusion

The long term goal of our research is to design small and conceptually clean programming language features that are dedicated to the construction of distributed and strong mobile systems in the context of Ambient Intelligence. Having established an initial design of a language, our experimental vision on language design demanded us to construct an experimental interpreter for it as soon as possible. Even though we were willing to make some performance sacrifices as a trade-off for portability and simplicity, we wanted our implementation to be really usable on small mobile devices. Although we do not claim to be experts in middleware technology, the available (commercial) literature led us to using Java and SOAP. Unfortunately, SOAP did not prove to be suitable in this context due to its inherent client-server architecture which requires deploying program classes on a separate web server, and due to the inherent weaknesses of XML when it comes to performance and expressivity. In the context of our restrictions we cannot help but conclude that SOAP is not only a simple but also a simplistic object access protocol.

References

[1]   Abelson, H. and Sussman, G. J. (1985). *Structure and Interpretation of Computer Programs*. MIT Press, Cambridge, MA.
[2]   Cardelli, L. and Gordon, A. D. (1998). Mobile ambients. In *Foundations of Software Science and Computation Structures: First International Conference, FOSSACS '98*. Springer-Verlag, Berlin Germany.
[3]   Caromel, D. (1993). Toward a method of object-oriented concurrent programming. *Communications of the ACM*, 36(9):90–102.
[4]   De Meuter, W., D'Hondt, T., and Dedecker, J. (2003). Intersecting classes and prototypes. In *Proceedings of PSI-Conference*. Springer-Verlag.
[5]   D'Hondt, T. (1996). The pico programming language project. http://pico.vub.ac.be.
[6]   ISTAG (2003). Ambient intelligence: from vision to reality. Draft report.
[7]   Snell, J., Tidwell, D., and Kulchenko, P. (2001). *Programming Web Services with SOAP*. O'Reilly.
[8]   The Apache Software Foundation (1999-2003). The tomcat 5 servlet/jsp container. http://jakarta.apache.org/tomcat/tomcat-5.0-doc/index.html.
[9]   The Apache Software Foundation (2001). Apache soap v2.3.1 documentation. http://ws.apache.org/soap/docs.
[10]   Ungar, D. and Smith, R. B. (1987). Self: The power of simplicity. In *Conference proceedings on Object-oriented programming systems, languages and applications*, pages 227–242. ACM Press.
[11]   Van Belle, W. and D'Hondt, T. (2000). Agent mobility and reification of computational state, an experiment in migration, in: Infrastructure for agents, multi-agent system, and scalable multi-agent systems. *Springer Verlag Lecture Notes in Artificial Intelligence nr. 1887*.
[12]   World Wide Web Consortium (2000). Extensible markup language (xml) 1.0 (second edition). http://www.w3.org/TR/REC-xml.
[13]   World Wide Web Consortium (2003). Simple object access protocol (soap) 1.2 w3c note. http://www.w3.org/TR/SOAP/.

A Flexible and Secure Deployment Framework for Distributed Applications

Alan Dearle, Graham Kirby, Andrew McCarthy, and Juan Carlos Diaz y Carballo

School of Computer Science, University of St Andrews,
North Haugh, St Andrews, Fife KY16 9SS, Scotland, U.K.
{al, graham, ajm, jcd}@dcs.st-and.ac.uk

Abstract. This paper describes an implemented system that is designed to support the deployment of applications offering distributed services, comprising a number of distributed components. This is achieved by creating high level placement and topology descriptions that drive tools to deploy applications consisting of components running on multiple hosts. The system addresses issues of heterogeneity by providing abstractions over host-specific attributes yielding a homogeneous run-time environment into which components may be deployed. The run-time environments provide secure binding mechanisms that permit deployed components to bind to stored data and services on the hosts on which they are running.

1 Introduction

This paper describes an implemented system that is designed to support the deployment of applications offering distributed services, comprising a number of distributed components. A number of requirements for flexible service deployment may be identified, including:

- an architectural description of software components, the hosts on which they are to execute, and the interconnections between them [1]
- the ability to enact the architectural description to obtain a running deployment consisting of the specified set of components—requiring:
  - the ability to install and execute code on remote hosts
  - a security mechanism to prevent malicious parties from deploying and executing harmful agents, and deployed components from interfering with each other, either accidentally or maliciously
- support for component implementation using standard programming languages and appropriate programming models
- the ability for components to interface with off-the-shelf (COTS) components already deployed

Clearly, security considerations are a major issue in any flexible deployment infrastructure. Our system introduces new security domains, called *thin servers*, which can be placed within an existing network. Thin servers permit flexible and dynamic

W. Emmerich and A.L. Wolf (Eds.): CD 2004, LNCS 3083, pp. 219-233, 2004.

placement of both code and data by authorised users, in a secure and simple manner. They support a model of global computation in which objects have global identity, and the programmer may define the physical domain in which code is executed. Thin servers do not replace existing hosts, but are instead used to complement existing infrastructure to increase its usability and effectiveness. Indeed, thin servers can be co-hosted on conventional servers, and the services offered by them may be indistinguishable from conventional services.

In order to permit deployed components to be assembled into appropriate topologies and communicate with each other, the components must exhibit some degree of interface standardisation. In the implementation described here, communication is via asynchronous channels that may be dynamically rebound to arbitrary components either by the components themselves or by suitably privileged external parties.

All software applications are subject to evolutionary pressure. In order to respond to these pressures, it may be necessary to adapt parameters of the deployed services, including, but not limited to, the placement of components and data on machines and the components' interconnection topology.

This paper describes a framework that permits distributed services to be described, deployed and evolved in distributed contexts. It provides binding mechanisms that permit components to bind to local code, data and processes, including inter-node, inter-component bindings. When combined, these provide a run-time environment within which a deployed application may evolve. The framework contributes to the state of the art in six areas, providing:

1. mechanisms for deploying code and data in a distributed environment
2. abstractions over node specific attributes yielding a homogeneous run-time environment for deployed components
3. safe binding mechanisms so that deployed components can bind to stored data and services on the nodes on which they are running
4. mechanisms for describing and deploying distributed applications consisting of components running on multiple nodes
5. the ability to evolve the topology of deployed applications and components
6. security mechanisms that permit a wide range of policies to be implemented ranging from liberal to draconian

The deployment framework described here is based on an enabling infrastructure called Cingal[1] [2, 3]. Cingal itself addresses points 1-3 above, while the deployment infrastructure adds support for points 4-6.

2 The Cingal Computational Model

Cingal supports a conceptually simple computational model in which each thin server provides the following:

- a port to which a *bundle* of code and data may be sent for execution
- authentication mechanisms, preventing unauthorised code from executing

---

[1] *Computation IN Geographically Appropriate Locations*

- a content addressable store
- symbolic name binders for data and processes
- an extensible collection of execution environments called *machines*
- channel-based asynchronous inter-machine communication
- a capability system controlling access to stored data, machines and bindings.

The computational model is illustrated in **Fig 1**, which shows two hosts: a conventional host that might be running Windows or MacOS, and a thin server running the Cingal infrastructure. In order to execute code on a thin server, an OS process on the conventional host sends a bundle of code and data to the thin server where it is received by a daemon known as the *fire daemon*.

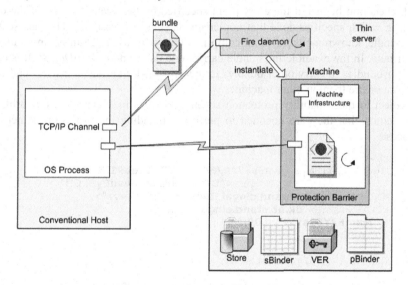

Fig 1: Cingal computational model

The fire daemon authenticates the bundle using mechanisms described later and, provided that it is authenticated, the bundle is *fired*. This causes a new operating system process to be created, which executes the code in the bundle. This process, which we term a *machine*, contains the code in the bundle and *machine infrastructure* containing code and data structures provided by the thin server. The infrastructure provides mechanisms to allow executing bundles to access the services provided by thin servers, to interface with the protection mechanisms, and to permit inter-machine communication channels to be established. The infrastructure may be invoked from other processes via an interface called the *machine channel* and from the executing bundle via an API (called the *machine API*) provided to the bundle when it is initialised[2].

The thin server infrastructure includes a number of services that may be invoked from bundles executing within machines. These are the *store, store binder, process binder* and *valid entity repository* (VER), providing storage, binding and certificate

---

[2] API documentation is available at *http://www-systems.dcs.st-and.ac.uk/cingal/docs/*.

storage respectively. A running bundle's interactions with these services are restricted via a capability protection scheme mediated via library code in the infrastructure.

The *bundle* is the only user-level entity that may be executed in Cingal. It is passive, consisting of a closure of code and data and a set of bindings naming the data. In the current implementation bundles are XML-encoded, as illustrated in **Fig 2**. Each bundle carries an *authentication* element with attributes *entity* and *signature*. The *entity* identifies the bundle using a globally unique identifier (GUID) implemented via an MD5 key. The *signature* is used by the security infrastructure. In the current implementation, code may be either MIME-encoded Java classes or JavaScript source. In principle, any programming language could be used for encoding components, provided that the appropriate run-time support was provided. When a bundle is fired, execution begins at the entry point specified by the *entry* attribute of the code element, which specifies code that implements a standard interface. The data section of a bundle, known as its *payload*, comprises data with each datum having a unique *id* attribute. In the example the bundle carries one datum named *ToDoList*. It is common for bundles to carry other bundles in their payload, in order to install bundles in the store or fire them in other machines.

Subject to the capability protection scheme, bundles may carry out any arbitrary computation that they are encoded to perform, including the provision of network services.

```
<BUNDLE>
    <AUTHENTICATION        entity="19730129df7447eb91509"
                           signature="DQoew3rasZ...9wu9ySLGU"/>
    <CODE entry="uk.ac.stand.cingal.Runner" type="java">
        <CLASS name="uk.ac.stand.cingal.Runner">
            MamF2YS9sYW5nL09ia...
        </CLASS>
    </CODE>
    <DATA><DATUM id="ToDoList">
        <TODOLIST>
            <TASK guid="urn:cingal:325444" type="RUN">
                <DATUM id="StoreGuid">
                    Lvcxk3wnAIUN...
                </DATUM>
            </TASK>
        </TODOLIST>
    </DATUM></DATA>
</BUNDLE>
```

Fig 2: An example bundle

The store provided by each machine is a collection of passive data and supports the storage of arbitrary bundles. So that a bundle may be retrieved, a *key* in the form of a GUID is returned by the store on its insertion. If that key is later presented, the original bundle is returned. Stores do not support any update operations. Where the effects of update are required by an application, these may be obtained using *binders*.

Cingal thin servers provide two kinds of symbolic name binders: a *store binder* for naming entities in the store and a *process binder* for naming active machines. Both provide the ability to manipulate bindings though symbolic names and provide standard *put*, *remove* and *get* operations.

Cingal supports asynchronous message-oriented inter-machine communication. All communication is via *channels* that support conventional *read* and *write* operations. Each machine has associated with it a minimum of two channels as shown in **Fig 1**. The first is called the *machine channel* and is used to communicate with the machine infrastructure. The second is called the *default channel* and is used to communicate with the bundle running within the machine. An interface to the default channel is returned to its progenitor whenever a bundle is fired. The fired bundle may access the default channel via the machine API.

The channel established between a bundle and its progenitor is normally used for diagnostics and the passing of parameters. In order to accommodate change and dynamic deployment, the Cingal computational model supports named channels between entities. This idea stems from Milner's π-calculus [4]. Using named channels, individual executing bundles are isolated from the specifics of what components are connected to them. This isolation permits channels to be connected, disconnected and reconnected independently of the running program. Connections may be manipulated by the connected bundles or by third parties. This ability is necessary for the orchestration, evolution and autonomic management of deployed applications [5].

Within the machine infrastructure a component called the *connection manager* is responsible for the management of named channels. It maintains an associative mapping of names to channels. This mapping may be manipulated by other machines via the machine's machine port and by the bundle being executed via the machine API.

The model described thus far is a perfect virus propagation mechanism. Code may be executed on remote nodes and that code may create new processes, update the store, create name bindings and fire bundles on other thin servers. Cingal implements a two-level protection system. The first level of security restriction is on the firing of bundles. A conventional Unix or Windows style security model is not appropriate for thin servers, which do not have users in the conventional sense. Instead, security is achieved by means of digital signatures and certificates. Each thin server maintains a list of trusted *entities*, each associated with a security certificate. Entities might correspond to organisations, humans or other thin servers. This data structure is maintained by a process called the *Valid Entity Repository* (VER).

Bundles presented for firing from outwith a thin server must be signed by a valid entity stored in the VER. The VER maintains an associative data structure indexed by the entity *id* and mapping to a tuple including certificates and rights. Operations are provided for adding and removing entities from the repository. Of course these operations are subject to the second protection mechanism, which is capability-based. An example of a signed bundle was shown in **Fig 2**.

The *entity* attribute of the *authentication* element represents the name of an entity in the VER of the thin server on which the bundle is being fired and the *signature* is the signed body of the bundle's code payload. The thin server deployment infrastructure for deploying bundles from conventional machines provides programmers with methods that simplify the signing of bundles.

The signing of bundles and their authentication on arrival at thin servers prevents the misuse of thin servers by unauthorised entities. However it does not prevent a bundle from interfering with other bundles or entities in the binder or store. It is possible for bundles to be totally isolated, giving the illusion that each is the only entity running on a thin server. Conversely, bundles may share resources when appropriate.

To address these needs, the second protection mechanism provided by thin servers is capability-based. In addition to the signatures stored in the VER, thin servers store segregated capabilities for entities stored in the *store*, *sBinder*, *pBinder* and the VER itself. Whenever a running bundle attempts an operation, the capabilities stored in the VER associated with the entity that invoked the operation are checked. The operation only proceeds if the entity holds sufficient privilege.

3 Application Deployment

The Cingal system provides the infrastructure for deploying components on arbitrary suitably enabled hosts. However, additional infrastructure is needed to *a)* describe distributed architectures, and *b)* deploy components from the descriptions. This infrastructure comprises a *description language*, a *deployment engine*, and various mobile code documents and tools.

The description language is an XML schema, instances of which are *Deployment Description Documents* (DDDs). Each DDD contains an architectural description of an application, comprising a set of autonomous software components, the hosts on which they are to execute, and the interconnections between them.

The deployment engine takes a DDD as input and deploys the components described in it on the appropriate hosts. These components are pushed to the hosts as Cingal bundles; every participating host is Cingal-enabled. The deployment engine also pushes various tools to the hosts to carry out local deployment tasks *in situ*, principally installing and initialising the components, and configuring the interconnection topology of the deployed application. These tools are also transferred as bundles.

The data element of a tool bundle includes a control document called a *to-do list*. This contains a set of tasks to be attempted by the tool when it arrives and is fired on the destination thin server. When the tool completes these tasks, it sends a *task report* document back to the deployment engine, listing the outcomes of each task and any other associated information. Examples of associated information might include the GUIDs of stored bundles, or the names of channels and machines.

The three primary tools are *installers*, *runners* and *wirers*. An *installer* installs an arbitrary number of payload bundles into the store of the destination thin server. A *runner* starts the execution of a number of bundles previously installed in the store. A *wirer* is responsible for making concrete connections between pairs of components using the named channel mechanism.

Under control of these tools, each application component on a thin server moves between the following states:

- **installed**: when the bundle has been installed into the store
- **running**: when the bundle has been fired and started computation; any reads or writes on named channels will block since they are not connected
- **wired**: when the bundle has started computation and all named channels have been connected to other components

During initial deployment of an application the constituent components move from *installed* to *running* to *wired*. During subsequent evolution the components may move from *wired* to *running* to *wired* again, in cases where only the interconnection topology needs to change, or from *wired* to *running* to *installed* to *running* to *wired* again, in cases where components need to be moved to different hosts in the network.

Each instance of a deployment tool is pushed to the appropriate host as a bundle containing a fixed code element depending on its type (i.e. installer, runner or wirer), and a data element configured to its particular role. Thus every installer bundle contains the same generic installer implementation (currently a Java class), which is specialised by the bundle payload—and similarly for runners and wirers.

The example installer bundle shown in **Fig 3** contains the installer code: the class *uk.ac.stand.cingal.Installer*. The payload carries another bundle, itself containing the classes *Server* and *CacheUpdater*, and a *to-do list* specifying that that bundle (identified by the *id* attribute value `"urn:cingal:a222jdjd2s"`) should be installed.

```
<BUNDLE>
    <AUTHENTICATION     entity="197301m7wWwrPxX9..EySLGU"
                        signature="kUdzrv6T..fFNn5Kap" />
    <CODE entry="uk.ac.stand.cingal.Installer" type="java">
        <CLASS name="uk.ac.stand.cingal.Installer">
        5leLKJJbnQBAAMoKU...
        </CLASS>
    </CODE>
    <DATA>
        <DATUM id="urn:cingal:a222jdjd2s">
            <BUNDLE>
                <AUTHENTICATION     entity="1973012..91509"
                                    signature="DQowLAIUNs..if1Dn5Kap" />
                <CODE entry="Server" type="java">
                    <CLASS name="Server">
                    5lHRHAJMnQDD43MoKU...
                    </CLASS>
                    <CLASS name="CacheUpdater">
                    5leHdkvjidfjFFFDDEEU...
                    </CLASS>
                </CODE>
                <DATA />
            </BUNDLE>
        </DATUM>
        <DATUM id="ToDoList">
            <TODOLIST>
                <TASK guid="urn:cingal:aEcncdeEe" type="INSTALL">
                    <DATUM id="PayloadRef">
                    urn:cingal:a222jdjd2s
                    </DATUM>
                </TASK>
            </TODOLIST>
        </DATUM>
    </DATA>
</BUNDLE>
```

Fig 3: An installer bundle

Examples of runners and wirers are shown in **Figs 2** and **6** respectively.

A DDD is a static description of a distributed graph of components; an example is shown in **Fig 4**. It specifies the locations of the required components (bundles), the hosts available, the mapping of components to hosts (deployments) and the connections between named channel pairs.

```
<DDD name="ServerAndCacheApplication">
   <BUNDLES>
      <BUNDLE name="Server" source="file://C:\bundles\server.xml" />
      <BUNDLE name="Cache" source="file://C:\bundles\cache.xml" />
   </BUNDLES>
   <HOSTS>
      <HOST id="A" address="129.127.8.34" />
      <HOST id="B" address ="129.127.8.35" />
   </HOSTS>
   <DEPLOYMENTS>
      <DEPLOYMENT name="PrimaryServer" bundle="Server" target="A" />
      <DEPLOYMENT name="CachingServer" bundle="Cache" target="B" />
   </DEPLOYMENTS>
   <CONNECTIONS>
      <CONNECTION>
         <SOURCE          deployment="PrimaryServer"
                          channel="DownstreamCache" />
         <DESTINATION  deployment="CachingServer"
                          channel="UpstreamServer" />
      </CONNECTION>
   </CONNECTIONS>
</DDD>
```

Fig 4: A Deployment Description Document

The first phase of application deployment involves installation of component bundles on appropriate hosts. The deployment engine reads a DDD and retrieves the specified bundles from their given locations (which may be within a local file-based component catalogue or elsewhere on the network). It then configures an installer bundle for each host by generating an appropriate to-do list. These installers are fired as illustrated in **Fig 1** on the participating thin servers throughout the network. The action of each executing installer bundle on arrival is to extract its payload component bundles and add them to the local store. It then sends a task report back to the deployment engine listing the resulting store keys of the installed bundles, and terminates.

The second phase of application deployment involves starting execution of the previously installed 'dormant' component bundles on the appropriate thin servers. The deployment engine configures a runner bundle for each thin server, by generating an appropriate to-do list, and fires it on that thin server. The action of each executing runner bundle on arrival is to extract the relevant bundle(s) from the local store, and to fire these in turn. **Fig 2** shows an example runner bundle, containing the store key (labelled as *StoreGuid*) of the bundle to be extracted and fired. As with the installation process, the runner sends a task report back to the deployment engine, in this case listing the connectors of the enclosing machine for each fired bundle. This will enable the deployment engine to communicate with the newly running bundles in the final wiring phase. The process is illustrated in **Fig 5**, in which a runner is fired on thin server *A*. The runner retrieves the *Server* bundle from *A*'s store and fires it in a new machine, and returns a task report to the deployment engine.

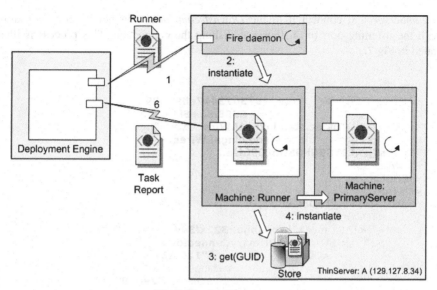

Fig 5: The running process

The final phase of application deployment involves connecting (termed *wiring*) the named channels on the running bundles to assemble the global application topology. The deployment engine configures a wirer bundle for each connection, by generating an appropriate to-do list. The wiring process will begin on one of the thin servers selected arbitrarily. Each wirer created is configured with a to-do list describing:

1. The connector for each machine—this contains the IP address of the machine and the machine and resource ports.
2. The name used by the executing bundle to reference the channel in both machines (this may be different for each machine).

Fig 6 shows an example wirer bundle for thin server *A*, which is (arbitrarily) chosen as the initiating thin server for the connection between the named channels *DownstreamCache* and *UpstreamServer*. Note that this bundle cannot be generated by the deployment engine until it has received the task reports from the runner bundles, since those contain the necessary port numbers.

The executing wirer bundle is able to communicate with the relevant machine's connection manager via its machine channel. In the example, the wirer executing on thin server *A* requests that the machine containing the running *Server* bundle create a new named channel with the name *DownstreamCache*. In response to this request, the machine's connection manager also starts a thread listening for incoming TCP/IP socket connections, and returns the port number to the wirer.

The wiring must now be completed by having the machine containing the running *Cache* bundle on thin server *B* connect to *A* on that port. To achieve this, the wirer on *A* configures another wirer bundle (its 'offspring'), which is fired on *B*. The purpose of the offspring wirer is to connect the named channel on *B* to the waiting channel on *A*. When the offspring wirer arrives at *B*, it communicates with the connection man-ager of the appropriate machine and instructs it to create a new named channel *Up-*

streamServer and connect it to the *DownstreamCache* channel by communicating with the listening port on *A*, thus establishing the connection. This process is illustrated in **Fig 7.**

```
<BUNDLE>
   <AUTHENTICATION  entity="1973073447eb91509"
                         signature=" CS68m..+SLGU" />
   <CODE entry="uk.ac.stand.cingal.Wirer" type="java">
      <CLASS name="uk.ac.stand.cingal.Wirer">
         sdjskF2YS9GFGSDnL09fdsa...
      </CLASS>
   </CODE>
   <DATA>
      <DATUM id="ToDoList">
         <TODOLIST>
            <TASK guid="urn:cingal:322xf344" type="WIRE">
               <DATUM id="PrimaryConnector">
                  <CONNECTOR    host="129.127.8.34"
                                machinePort="30112"
                                resourcePort="29000" /></DATUM>
               <DATUM id="SecondaryConnector">
                  <CONNECTOR    host="129.127.8.35"
                                machinePort="47121"
                                resourcePort="26083" /></DATUM>
               <DATUM id="PrimaryNamedChannel">
                  DownstreamCache</DATUM>
               <DATUM id="SecondaryNamedChannel">
                  UpstreamServer</DATUM>
            </TASK>
         </TODOLIST>
      </DATUM>
   </DATA>
</BUNDLE>
```

Fig 6: A wirer bundle

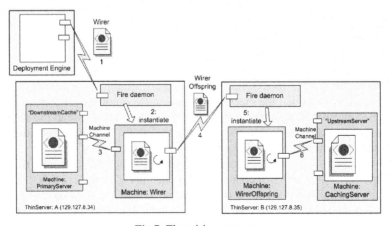

Fig 7: The wiring process

Once all the wirers have completed their (possibly parallel) computation, the wiring process is complete and the named channels are connected as shown in **Fig 8**. This completes the deployment of the distributed application.

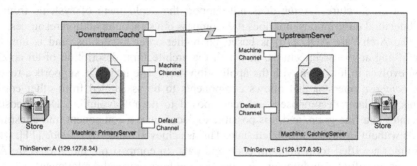

Fig 8: Result of wiring process

4 Related Work

The OSGi Service Platform [6] has perhaps the most in common with this work; it addresses similar issues of remote installation and management of software components, and (independently) adopts similar terminology for *bundles* and *wiring*. The most significant difference is the lack of high-level declarative architectural descriptions. This arises from it being targeted primarily at software deployment onto smart and embedded devices, whereas Cingal is aimed more generally at deployment and evolution of distributed applications on the basis of explicit architectural descriptions. As mentioned in Section 6, we are currently working on generating these descriptions automatically from high-level goals specified as constraints, to allow automatic reconfiguration and deployment in response to observed run-time problems such as host or network failure. Another difference is in the wiring model: a given OSGi bundle can be a producer and/or a consumer, and all its associated wires are conceptually equivalent. Cingal allows any number of symbolically named ports to be associated with a bundle, and the programmer may treat these differently. However, the two schemes have equivalent modelling power. Finally, Cingal is more flexible with regards to initial provisioning: its ubiquitous *fire* service allows bundles to be pushed to a new node from a remote management agent without any intervention required locally on the node. Initial provisioning in OSGi involves pull from a new node, which must be initialised somehow with an address from which to pull the code. The address may be provided by various means such as direct user intervention, factory installation, reading from a smartcard, etc.

A number of languages have been developed to describe software architectures, including [7-9]. Typical of these is Acme [1], which is intended to fulfil three roles: to provide an architectural interchange format for design tools, to provide a foundation for the design of new tools and to support architectural modelling. The Acme language supports the description of components joined via connectors, which provide a variety of communication styles. Components and connectors may be annotated with properties that specify attributes such as source files and degrees of concurrency, etc. Acme also supports a logical formalism based on relations and constraints, which permits computational or run-time behaviour to be associated with the description of architectures. Acme does not support the deployment of systems from the architectural descriptions, nor does it encompass physical computation resources.

The ArchWare ADL [10] is based on higher-order π-calculus, and is aimed at specifying active architectures, in which the architectural description of an application evolves in lock-step with the application itself. The language supports a reversible *compose* operator that allows components to be assembled from other components, and later decomposed and recomposed to permit evolution. Decomposition operates at a fine-grain, and it is possible to decompose a component into constituent parts without losing encapsulated state. This is achieved using *hyper-code* [11], which provides a reified form for both code and data. In comparison, the ArchWare ADL focuses on software architecture and does not address physical deployment.

The idea of installing components using agents has its roots in a number of places. Java Servlets were initially developed within Sun Labs with the express purpose of freeing the restrictions of a fixed repertoire service, allowing the client to modify the behaviour of the server. However, as they moved into a commercial product domain, this flexibility was removed as it was deemed to compromise the security of the underlying traditional operating system [12]. The Infospheres project from Caltech [13] has some overlap with the system described here. They propose a system of distributed Java processes (dapplets), which can be connected using asynchronous message passing.

The Tacoma system [14] uses agent technology to install software on remote machines and like our system uses digital signatures to verify the authenticity of agents. Tacoma introduces the notions of a *briefcase* to carry agent payloads, which may include components, and a *cabinet*, which is a persistent site bound briefcase, corresponding closely to our *store*. However, the Tacoma system appears to be aimed at installing non-distributed applications on remote nodes and does not include the notion of distributed components, communication channels nor high-level architectural descriptions.

5 Conclusions

At the start of this paper six claims were made about our deployment architecture[3]. In conclusion, these claims are critically re-examined.

Claim 1: The Cingal infrastructure permits bundles to be deployed in arbitrary geographic locations from conventional machines. Bundles may perform arbitrary computation and offer arbitrary network services.

---

[3] The current implementation may be downloaded from
 http://www-systems.dcs.st-and.ac.uk/cingal/downloads/.

Claim 2: The runtime infrastructure provided by Cingal thin servers abstracts over host-specific differences yielding a homogeneous run-time environment for deployed components.

Claim 3: The store and binder provided by thin servers support content-addressed storage, which permits code and data to be stored with no possibility of ambiguous retrieval. The binder permits objects to be symbolically named to facilitate the retrieval of components whose content keys are not known. The binder also provides an evolution point supporting update of component mappings.

Claim 4: Deployment Description Documents support the specification of distributed architectures. The deployment engine technology combined with the thin server infrastructure permits these distributed deployments to be realised into running instances of component based architectures. The process of deployment from specification through to having a connected collection of running components on distributed hosts is totally automated.

Claim 5: A number of novel evolution mechanisms are provided by the architecture. Firstly, the architecture supports the ability to remotely update components. Secondly flexible binding between components is made possible thorough the binder and store interfaces. Most importantly, distributed architectures may be re-arranged by unbinding and reconnecting named channels within machines running on thin servers.

Claim 6: The two security mechanisms provided by Cingal prevent unauthorised entities from firing bundles on hosts on which they do not have privilege. The ownership model which makes uses of standard cryptographic certificate techniques is well suited to distributed deployment. Tools (not described here) that operate in a similar manner to the deployment tool are provided for managing entity privileges and updating collections of machines. The capability protection system provided within Cingal thin servers prevents bundles being used for malicious or unintentional abuse of the thin server infrastructure.

6 Future Work

In the future we propose to expand the system in two primary ways. Firstly we would like to make the specification of distributed components more declarative. To this end we are currently investigating the use of constraint based specification languages. It is our intention to construct higher level specifications and a set of tools to support them and compile these specifications down to DDD documents. Secondly, we are investigating how evolution can be specified at the DDD level. Since we use DDDs to specify deployments, it seems natural to have high-level descriptions of evolution and automatically generate bundles to enact the necessary changes. Another interesting line of investigation is the use of a higher level specification of architectural intent from which DDDs may be generated. We are currently investigating the use of constraint based specification languages for this purpose [5]. We believe that this approach may be combined with the infrastructure described in this paper to yield systems that are capable of autonomic evolution in the face of perturbations such as host and link failure, temporary bandwidth problems, etc. We postulate that it will be feasible to implement an autonomic manager that will automatically evolve the deployed application to maintain the constraints while it is in operation.

7 Acknowledgements

This work is supported by EPSRC grants GR/M78403 "Supporting Internet Computation in Arbitrary Geographical Locations", GR/R51872 "Reflective Application Framework for Distributed Architectures" and by EC Framework V IST-2001-32360 "ArchWare: Architecting Evolvable Software".

The authors thank Richard Connor for his invaluable input to the Cingal project, on which he was a principal investigator, and Ron Morrison who read early drafts of this paper.

8 References

1. Garlan D., Monroe R., Wile D. ACME: An Architecture Description Interchange Language. In: Proc. Conference of the Centre for Advanced Studies on Collaborative Research (CASCON'97), Toronto, Canada, 1997, pp 169-183
2. Diaz y Carballo J.C., Dearle A., Connor R.C.H. Thin Servers - An Architecture to Support Arbitrary Placement of Computation in the Internet. In: Proc. 4th International Conference on Enterprise Information Systems (ICEIS 2002), Ciudad Real, Spain, 2002, pp 1080-1085
3. Dearle A., Connor R.C.H., Diaz y Carballo J.C., Neely S. Computation in Geographically Appropriate Locations (CINGAL). EPSRC, 2002. *http://www-systems.dcs.st-and.ac.uk/cingal/*
4. Milner R., Parrow J., Walker D. A Calculus of Mobile Processes. Information and Computation 1992; 100,1:1-77
5. Dearle A., Kirby G.N.C., McCarthy A. A Framework for Constraint-Based Deployment and Autonomic Management of Distributed Applications (Extended Abstract). To Appear: Proc. International Conference on Autonomic Computing (ICAC-04), New York, USA, 2004
6. OSGi Service Platform Release 3. Open Services Gateway Initiative, 2003
7. Garlan D., Allen R., Ockerbloom J. Exploiting Style in Architectural Design Environments. In: Proc. 2nd ACM SIGSOFT Symposium on Foundations of Software Engineering, New Orleans, Louisiana, USA, 1994, pp 175-188
8. Moriconi M., Qian X., Riemenschneider R.A. Correct Architecture Refinement. IEEE Transactions on Software Engineering 1995; 21,4:356-372
9. Shaw M., DeLine R., Klein D.V., Ross T.L., Young D.M., Zelesnik G. Abstractions for Software Architecture and Tools to Support Them. IEEE Transactions on Software Engineering 1995; 21,4:314-335
10. Morrison R., Kirby G.N.C., Balasubramaniam D., Mickan K., Oquendo F., Cîmpan S., Warboys B.C., Snowdon B., Greenwood R.M. Constructing Active Architectures in the ArchWare ADL. University of St Andrews Report CS/03/3, 2003
11. Kirby G.N.C. Reflection and Hyper-Programming in Persistent Programming Systems. PhD thesis, University of University of St Andrews, 1992
12. Jordan M. Java Servlets Discussion. Personal Communication, 1998

13. Chandy K.M., Rifkin A., Sivilotti P.A.G., Mandelson J., Richardson M., Tanaka W., Weisman L. A World-Wide Distributed System Using Java and the Internet. In: Proc. International Symposium on High Performance Distributed Computing (HPDC-5), Syracuse, New York, 1996
14. Sudmann N.P., Johansen D. Software Deployment Using Mobile Agents. In: Proc. 1st IFIP/ACM Working Conference on Component Deployment (CD 2002), Berlin, Germany, 2002, pp 97-107

Deploying Agents with the CORBA Component Model

Fabio Melo[1], Ricardo Choren[1], Renato Cerqueira[1],
Carlos Lucena[1], and Marcelo Blois[2]

[1] Pontifícia Universidade Católica do Rio de Janeiro (PUC-Rio)
Computer Science Department
Rua Marquês de São Vicente, 225 - Gávea, Rio de Janeiro/RJ, 22451-900, Brazil
{fabio, choren, rcerq, lucena}@inf.puc-rio.br
[2] Pontifícia Universidade Católica do Rio Grande do Sul (PUCRS)
Informatics Faculty
Av. Ipiranga, 6681, Prédio 30, Bloco 4 - Partenon, Porto Alegre/RS, 90619-900, Brazil
blois@inf.pucrs.br

Abstract. In the past few years, the multi-agent systems (MAS) area
has presented an accelerated growth. New techniques and tools are constantly being proposed and several methodologies have been published to
support the development of MAS. Most of these methodologies concentrate on the system analysis phase, giving almost no support for MAS implementation. Since agents can be seen as sort of specialized distributed
components, in this paper we propose an agent deployment model based
on the CORBA Component Model. We also describe a case study to
show the potential of an agent-based application development using this
model.

1   Introduction

The term large-scale application applies to a class of applications that perform
important business functions, such as automating key business processes. Usually, a large-scale application is distributed and is composed of several parts
implemented with different types of technologies.

Multi-agent systems (MAS) development has promoted new ways of building large-scale applications that foster features such as autonomy, modularity,
openness and distribution [8]. Software agents offer great promise as an abstraction that can be used by developers as a way to understand, model and develop
software that operates in adaptive, flexible, large-scale environments [23].

Agent-oriented software design and programming [15] decomposes large distributed systems into autonomous agents, each driven by its goals. This decomposition is done with specification languages such as AUML [13], MESSAGE
[3], AORUML [21], ANote [4] and MAS-ML [16] and it helps developers create
a set of agents that collaborate among themselves, using structured high-level
messages to achieve the system's goals.

W. Emmerich and A.L. Wolf (Eds.): CD 2004, LNCS 3083, pp. 234–247, 2004.
© Springer-Verlag Berlin Heidelberg 2004

After modeling a multi-agent system, developers face the challenges of implementing it. Despite the evolution of new platforms such as [2], [18], [20], currently there is no widely accepted agent-oriented language or architecture to support agent-based software development. Thus developers need to look for other ways to transform an agent system specification into a concrete robust implementation.

Software components show much promise at satisfying the demands of inherent modularity on which agents need to be added and recombined to form new applications. Moreover, component middleware, such as the CORBA Component Model (CCM) [11], J2EE [17] and emerging web services middleware, e.g. .NET [10], have shown great potential for the development of improved component-based solutions.

Agent-oriented software development can extend the conventional component development, offering more flexibility, less design and implementation time and less coupling between agents [9]. In fact, an agent can be seen as a complex component, composed of several simpler ones.

In this paper, we address some of the above issues and our work in progress on creating an implementation model to build scalable, large-scale, distributed agent systems using a component model. The rest of the paper is structured as follows. We begin with a review of components, middleware and how they impact on agent-based development. Section 3 describes the CCM in more detail. Section 4 presents a brief description of the proposed Agent Deployment Model. Section 5 presents a sample case study. Section 6 discusses some related work. We conclude in Section 7.

2   Components, Middleware, and Agents

A software component is defined as a self-contained, customizable and large-grain building block for (possibly distributed) application systems [19]. Some of the common characteristics of components are their ability to communicate by sending and receiving messages, the possibility of having multiple components of the same type in a system, and the description of their state consisting of attributes and other aggregated components [22].

Middleware is reusable software that resides between the applications and the underlying operating systems, network protocol stacks and hardware [14]. It works as a bridge between application programs and the basic lower-level hardware and software infrastructure that deals with how the parts of these applications are connected and interoperate.

From the development point of view, a middleware decouples application-specific functionality from the inherent complexities of the infrastructure. Thus it enables developers to concentrate on programming application-specific functionality instead of being concerned about low-level infrastructure problems. Several technologies, such as CORBA, .NET and J2EE, emerged to decrease the complexities associated with developing distributed large-scale software. Their successes have been a key factor to the spread of the middleware paradigm.

An agent, like a component, is a high-level abstraction. Agents have been used by software developers as a new way to understand, model, and develop software that operates in dynamic, open, and often unpredictable environments [23].

Components and middleware can be used to develop agent-oriented software. Some advantages [9] include:

- Loose coupling since components are not built assuming the existence of other components, as it must be with agents. Dynamic registration and discovery by name and features, and the loose coupling offer a greater degree of independent development. For example, agents can be loaded and activated while the system is running.
- Components offer services that are invoked by messages. Agents also respond to messages and offer services. Thus, agent infrastructures can be built over current component standard infrastructures such as J2EE, .NET and CORBA.
- Techniques of component coordination can be used to choreograph a society of agents. These include workflow and contracts for agent action execution and delegation or multi-agent system management.

3 The CORBA Component Model

CORBA Component Model (CCM) is a server-side component model for building and deploying CORBA applications. It uses accepted design patterns and facilitates their usage, enabling a large amount of code to be generated and allows system services to be implemented by the container provider rather than the application developer.

CCM introduces the concept of component and the definition of a comprehensive set of interfaces and techniques for specifying implementation, packaging and deployment of components [1]. A component is a basic meta-type in CORBA that is an extension and specialization of the object meta-type [12]. As seen in Fig. 1, components support four kinds of ports through which clients and other elements of an application may interact: facets, receptacles, event sinks and event sources. They also support attributes, which represent their properties.

Facets are the interfaces that the component exposes. Facets are object references for the many different interfaces a component may support. The component has a main reference and may have many facets, supporting distinct interfaces and representing new references. It is possible to navigate from the component's main reference to a facet's reference and vice-versa.

Component systems contain many components that work together to provide the client functionality. The relationship between components is called a connection and the conceptual point of connection is called a receptacle. The receptacle allows a component to declare its dependency to an object reference that it must use. Receptacles provide the mechanics to specify interfaces required for a component to function correctly.

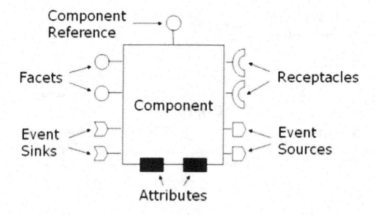

Fig. 1. CORBA component.

CCM also provides a publish-subscribe event mechanism that allows components to work with each other without being tightly linked. A component is an event source when it declares its interest in publishing or emitting an event. The difference between publishing and emitting is that a publisher can send events to multiple destinations (consumers), while an emitter has only one event consumer.

Other components become subscribers or consumers of those events by declaring an event sink. Components that want to be notified when a certain event occurs must connect its event sink to the event source of the component where the event might occur. When the event is generated, the component notifies all components that connected to its event source.

4   The Agent Deployment Model

In a multi-agent system, an agent is an active entity that, in some point of the system execution, may do activities, respond to some events, and generate some new events. The Agent Deployment Model (ADM) we propose combines component and middleware technologies for the development of agent-based systems. The ADM describes an agent similar to a CORBA component defined in the CCM. The model (see Fig. 2) shows a generic agent composed of two basic components: core and plan.

An agent is an entity. Thus it needs an identity and a self-representation on the system. The ADM core component is responsible for being the body of the agent. It has an interface that holds the main reference of the agent in the system and it also stores the agent's attributes. The core component keeps track of the agent current state and it is accountable for the agent's reasoning, i.e. for properly handling message receiving, message sending and plan management (start, stop, resume, cancel, etc.).

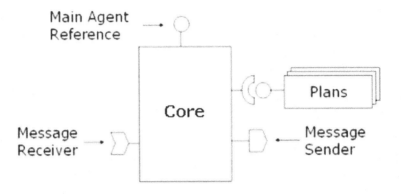

Fig. 2. The agent deployment model (ADM).

An agent does activities. The activities of an agent are carried out by their action plans. Therefore, the set of action plans describes the agent dynamic behavior. The ADM plan component is responsible for representing the agent's action plans. A plan component is accessed by an agent (core component) through receptacles. When something (a service) is required from an agent, it must execute at least one action plan, i.e. instantiate a plan component, to deliver it.

An agent responds to some events and generates some new ones. In other words, an agent is a highly interactive entity. It interacts with its environment and with other agents to perform its activities. In ADM, the interfaces through which an agent sends and receives events are event senders and event sinks. They are particularly fit to manage agent messages since conversations between agents are usually asynchronous. There must be an event sender for any message an agent has to send (from the system specification). Likewise, there must be an event receiver for every message an agent has to receive.

The ADM offers a model for a single agent. However, multi-agent systems may gather several agents that can be grouped in organizations. An organization defines a boundary around a set of agents, delimiting the set of services it provides. In ADM, an organization is implemented the same way as an agent, i.e. with a core component that identifies the organization in the system. An organization has a receptacle for each agent it encompasses, allowing the dynamic registration of agents in the organization. The communication between agents inside an organization is done through the message senders and receiver of the agents. When an agent has to communicate with an agent that is in another organization, the messages must also go through the message senders and receiver of the organizations.

In a multi-agent system, there are other kinds of entities that do not have active behavior. These are the system resources (non-agent artifacts) that encompass and operate data or information on their own. Examples of resources are databases and objects, and they are part of the system ontology, i.e. concepts that form the agent knowledge about the system. In ADM, resources do not have a particular way to be implemented. They should be developed as simple components that will be used by agent components.

The ADM relies on the CCM in a pretty straightforward way. The component and its reference are suitable to represent the core and the identity of an agent. Developing action plans as components allows for the reuse of agent functionality. If a multi-agent system requires two or more agents to provide a same service, the developer does not need to write code again. The developer deploys an action plan component and configures the receptacles of the core components of the agents that will deliver the service to that component. This also allows for agent evolution and adaptation. If an agent evolves or adapts, it can dynamically add, change or remove action plans from its plan component library.

The publish-subscribe model of communication allows for the use of any agent communication language. Developing the agent as a set of components also eases the question of learning other communication languages. For instance, if an agent currently understands a message in a format A and it needs to understand a new format B, it will be necessary to add a new component for format B to the agent.

ADM also benefits from the CCM in the architecture of the agent system solution. Since ADM does not classify nor offer predefined agents, it does not come with administrative, matchmakers or yellow pages agents. Administrative functions such as agent registration and discovery are directly dealt with by the middleware infrastructure since components already need to register and find themselves. This diminishes the administrative load the developers put on the system agents. Also, the developers only have to build agents that are related to the application solution.

The CCM brings other advantages to ADM as an infrastructure for agent systems. The CCM defines features and services in a standard environment, enabling the implementation, management, configuration and deployment of components that integrate with commonly used CORBA services. These server-side services add other facilities to agent-based applications, including transactions, security, persistence and events.

5   Implementing a MAS Using ADM

In order to better understand the ADM approach, this section describes a case study based on a marketplace application. The functionality required for this example can be described as follows. The application defines a model structured trading of products. During its lifecycle, a negotiated product typically goes through a number of states. Initially, the product has to be announced by sellers, waiting to be traded. Buyers check the announcements to find out if there are products they want acquire available in the marketplace. If so, every buyer potentially interested in a product can make an offer on it. Additionally, buyers can form groups to make an offer on a larger quantity of the product. The seller analyzes each offer, starting negotiation rounds with buyers. A negotiation round can lead to both successful (trade operation accomplished) or unsuccessful (trade not done) states.

This application was modeled using ANote [4] to define the system's goals and the agents that would carry out those goals. With ANote the designer captures and analyzes the intentions of the stakeholder, modeling them as goals, which eventually lead to the functional requirements of the system. These functional requirements are further detailed using scenarios so that the designer can define the actors in the system, i.e. the agents, and the social dependencies among these actors, including action plans, actions, interactions and resources.

For the case study, the modeling phase depicted three classes of agents: sellers, buyers and managers. Sellers announce and trade products for selling, buyers search, form groups and trade products for buying and managers manage groups of buyers. Those are their goals in the multi-agent system. Each agent has action plans to accomplish those goals. Moreover, the agents interact and manipulate resources such as products, announcements and groups.

Every agent class must be described as a specialization of the ADM core component. For instance, a buyer agent will have a core component that will have its identity (facet), a holder for its plans (receptacles) and its communication features (event senders and sinks). The agent's action plans are specializations of the ADM plan component. Each agent action plan must have a receptacle to store the reference to the agent (core component) that can perform it in the system, see Fig. 3.

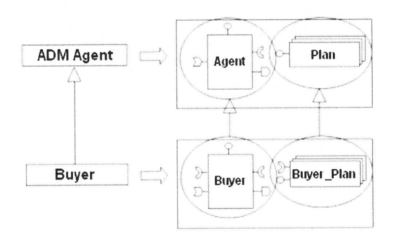

Fig. 3. The buyer agent in ADM.

Interactions between agents are carried out by messages. Messages are mapped to an event called Message. In the case study, this event was structured according to the definition proposed by FIPA-ACL [6], [7]. A Message event contains all the message data. A message is transmitted when the sender agent notifies the receiver agent that a Message event has occurred. These notifications are made through the event source and sink ports. The Message event is passed as a parameter of this notification, see Fig. 4.

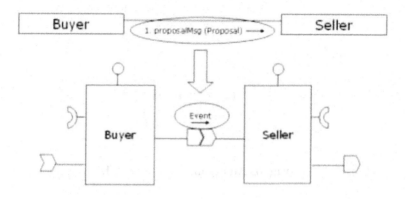

Fig. 4. A message in ADM.

It is also necessary to develop the resources (the non-agent artifacts) that are present in the multi-agent application. These resources are mapped to CORBA interfaces or structs. The mapping is based on one simple rule. If the resource presents data and behavior, it is mapped to a CORBA interface. Behaviors are mapped to operations and the data are mapped to interface attributes. On the other hand, if the resource works only as a data repository and it does not have specific behavior, it is mapped to a struct, where its attributes represent the element's data.

In the case study, resources include products, proposals and advertisements. For instance, a proposal holds attributes such as the product, its type, the quantity to be negotiated and the total price. The proposal was mapped to a struct because it did not need operations; it only needed to store data.

To develop the system organization, it is necessary to create another component to hold the references of the organization members, i.e. agents. In the case study, a MarketPlace core component was created to define the organization of sellers, buyers and manager agents (Fig. 5).

The modeling process identified aspects that are strongly connected to the ADM features. For example, action plans are directly mapped to plan components in ADM, and interactions are mapped to messages in event sources and sinks. Agents, goals, interactions, and plans are generally relevant to model multi-agent systems and thus they are specified not only by ANote but also by other agent-oriented analysis and design methodologies. Therefore, modeling these aspects of multi-agent systems as directly as possible can significantly favor the ADM characteristics such as ease of usage and reusability.

Fig. 5. An organization in ADM.

5.1   Some Implementation

In this section we show some code templates to illustrate (partially) how the ADM would implement a multi-agent system. An agent is initially implemented with a core component that implements a basic IAgent interface in the ADM. The IAgent interface creates all the features responsible for the agent lifecycle such as start up, plan instantiation and message dispatching. So, the ADM core component is implemented as a template that defines that an agent can perform a set of action plans and it can publish and consume messages.

```
interface IAgent {
  agent_name get_name ();
  void send_msg (in Message msg);
  IPlan get_plan (in string plan_name) raises (PlanNotFound);
  void start_agent ();
};
component Agent {
  /* Agent plans */
  uses multiple IPlan plans;

  /* Agent interaction */
  publishes Message emitter;
  consumes Message receptor;
};
```

An agent action plan is implemented by extending a plan component that implements a basic IPlan interface in the ADM. The IPlan interface is a definition of the plan method that will actually execute the action plan. The plan component must have a reference for the core component of all the agents that perform the action plan it implements.

```
interface IPlan {
  AnySeq execute_plan (in AnySeq param);
};
component Plan supports IPlan {
};
component Buyer_Plan : Plan {
  /* Reference to Buyer agent receptacle */
  uses IBuyerAgent agent;
  ...
};
```

From the case study, the buyer agent looks like the following.

```
interface IBuyerAgent : IAgent {
  ...
};
component BuyerAgent : Agent supports IBuyerAgent {
  ... /* logic for BuyerAgent */
};
```

A message is implemented as an event type in the ADM. In the case study, the event type conforms to the FIPA ACL message. Thus, it defines all the parts of an ACL message, such as performative, sender and receiver. The ADM does not make any assumptions about the message format the multi-agent system will use, i.e. a system can use message implementations other than the FIPA ACL. This is a development decision.

```
eventtype Message {
  /* Conforms to FIPA ACL (from the Case Study) */
  public string performative;
  public string sender;
  public string receiver;
  public string reply_to;
  public string content;
  ... /* other FIPA ACL attributes */
};
```

Finally, the resources should also be implemented. In the case study, the proposal resource was implemented as a struct.

```
struct Proposal {
  string proposal_type;
  string product;
  float price;
};
```

6 Related Work

Several agent-based infrastructures have been proposed and, also, a number of techniques for building agents based on these infrastructures have been developed. Sycara and her group have developed RETSINA [18], a MAS infrastructure composed of a set of services and conventions that allow agents to interoperate. It provides a layered model in which its various components, such as a Communication Infrastructure, are organized. So, in RETSINA, the components are part of the platform, which is different from the ADM - the components build the agents, and the platform is the component middleware. This does not allow the easy reuse of components of agents such as action plans.

The RETSINA infrastructure supplies a MAS Management Service to provide agent registration and discovery. In ADM, this is done directly by the component middleware, requiring no extra programming effort. RETSINA also deals with agent security, a major issue in mobile agents. In ADM this is also left to the component middleware; however, since the used component middleware (CORBA) is not meant for agents, some security issues such as authenticity are not present in ADM.

ZEUS [2] is a toolkit for constructing collaborative multi-agent applications. The ZEUS toolkit consists of a set of components that can be categorized into three functional groups (or libraries): an agent component library, an agent building tool and a suite of utility agents comprising nameserver, facilitator and visualize agents.

The component library is composed of planning, communication, social interaction, data structures and user interface components. Planning, communication and social interaction components are also supported by ADM. However, the ZEUS toolkit is not open, not offering support for the maintenance, change and addition of these components. For instance, ZEUS offers scheduling and coordination engine components, but a developer can only use those provided by the toolkit.

JADE (Java Agent Development Framework) [20] is a software development framework aimed at developing multi-agent systems and applications conforming to FIPA standards for intelligent agents. It includes two main products: a FIPA-compliant agent platform and a package to develop Java agents. JADE has two main components: Agent and Behavior. The Agent component is the class that must be extended by application programmers to create agents, a mechanism similar to ADM. The Behavior components implement the tasks, or intentions, of an agent. They are logical activity units, similar to the ADM plan components, that can be composed in various ways to achieve complex execution patterns and that can be concurrently executed. However, JADE offers a limited set of Behavior components, reducing the reuse potential, such as ZEUS.

Unlike these works, ADM does not make any platform classification of components (e.g. communication, interaction). It only classifies components into agent capabilities so that these components can be more easily reused in different agent-based systems. Also, ADM does not classify agents (e.g. nameserver, facilitator). The idea is that specific agents developed using the component model build an agent library in order to create an agent reuse repository.

Another issue is the communication language. All the above works use only languages based on FIPA ACL, such as KQML [5], for agent communication. This feature is bound to the platform. In ADM, agent communication is done through a publish-subscribe mechanism. It does not predefine any agent communication language. This allows for extensibility, since other languages can be used, and reuse, since a component that deals with a language can be reused in other MAS that utilize this language.

7 Conclusion

We have presented a deployment model for multi-agent systems in terms of components. We have defined and implemented a set of components and illustrated, with an example, how they can be used to support the implementation of MAS. Using the model, we help to manage the complexity of MAS specifications, promoting agent reuse, and providing a simple, operational way of showing how the component technology relates to agent-based development. Using components to develop agents we help developers make an explicit correlation between domain-specific or general assumptions in agent specifications to an implementation model.

The model allows for the development of single agents and a way for them to work together. It provides a way to implement agent capabilities - core, action plans and interaction. Moreover, since it is based on a standard component middleware, it can take advantage of all middleware services, such as location services, security mechanisms, communication platform, and deployment tools, and it provides a better interoperability of MAS applications with legacy components.

In addition to a mapping model of a MAS specification to a standard deployment and implementation infrastructure, our work also provides an evaluation of the CCM' applicability, since it uses this infrastructure to support abstractions different from the ones CCM was originally designed to support.

One direction for future work is to study how MAS specification languages and methods can be integrated into our approach. Use of a variety of languages for describing agent capabilities and system specifications should show us how to improve the current model. Another direction is that of experimenting with component platforms other than CORBA.

Finally, to help make multi-agent technologies adoption happen, there is a need to build agent platforms, models and implementation toolkits to ease the generation of individual agents and multi-agent systems. Components have proven to be a good technique for bridging the gap between agent specifications and agent implementations. We believe an important direction of future work should focus on building mechanisms to provide feedback to system designers about the implementation's world. It would be very desirable to automate the construction of some components of the agent system from synthesized agent models. This can allow designers to gain more insight into the specification and to show its impact in the actual system construction.

Acknowledgements. This work has been partially supported by the ESSMA Project under grant 552068/2002-0 (CNPq, Brazil).

References

1. Bartlett, D.: CORBA Component Model (CCM): Introducing next-generation CORBA. Available at:
   http://www-106.ibm.com/developerworks/webservices/library/co-cjct6/ (2001).
2. British Telecommunications: BT Intelligent Agent Research. Available at: http://more.btexact. com/projects/agents/zeus/index.htm (2002).
3. Caire, G.: MESSAGE: Methodology for Engineering Systems of Software Agents Initial Methodology. Technical Report, EDIN 0224-0907, Project P907, EU-RESCOM (2001).
4. Choren, R., Lucena, C.J.P.: An Approach to Multi-Agent Systems Design Using Views. Technical Report, DI / PUC-Rio (2003).
5. Finin, T., Fritzson, R., McKay, D., McEntire, R.: KQML as an Agent Communication Language. Proceedings of the 3rd International Conference on Information and Knowledge Management (CIKM'94), Gaithersburg, Maryland. ACM Press (1994) 456–463.
6. Foundation for Intelligent Physical Agents: FIPA ACL Message Structure Specification. Available at: http://www.fipa.org/specs/fipa00061 (2002).
7. oundation for Intelligent Physical Agents: FIPA Communicative Act Library Specification. Available at: http://www.fipa.org/specs/fipa00037 (2002).
8. Garcia, A.F., Lucena, C.J.P., Zambonelli, F., Omicini, A., Castro, J. (eds.): Software Engineering for Large-Scale Multi-Agent Systems, Research Issues and Practical Applications. Lecture Notes on Computer Science, Vol. 2603. Springer-Verlag, Berlin Heidelberg New York (2002).
9. Griss, M.L., Kessler, R.R.: Achieving the Promise of Reuse with Agent Components. In: Garcia, A.F., Lucena, C.J.P., Zambonelli, F., Omicini, A., Castro, J. (eds.): Software Engineering for Large-Scale Multi-Agent Systems. Lecture Notes on Computer Science, Vol. 2603. Springer-Verlag, Berlin Heidelberg New York (2002) 139–147.
10. Microsoft Corporation: Microsoft .NET. Available at:
    http://www.microsoft.com/net/ (2003).
11. Object Management Group: CORBA Component Model, v 3.0 (2002).
12. Object Management Group: CORBA Components, v 3.0 (2002).
13. Odell, J., Parunak, H., Bauer, B.: Extending UML for Agents. Proceedings of the Agent-Oriented Information Systems Workshop at the 17th National Conference on Artificial Intelligence (2000) 3–17.
14. Schantz, R.E., Schmidt, D.C.: Middleware for Distributed Systems: Evolving the Common Structure for Network-centric Applications. In: Marciniak, J., Telecki, G. (eds.): Encyclopedia of Software Engineering. Wiley & Sons (2002).
15. Shoham, Y.: Agent-Oriented Programming. Artificial Intelligence, Vol. 60, N. 1 (1993) 139–159.
16. Silva, V.T., Choren, R.: Using the MAS-ML to Model a Multi-Agent System. Technical Report 24/03, DI / PUC-Rio (2003).

17. Sun Microsystems: Java 2 Platform Enterprise Edition Specification, v 1.4 (2004).
18. Sycara, K., Paolucci, M., van Velsen, M., Giampapa, J.: The RETSINA MAS Infrastructure. Technical Report CMU-RI-TR-01-05, Carnegie Mellon (2001).
19. Szyperski, C.: Component Software: Beyond Object-Oriented Programming. Addison-Wesley (1998).
20. Telecom Italia Lab: JADE Programmer's Guide. Avaliable at: http://sharon.cselt.it/projects/jade/doc/programmersguide.pdf (2003).
21. Wagner, G.: Agent-Object-Relationship Modeling. Proceedings of the 2nd International Symposium: From Agent Theory to Agent Implementation (2000).
22. Wienberg, A., Matthes, F., Boger, M.: Modeling Dynamic Software Components in UML. Proceedings of the Second International Conference on UML (UML'99), Fort Collins, Colorado. Springer-Verlag (1999) 204–219.
23. Wooldridge, M.: Intelligent Agents. In: Weiss, G. (ed.): Multiagent Systems. The MIT Press (1999) 3–51.

Author Index